ISBN: 9781313051514

Published by:
HardPress Publishing
8345 NW 66TH ST #2561
MIAMI FL 33166-2626

Email: info@hardpress.net
Web: http://www.hardpress.net

INSULATION AND DESIGN OF
ELECTRICAL WINDINGS

INSULATION AND DESIGN
OF
ELECTRICAL WINDINGS

BY

A. P. M. FLEMING, M.I.E.E.
AND
R. JOHNSON, A.M.I.E.E.

WITH DIAGRAMS

LONGMANS, GREEN, AND CO.
39 PATERNOSTER ROW, LONDON
NEW YORK, BOMBAY, AND CALCUTTA
1913

PREFACE

IT is generally recognised that insulation constitutes the most vulnerable part of electrical machinery, and manufacturers and users alike are confronted with the problem of how to ensure the maintenance of electrical service while dependent on materials known to be of an unreliable character.

The extremely unmechanical nature and general unsuitability of the commercial insulating materials for withstanding the high temperatures and stresses occurring in service, has discouraged any wide-spread scientific investigations of directly practical application. As a result, therefore, insulation problems have in the past been solved largely by process of trial and error.

The necessity for greater attention to these problems has been forced upon engineers by the advent of high voltages and larger and more costly units.

Modern scientific research has thrown much light on the electrical behaviour of dielectrics, and much scattered data has been published dealing with the properties of insulating materials. This information, however, has not been available heretofore in a co-related form whereby it can be used as a fundamental basis for the practical insulation of electrical apparatus.

In this treatise the authors have endeavoured to set forth the underlying principles and methods whereby the design of insulation can be carried out with precision, and have embodied the results of many years of practical experience in connection with insulating problems.

CONTENTS

CHAPTER I

PHYSICAL CHARACTERISTICS OF DIELECTRICS

Introduction.—In considering the physical characteristics of insulating materials it is important to appreciate that all matter to some extent possesses the property of electrical conductivity, and that in this respect the difference between " conductors " and " insulators " is not so much one of kind as of degree.

The exhaustive investigations of Sir J. J. Thompson and others show that the conductivity of gases is explained by the presence and motion of infinitely small electrically charged particles termed " ions," which may be considered to consist of atoms or groups of atoms, or of very much smaller negatively charged particles known as " electrons." Largely as a result of these investigations the " electron theory " has been developed, which has served to throw much light on the electrical behaviour of matter.

In applying this theory to the study of electrical conductivity it is assumed that every atom has associated with it one or more detachable electrons whose aggregate negative charge is balanced by an equivalent positive charge on the atom, and that an ion possessing a definite positive or negative charge is formed by the addition of an electron to, or its removal from, one of these neutral atoms or combinations of atoms.

If the cohesion between atoms and their electrons is overcome, the ions thus formed are free to move under the influence of an electric force, and when in motion in a definite direction constitute what is ordinarily termed an electric current, the magnitude of which is determined by the number of the ions and the velocity with which they move.

The theory thus presents a mental picture of the conducting

process which, in so far as it is at present understood, is the same for all matter, whether in a solid, liquid, or gaseous form.

The relatively high conductivity of so-called conductors may be explained by assuming that the cohesive force between their atoms and electrons is very weak, and consequently there are always a large number of ions free, whereas in dielectrics comparatively few ions are normally free and considerable force is required to liberate the electrons.

When a difference of potential exists between two electrodes separated by a dielectric, a stress is set up in the latter the intensity of which is dependent on the size and shape of the electrodes and the distance separating them. The effect of this stress is to distort the molecular structure of the dielectric and tend to liberate some of the electrons, and these, together with any ions already existing in the medium, are propelled—as in the case of all charged moveable bodies when placed in an electrostatic field—in the direction of the lines of force, and thread their way through the interatomic space with a velocity depending on their mass, charge, and strength of the field. The transference of ions in this way constitutes a flow of electricity from one electrode to the other, and the magnitude of the operation represents the conductivity of the medium.

In materials, such as metals, having a high conductivity, the current at a given temperature increases directly as the applied voltage, that is to say, the "resistance" to the motion of the ions is constant. In dielectrics, however, the resistance is constant probably only as long as conduction is due solely to the initially free ions, and when the field is intense enough to liberate electrons, the resistance rapidly decreases, and ultimately the disruption of the molecular structure occurs, and the dielectric is then said to have "broken down."

The property possessed by a material whereby it is able to resist this disruption of its molecular structure is known as its *dielectric strength*.

The distortion of the structure prior to actual disruption, whatever its precise nature may be, accounts for the charging or displacement current familiar in condenser work, the magnitude of which for a given area of electrodes and thickness of dielectric depends on the property of the material known as its *specific inductive capacity.*

When the electrostatic field is the result of an alternating E.M.F., a certain amount of energy is expended in producing periodic molecular distortions of this nature, which, in the case of solid dielectrics, manifests itself in the form of heat.

The conditions which enter into the conduction and ultimate breakdown of dielectrics will be considered separately for gases, liquids, and solids.

GASES.

Nature of conduction.—The fact that gases can be obtained in a very pure state, and their condition as regards temperature and pressure closely controlled, renders them of particular value for the investigation of the properties of dielectrics. Until comparatively recent years it was thought that gases were perfect insulators. It is now, however, quite definitely established that gases conduct electricity, although in many cases so poorly under normal conditions that to facilitate investigations it is necessary to improve their conductivity by means of artificial ionisation.

This can be accomplished by exposing the gas to the action of an ionising agent producing electrons, such as radium, certain incandescent solids, an electric discharge, or ultra-violet light.

A gas which has been ionised in this way does not retain its conductivity permanently after the removal of the ionising agent, owing to the recombination of the positive and negative ions which neutralise each other. Also the ionising process will not go on increasing indefinitely if the ionising agent is continuously applied, owing to the fact that as more and more ions are formed the chances of recombination are greater, and a stage may be reached when the ions recombine at the same rate as they are produced.

A typical conduction curve for gases is shown in Fig. 1. This can be divided into two distinct stages.

In the first stage, as shown by the full-line part of the curve, the conductivity is due to the ions which are already in a free state, the current increasing in proportion to the applied voltage.

It is thus seen that over a certain range the "resistance," i.e. $\frac{\text{voltage}}{\text{current}}$, may be considered constant.

If the gas is already ionised from an external source the curve will take the form shown by the dotted portion, and, as indicated, the current reaches a steady value beyond which it does not appreciably increase even for considerable increase in voltage. This steady value is known as the "saturation" current, and is reached

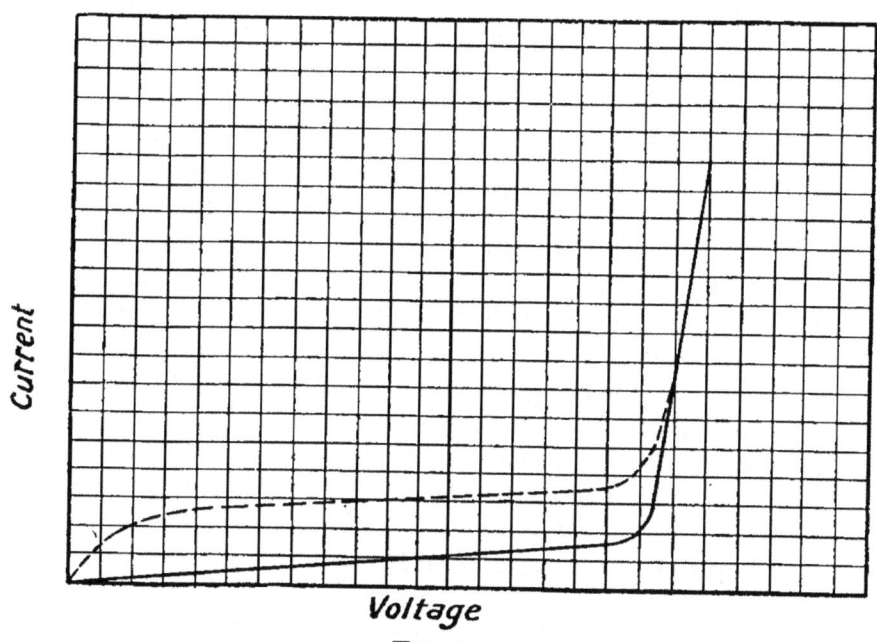

FIG. 1.

when ions are utilised in transmitting the current, at the same rate as they are supplied from the external source. In such an ionised gas the current depends on the number of ions present which increases with the distance between the electrodes, so that under these conditions the term "resistance," as ordinarily indicated by $\frac{E}{C}$, does not apply.

During the first stage, except in rarefied gases, the flow of current is not accompanied by any visible or audible discharge, and, until the second stage is reached when the field is strong enough to continue and accelerate the ionising process, the amount of current that can be transmitted is too insignificant to be of practical interest.

In the second stage the current is practically independent of the initially ionised condition of the gas, and its magnitude is mainly determined by the ionisation produced by the electrostatic field, the voltage required to produce ionisation depending on the shape of electrodes, the space by which they are separated, and nature and density of the gas. When this voltage is reached the conductivity very rapidly increases until disruption of the dielectric occurs.

This increase in current is first indicated by a glow, and as the voltage increases, by a brush discharge which forms a conducting envelope or corona around the opposing faces of each electrode, and thereby virtually reduces the effective thickness of the dielectric. The field between these two points is thus concentrated, and its intensity increases as the distance between the conducting envelopes is reduced, until eventually the disruption of the medium occurs, as shown by the passage of a spark between the electrodes. After the passage of the first spark, if the voltage applied is sufficient to maintain the sparking, the heating produced at the faces of the electrodes apparently causes the emission of metallic ions which increases the conductivity until the passage of the current is indicated by a continuous arc. The potential across the gap then falls considerably, and the arc behaves somewhat as a metallic conductor of more or less constant resistance.

Spark potential.—The greatest potential difference that can be maintained indefinitely between two electrodes without causing the intervening gap to break down has been termed the " spark potential." It does not follow, however, that a voltage slightly in excess of this will, under all conditions, cause a spark to pass.

If applied only for a very short period of time the gap will sustain a much higher voltage, and there is a definite element of time required to produce a breakdown under given conditions. On the other hand, when the gap is once broken down, a number of sparks may quickly follow at a much lower voltage, due to the ionisation produced by the first discharge.

Again, if the gas is very carefully dried it will sometimes

withstand several times the normal spark potential, although this high insulating condition is extremely unstable and the gas quickly reverts to its normal state, especially if ionising agents are present.

Under certain conditions the influence of an ionising agent may be sufficient to considerably reduce the spark potential, and this is especially noticeable where needle-point electrodes exposed to ultra-violet light are used.

The distance through which a given voltage will spark depends on the facility with which the gas separating the electrodes is ionised, this being determined mainly by the pressure of the gas and the shape of the electrodes, the latter governing the distribution of the electrostatic field.

For very short spark lengths of the order of one or two thousandths of an inch the spark potential is independent of the pressure of the gas, but is influenced by the nature of the metals used for the electrodes, and it would appear that for such short gaps the current is transmitted by ions derived from the electrodes rather than from the gas.

Fig. 2 shows the relation between spark potential and spark length in air at normal pressures, when the spark length is very small. This curve is typical for most gases, and the important point to note is the abrupt change in slope when a certain spark length is reached.

Effect of pressure on spark length.—For a given spark length that is greater than a few mils, the spark potential for a very wide range in pressure varies as the product of pressure and spark length, *i.e.* on the mass of gas between the electrodes. This law has been verified experimentally by Paschen for pressures up to several atmospheres.

At low pressures the number of atoms, and consequently the number of available electrons, is less than at high pressures; on the other hand, owing to the greater interatomic space at the lower density, less obstruction is offered to the ions in their passage and they consequently attain a higher velocity, hence the conductivity of the gas increases as the pressure is reduced.[1]

The luminous strata between the electrodes in rarefied gases

[1] See " Conduction of Electricity through Gases," J. J. Thompson.

indicates the region where ,the ions, having acquired sufficient energy by virtue of their high velocity, expend their energy by colliding with and ionising the neutral atoms of the gas.

At very low pressures, however, of the order of $\frac{1}{10}$ to $\frac{1}{100}$ of an atmosphere, depending on the spark length, a critical point is reached below which the conductivity decreases, and if a perfect vacuum could be obtained this would be found to be a perfect insulator, since there would be no available electrons in the

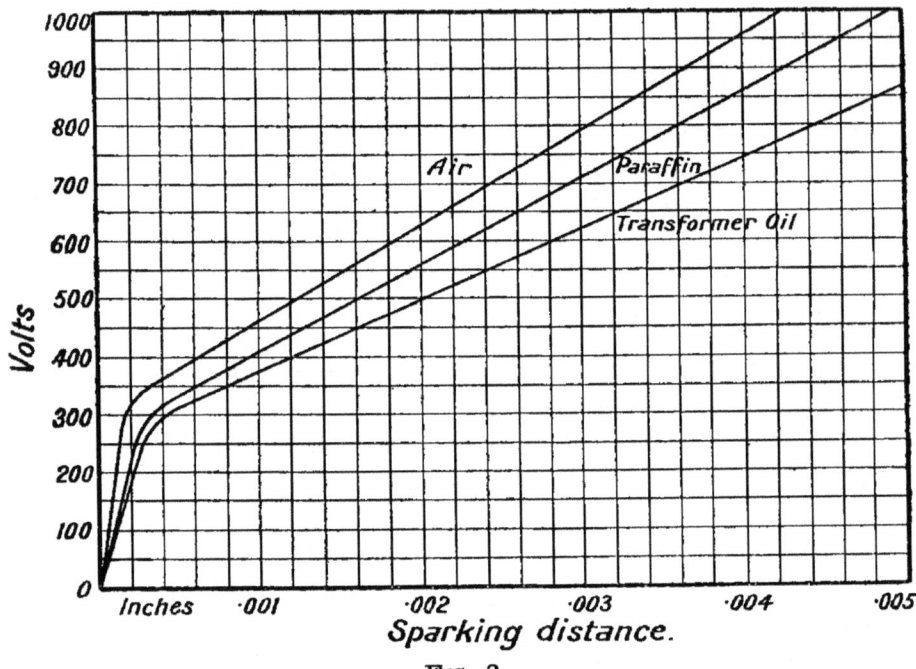

FIG. 2.

medium and no current could be transmitted until possibly at a high voltage ions might be dragged from the electrodes.

Distribution of electrostatic field with different shapes of electrode.—As already noted, the shape of the electrodes determines to a large extent the distribution of the electrostatic field between them. If flat plates of considerable size, or very large spherical electrodes are used, the field is approximately uniform in intensity. On the other hand, if the electrodes consist of needle points or very small spheres, the intensity of the field will be far from uniform and will have a maximum value near the electrodes and a minimum midway between them.

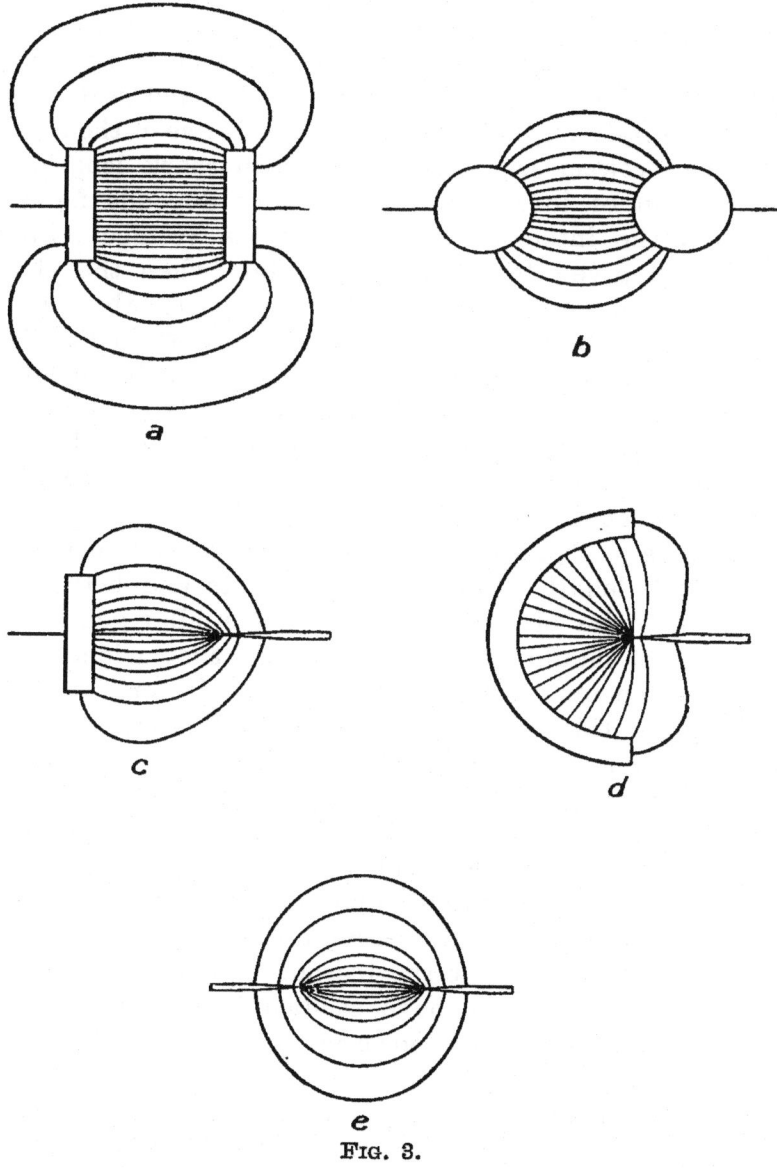

FIG. 3.

In Fig. 3 the distribution of field between various-shaped electrodes is diagrammatically set forth, the lines of force leaving each electrode normal to its surface. From these figures the similarity between the electrostatic and the magnetic field will be readily seen, and for any particular shape of electrodes the distribution of the electrostatic field can be experimentally illustrated by employing similar-shaped magnetic poles and scattering iron filings on a supporting non-magnetic plate between them.

Relation between sparking voltage and spark length.—Since the production of ions and their velocity depends for a given pressure on the intensity of the field, the voltage required to break down a given length of gap is less when the electrodes consist of sharp points, as shown in Fig. 3 (*e*), than when, for instance, larger spherical electrodes, such as shown in Fig. 3 (*b*), are used. For example, it is found that a voltage of 250,000 will spark across a gap of about 25 inches between needle points, but only across a gap of about 10 inches between equal spherical electrodes of 10 inches diameter, when the tests are carried out under otherwise identical conditions.

The curves in Fig. 4 show the relation between sparking voltage and spark length between needle points and between equal spherical electrodes of various sizes under similar general testing conditions. It should be noted, however, that widely different results are often obtained by different investigators, and some of the reasons for this difference are discussed later. Under most testing conditions the relation between sparking voltage and spark length is not, strictly speaking, indicated by a regular curve, as shown in Fig. 4, but a variation is found at some point on the curve, the position and magnitude of which appears to depend on the size and shape of electrodes, and the capacity, frequency, and other conditions of the testing circuit. No satisfactory explanation has been advanced as to the reasons of this variation, by the different investigators who have studied it, and, as far as most practical considerations are concerned, no great importance need be attached to it.

Conditions affecting sparking voltage.—An important factor governing the sparking voltage for a given air-gap, apart from such considerations as the shape of electrodes and the pressure, is the relative potential of the two electrodes.

There are two principal conditions to be considered, viz. (*a*) where the electrodes are of equal and opposite potential, as when they are connected to the terminals of the high tension winding of a transformer, the middle point, *i.e.* the point of zero potential, being earthed; or the whole of the circuit connected with the electrodes symmetrically insulated in respect to earth, and (*b*), where the potential of one electrode is zero, such as when one terminal of the testing transformer is earthed. In the former case, where the electrodes are of equal and opposite potential, the voltage

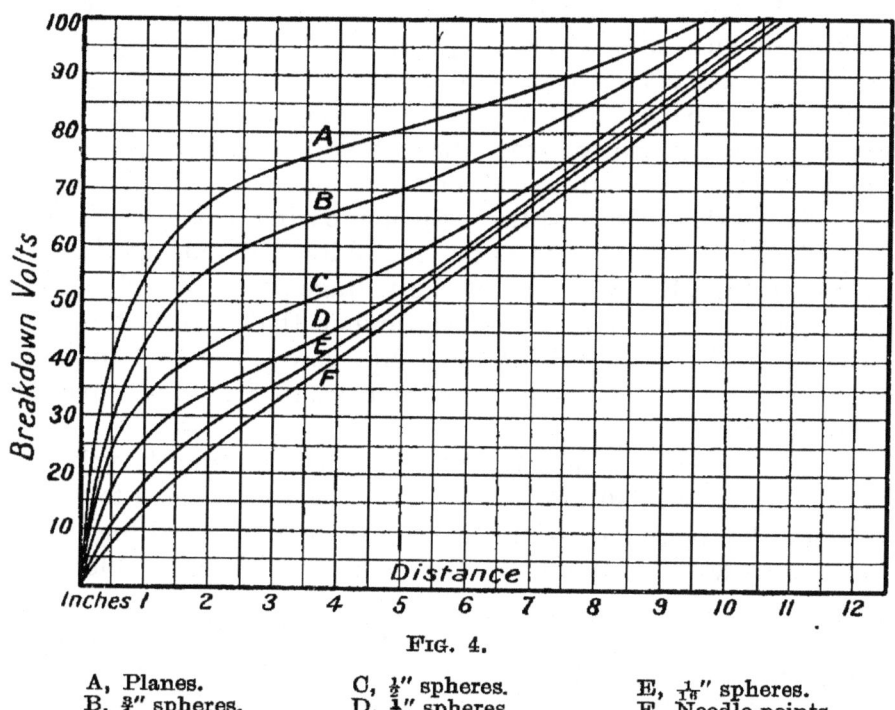

Fig. 4.

A, Planes.
B, ¾" spheres.
C, ½" spheres.
D, ¼" spheres.
E, ⅟₁₆" spheres.
F, Needle points.

required to break down a given length of gap is much higher than when one electrode is at zero potential. Similarly, if the distribution of the electrostatic field is altered by any other means, as by the proximity of bodies which would have an electrostatically inductive effect, the sparking voltage may be considerably altered.

For these reasons it is usual to carry out spark gap investigations with the middle point of the high-tension winding of the testing transformer earthed, and to connect the testing terminals to the electrodes by short lengths of line, carefully spaced from neighbouring bodies and in such a manner that the electrostatic field set up by the lines themselves exercises the minimum distorting effect on the field between the electrodes.

The presence of inductance or capacity in the high voltage testing circuit, unless symmetrically disposed in respect to each electrode, introduces a source of error, and, moreover, unless under such conditions the voltage is applied and raised gradually to the breaking-down value, a rise in pressure above that indicated by the transformer ratio may be obtained.

The wave-shape of the voltage of supply is an important consideration, since the voltage that should really be taken into account is the maximum attained during the cycle, while that measured is the R.M.S. value. In comparing the results, therefore, of sparking voltages obtained under different testing conditions, the amplitude factor of the voltage-wave should be taken into account. It should be noted further that, unless the source of the supply voltage is of considerable power, the load impressed by the testing apparatus may be such as to alter the wave-form of the generator.

The effect of varying the frequency of the supply voltage is not very important, although certain investigators [1] have found that it alters the position on the curve connecting sparking voltage and spark length, at which the variation already referred to occurs.

As regards the condition of the air, the effect of pressure has already been noted, and in this connection temperature has also some bearing, although for all practical purposes the variation in value due to the comparatively limited range of temperature variation usually met with, does not introduce errors of any great magnitude. The effect of humidity also on the sparking voltage has not been found in practice of any great importance.

When air under rarefied conditions is tested, the sparking voltage for a given length of gap is liable to be seriously affected by ultra-violet light, and while at normal pressure this effect is

[1] Kemp and Stephens, *Journal of the Institution of Electrical Engineers*, Vol. xlv., No. 204.

not so marked, it is advisable, when testing under artificial light, such as an arc light, to shield the electrodes from direct rays.

Where spherical electrodes are employed, these must be kept clean and free from the burning effects of the arc, and it has been recommended that brass electrodes, having their surfaces amalgamated, be used and polished after each breakdown with cloth moistened with mercurous nitrate. Where needle-point electrodes are used, these should be carefully selected as regards uniformity of sharpness and be replaced after each breakdown.

Dielectric strength of air.—From the results of breakdown tests obtained between spherical electrodes by various investigators, the dielectric strength of air, *i.e.* its breakdown value when the electrostatic field between the electrodes is absolutely uniform,

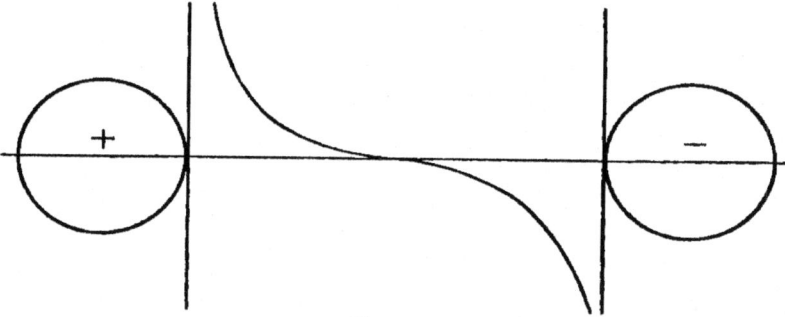

FIG. 5.

has been computed to be of the order of 38 kilovolts per centimeter,[1] *i.e.* about 100 volts per mil, the voltage given being the maximum and not the R.M.S. value.

It must be remembered, however, that in applying this value, the actual voltage required to breakdown a given length of gap will depend, as already pointed out, on the shape of electrodes and other considerations, since the voltage is not necessarily distributed uniformly across the entire gap. This can be judged for instance by referring to Fig. 3 (*b*), in which it is seen that the field is concentrated very much at the opposing faces of the electrodes, and, for such conditions, the voltage distribution between them would be as represented by the curve in Fig. 5.

[1] See *Journal of the Institution of Electrical Engineers*, No. 187, Vol. xl., Paper by Dr. A Russell.

Taking the dielectric strength of air as a standard, that of any other insulating medium can be obtained by making comparative breakdown tests under identical testing conditions, the electrodes in each case being completely surrounded with the medium under test.

Practical considerations in the use of gaseous dielectrics.—Air is the only gaseous dielectric of practical value for insulating purposes, and as it is most generally employed together with solid

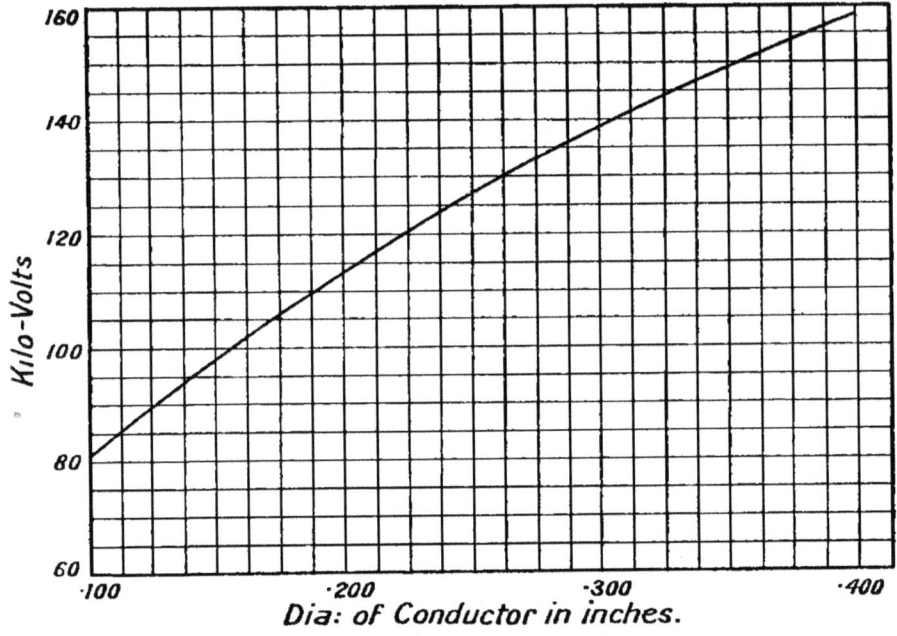

FIG. 6.

insulating media, its specific applications in the insulation of windings will be dealt with in Chapter IV.

On high voltage transmission lines an important consideration in connection with the insulating value of air lies in the corona formation around the line conductors. This represents a loss of energy which at voltages of the order of 100,000 may be of very considerable magnitude, and this introduces one of the limiting factors in regard to the highest voltage that can be employed. As the size of conductor is increased the voltage at which the energy loss suddenly becomes excessive is also increased, as shown in the curve in Fig. 6.

The use of compressed air has been suggested for insulating purposes in connection with such apparatus as transformers and even cables, on account of its increased dielectric strength. Except in connection with certain instruments, however, no practical use has been made of this means of insulating.

For many years the sparking voltage in air between needle points has been employed for measuring high voltages. On account, however, of the many variables that have to be considered, the method has not been entirely satisfactory, especially for voltages upwards of about 75,000. For very high voltages it has been proposed[1] that spherical electrodes be used, with which very consistent results are obtainable so long as the gap does not exceed about the diameter of the sphere, within which limits no corona is formed. The following diametres of spheres have been recommended for various ranges of voltage :—

Diameter of spherical electrode.	With one electrode grounded.	With middle point of testing transformer grounded.
25·0 cms.	up to 275,000 volts	330,000
37·5 ,,	,, 412,500 ,,	440,000
50·0 ,,	,, 550,000 ,,	650,000

When an electrical discharge takes places in air certain chemical effects are produced, which appear to be inseparably connected with the changes that occur in the character of the discharge at different voltages. If the intensity of field is such as to produce merely a violet glow, ozone is formed. When the field is intense enough to produce a " brush discharge," oxides of nitrogen are formed, and under certain conditions of temperature and moisture, nitric acid. These chemical effects produced by an intense electrostatic field are employed as a basis for certain commercial methods of producing ozone and nitrates. They also have important bearing in connection with the insulation of high voltage windings, and will be further discussed in connection with the design of insulation in Chapter IV.

[1] See *Proceedings of the American Institute of Electrical Engineers*, Vol. xxxii., No. 2. The " Sphere Spark Gap," Farnsworth and Fortescue, p. 301.

LIQUIDS.

Investigations on the characteristics of liquids have in the main been confined to a few grades of oils of mineral or vegetable origin, these being the only liquid insulators that have been employed to any extent in the commercial insulation of electrical apparatus.

Nature of conduction.—There is good reason to consider that the process of conduction in liquid dielectrics takes place on the same general lines as in gases, that is to say, current is transmitted through them by means of ions which already exist in a free state in the dielectric or which are produced therein by the electrostatic field.

With weak electrostatic fields, and at a given temperature, the current transmitted in the case of dielectrics of the type already referred to, increases in proportion to the voltage, and in this respect the behaviour of the dielectric is represented by the full-line first portion of curve in Fig. 1, that is to say, under certain conditions the resistance as computed from $\frac{E}{C}$ is constant. In this connection the curves[1] in Fig. 7 illustrate for a given oil how the specific resistance varies with temperature, the upper curve showing the results obtained when heating, and the lower one when cooling. These may be compared with similar curves for solid dielectrics shown in Fig. 11, the difference being, however, that in the case of oil the cooling curve shows lower values, due apparently to some physical change caused by the heating.

As the electrostatic field is made more intense, a point is reached at which something of the nature of ionisation of the dielectric occurs, the conductivity increases rapidly and the medium breaks down, the disruption being indicated by the passage of a spark, and in this respect the dielectric behaves as shown by the second portion of the curve for gases in Fig. 1.

Until the actual breakdown occurs there is no visible glow or brush discharge around the electrodes, but the medium is

---

[1] See *Journal of the Institution of Electrical Engineers*, Vol. xcv., No. 202. Paper by Digby and Mellis on "Physical Properties of Switch and Transformer Oils."

considerably agitated where the field is most intense, and the energy expended in this way probably corresponds to that which in gases produces the luminous effects.

As already pointed out, when a dielectric is subjected to alternating electrostatic stresses, a certain amount of energy is expended in producing the molecular distortions, which, in the case of solid dielectrics, shows itself in the form of heat. In the case of liquid dielectrics subjected to such stresses, while some

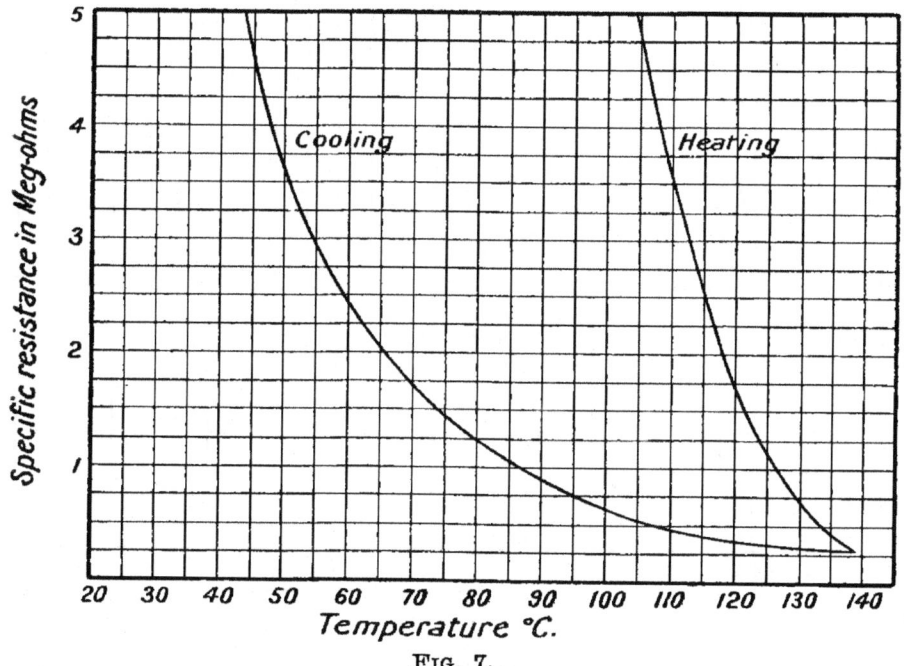

FIG. 7.

rise in temperature probably takes place quite locally at the time of disruption, the convection currents set up as soon as any temperature difference occurs, assisted by the agitation due to the electrostatic field, so circulates the oil as to prevent any marked local rise in temperature such as occurs with solid dielectrics, as noted later.

Spark voltage and spark length.—For very short lengths of gap, the relation between spark voltage and spark length for a given shape of electrode is practically the same for liquid as for gaseous dielectrics, and the curve shown in Fig. 2 is a typical one.

For spark lengths of more than a few mils, the relationship departs from a linear law, and a typical curve is that shown in Fig. 8. In the same figure is shown for the sake of comparison curves for air, liquid air, xylol and mineral oil, the electrodes used in each case consisting of a point and a plane.

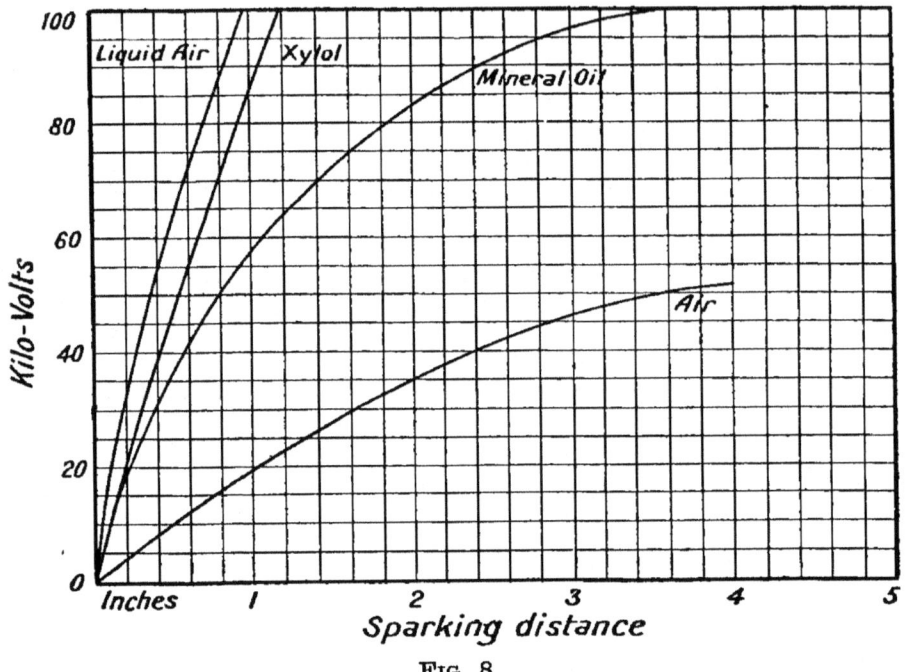

FIG. 8.

Conditions affecting sparking voltage.—As might be antici-pated from a consideration of the distribution of the electrostatic field, the shape of electrodes, as in the case of gases, is an important factor, and needle-point electrodes give a lower break-down voltage for a given length of gap than is the case, for instance, with large spheres. In practice, however, more reliable and consistent results are obtained by using either needle points, or point and plane electrodes, and most research work has been carried out with one of these two types of electrodes. The latter arrangement gives the minimum sparking voltage for a given

C

length of gap. The curves in Fig. 9 show the relation between sparking voltage and spark length for various kinds of electrodes.

The effect of moisture in suspension in the dielectric is very marked. The curve in Fig. 10 shows the reduction in breakdown voltage for definite percentages of moisture. It might be noted that an approximately steady minimum value is obtained when the dielectric becomes saturated, and any further addition of moisture is no longer held in suspension.

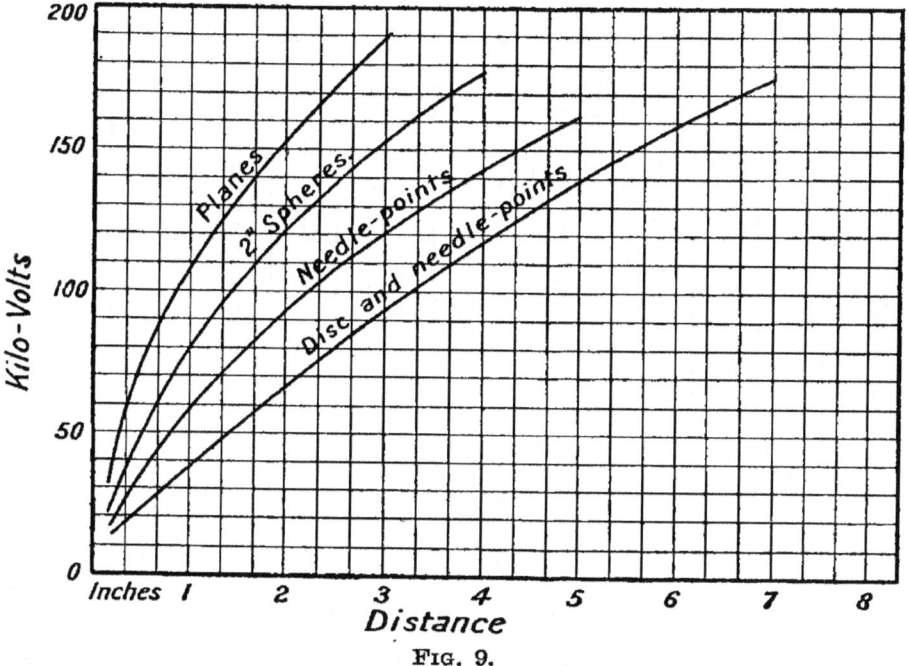

Fig. 9.

Contrary to the effects that will be noted later in connection with solid insulation, the voltage required to break down a given spark length in oil increases with the temperature. Over a range of at least from 15° to 100° C., this increase follows a linear law and appears to be about the same percentage for various oils, this increase being of the order of about ·4 to ·5 per cent. per degree centigrade.

It is interesting to note that as the temperature is reduced, the insulation value falls until the oil commences to congeal and solidify, when the breakdown voltage increases rapidly to a value considerably higher than that of the liquid state. In general, the more viscous the oil, the lower the breakdown value for a given length of gap. The dielectric strength of well-dried commercial oil varies from about 75 to 150 kilovolts per cm.

After the first spark has passed and the same oil is re-tested, the subsequent breakdowns usually require a higher voltage for a similar length of gap. This may be due to the presence of moisture or of foreign particles, which, due to the electrostatic attraction,

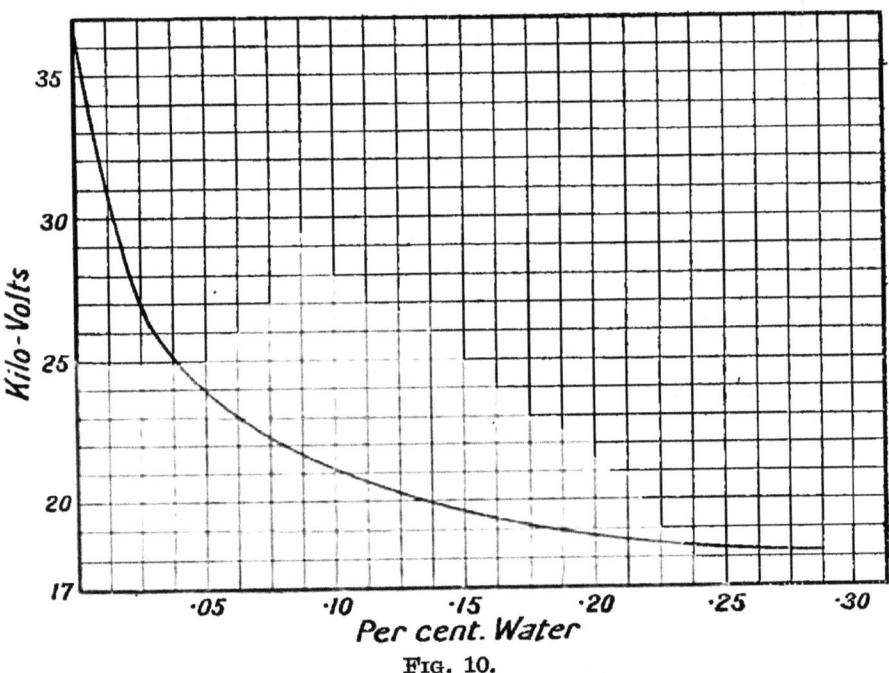

FIG. 10.

line themselves up in the most intense portions of the field and form a bridge, and are dispersed after the first failure. An alternative explanation is that the carbon formed by the passage of the spark when the first failure occurs absorbs the moisture which is almost always present in more or less minute quantities, and thereby improves the insulation value of the oil.

The effect of a head of oil above the electrodes is not very marked, since the density of the oil is increased very little by pressure.

It should be noted that the time lag in effecting the breakdown of liquid dielectrics is much greater than in the case of gaseous dielectrics.

There is a tendency for liquids, when subjected to intense electrostatic fields, to split up into component parts, which group themselves in the order of their respective specific inductive capacities. In the case of commercial oil insulators, however, this does not occur, although—as will be noted in Chapter III.—other chemical and physical changes occur connected with the formation of sediment.

The insulation resistance of an oil under all conditions is so high that for all practical purposes this characteristic can be ignored. From an insulation point of view the breakdown voltage is by far the most important feature, and in this connection the value of drying the oil should be kept in view, since the presence of even minute quantities of moisture may very seriously impair the insulation value.

Solids.

The full-line conduction curve in Fig. 1 applies generally to solid, as well as to liquid and gaseous dielectrics. The first stage of the curve indicates that over a certain range of voltage for given conditions of temperature, the resistance, *i.e.* $\frac{E}{C}$, is more or less constant, and the second stage, *i.e.* the portion beyond the upward bend of the curve, shows the rapid increase in current prior to disruption.

As regards the first stage, the results of some investigations on certain solid dielectrics which had been subjected to the influence of an external ionising agent, indicated that a temporary decrease in resistance occurred, that is to say, the conductivity was increased in a manner analogous to that of an ionised gas. Under practical conditions, however, in dealing with solid dielectrics, the only ionisation to be considered is that due to applied electrostatic forces.

When an alternating potential difference is applied to two conductors separated by a dielectric, a current flows in the circuit thus formed, of a magnitude depending, for a given voltage, frequency, area of electrodes and distance between them, on the property of the dielectric known as its *specific inductive capacity.* This so-called " displacement " or condenser current is apparently the result of some kind of molecular displacement, to produce which requires the expenditure of a certain amount of energy which may be termed the *dielectric loss.*

This loss is frequently referred to as *dielectric hysteresis,* but this term is misleading in that the loss is not a hysteresis loss in the sense in which it is applied to magnetic phenomena.

Taking the case of electro-magnets, in a core that is once magnetised and the magneto-motive force then reduced to zero, a certain amount of the molecular distortion still remains and can only be removed by the application of a counter magneto-motive force. In the case of a dielectric, however, that has been subjected to a difference of potential between its opposing faces, the normal molecular condition quickly readjusts itself if the potential difference between the faces is reduced to zero.

If the voltage between the conductors is raised sufficiently, the disruption of the dielectric takes place and a current flows limited only by the impedance of the circuit. Prior to disruption, in addition to the displacement current, there will be the ordinary conduction current, which is limited in amount by the resistance of the dielectric. The insulation resistance is, as already noted, constant only for a certain range of voltage and for definite conditions of temperature and moisture, and while the conductivity curve shown in Fig. 1 indicates in general the relation between current and voltage, the exact shape of the curve depends on these conditions and on the nature of the material. If the dielectric is very homogeneous and free from moisture, the upward bend of the curve indicating the voltage when disruption commences will be very abrupt. When the material is not homogeneous and is chemically unstable or contains a considerable amount of moisture, the change is much more gradual, this being particularly so when the temperature is raised. It must be remembered, however, that, as with gases and liquids, the two stages in the curve are quite distinct. In the first stage the conductivity is due to conditions already existing in the material, and is more or less independent of the voltage applied, whereas in the second stage the conductivity, while governed by inherent properties of the material, is due to electrostatic stresses produced by the applied voltage.

From this it follows that while a measurement of the insulation resistance indicates that certain conducting conditions exist, it does not afford any indication of the voltage required to bring about the disruption or breakdown of the dielectric, which is the

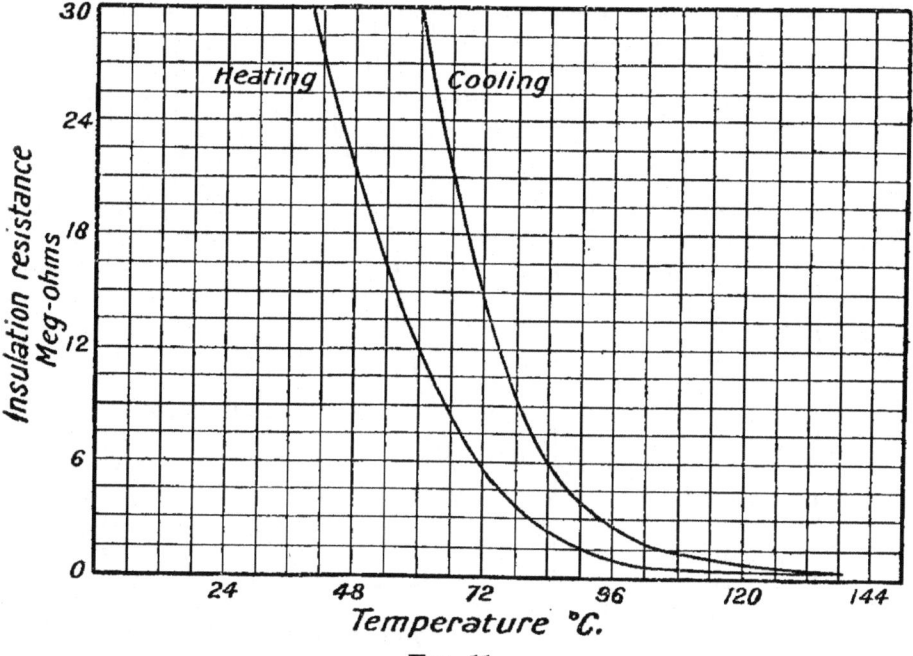

FIG. 11.

essential feature to be considered in dealing with the practical application of insulation.

Factors affecting conduction.—The principal conditions which influence the insulation resistance of solid dielectrics are temperature and moisture. The curve shown in Fig. 11 indicates the effect of temperature on the insulation resistance of cotton covering. The electrodes consisted of two sections, clamped side by side, of a transformer coil which had been thoroughly impregnated with an insulating varnish, and which had between copper and copper only the thickness of impregnated cotton covering on the conductors, amounting in all to about 0·03″. This coil, which had previously been thoroughly dried, was placed in an electrically heated chamber and the temperature varied over a wide range. The temperature of the coils was ascertained by measuring the increase in resistance of the winding.

As will be seen, the insulation resistance rapidly falls as the temperature increases and reaches a minimum value at about

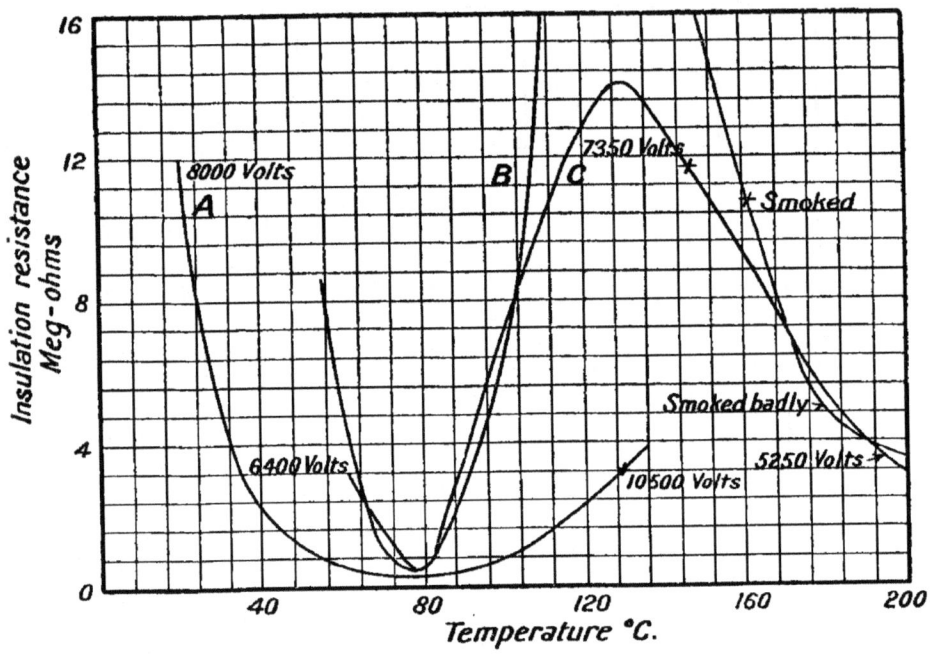

FIG. 12.

A, 0·04″ fishpaper.   B, 0·125″ fullerboard.   C, 0·025″ fishpaper.

140° C. The measurements were repeated as the coil cooled down, and indicate an increase in resistance, which may be accounted for partly by temperature lag and partly by a further oxidation of the impregnating varnish. Fig. 12 shows some characteristic curves for fibrous materials, such as papers and fabrics, on which the temperature has been carried higher than in the tests given in Fig. 11.

From these curves it will be noted that, after reaching a

minimum value at about 75° C., the resistance increases to a very high value.

This increase is due mainly to the expulsion of moisture from the fibres, after which the material begins to change in nature. Ultimately the insulation commences to carbonise and behaves as a high resistance conductor, the resistance then falling rapidly to a very low value. The figures marked on the curve show the voltage required to produce breakdown at the temperatures indicated.

While such curves are generally typical of all insulating materials, the exact temperatures at which the minimum and maximum values of the resistance occurs depend mainly on the area of the electrodes, the amount of moisture the materials contain, and the facility with which it can escape ; also on chemical and physical changes that occur due to the applied temperature or to the conduction current.

Factors affecting disruption.—The principal conditions which have to be considered in connection with the second stage of the conductivity curve, and which to a large extent determine the voltage required to break down the dielectric, may be classified as follows :—

Heating, either internal or external.

Chemical change.

Absorption of moisture.

Nature of surrounding medium.

The extent to which these conditions affect the dielectric strength depends mainly on the nature of the material. If the dielectric is not homogeneous in structure and composition the ultimate breakdown may be expected to be largely due to internal heating. If quite homogeneous and thoroughly dry the breakdown will probably be of the nature of a mechanical disruption. If the material contains oxidisable substances, such as certain varnishes, or if there is moisture present, or the insulation contains matter which is chemically unstable when subjected to electrostatic stress, the breakdown may be the result of a definite chemical change.

In most commercial insulating materials it is highly probable that all these conditions affect to some extent the disruptive voltage, and each will be considered separately more fully.

Heating, either internal or external.—As already pointed out, a certain amount of energy is expended in a dielectric when it is subjected to alternating electrostatic stresses. This energy loss manifests itself in the form of heat, and as the thermal conductivity of all insulating materials is very low, the internal heat thus produced may be sufficient to cause carbonisation before it can escape to the surface and be dissipated.

The dielectric loss depends to a large extent on the temperature of the material and increases rapidly as this is raised. From this it follows that if the external temperature is high the dielectric loss, and consequently the internal temperature tending to produce carbonisation, is also high, so that the voltage required to produce disruption may be much less when the material is hot than when cold. Moreover, if means are provided whereby the internal heat rapidly escapes to the surface and is dissipated, and the temperature at any point in the insulation kept low, the voltage required to produce a breakdown may be raised to an abnormally high amount.

This consideration is exceedingly important when dealing with insulation design, and also in connection with the conditions under which the insulation of electrical apparatus should be tested.

It is probable that in all cases of insulation breakdown internal heating occurs, although failure may not necessarily be due directly to this cause.

The internal heating varies considerably with different materials, but it does not follow that insulation having a higher dielectric loss will break down before one having a lower loss, when subjected to the same electrostatic stress, since the materials may not carbonise or disintegrate at the same temperatures, or their thermal characteristics may be different.

In the case of a few fibrous materials impregnated with certain compounds, it would appear that the voltage required to cause breakdown is to a large extent independent of temperature, but such cases are exceptional.

The conditions affecting the internal loss, and consequently the heating of a dielectric where moisture is not a serious factor, are, for a given external temperature and ventilation, the voltage, specific inductive capacity, and frequency.

If the insulation becomes heated internally the dielectric loss may increase rapidly until disruption occurs. This tendency is clearly indicated by the curves in Fig. 13, which show the relation between the dielectric loss and the time of application of the voltage for varnished paper insulation. The upward bend of the upper curve shows the increase in loss which occurs as the internal temperature increases.

The curves in Fig. 14 show how the loss in certain fibrous

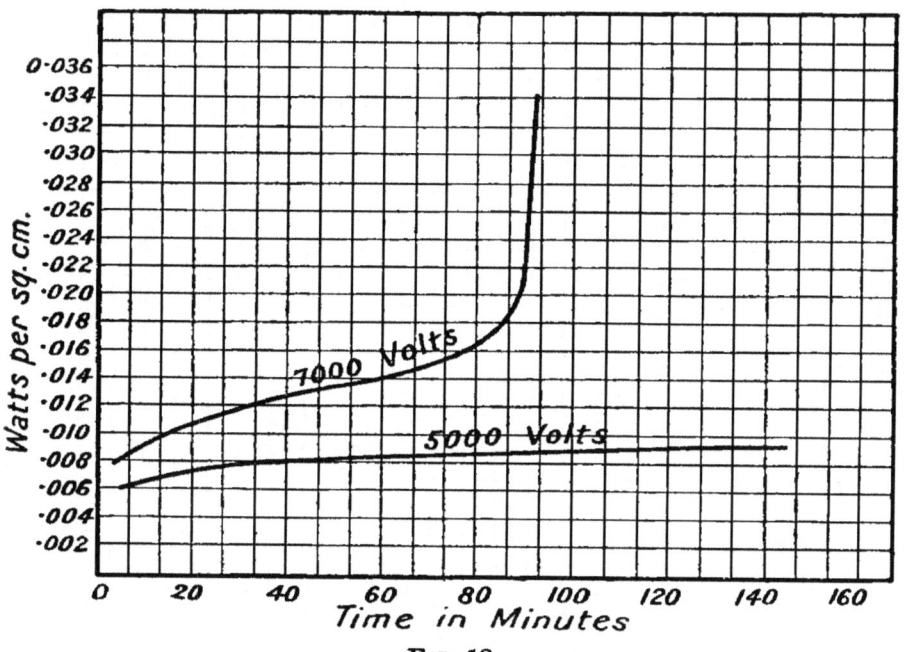

Fɪɢ. 13.

material increases with the frequency and at different temperatures, and Fig. 15 gives the curve of dielectric loss measured on a 10,000 K.V.A. 11,000 volt three-phase generator at various voltages.

The curves in Fig. 16 show the rate of heating in a piece of impregnated asbestos when tested between two electrodes at voltages approaching the breakdown point of the material.

These curves indicate that a steady temperature is attained for certain voltages at which the heating, due to the internal loss, is dissipated at the same rate as it is produced. It will be seen that for these particular conditions a voltage which will produce a steady temperature of about 45° to 50° C., as measured on the surface of the insulation, is the maximum that can for any length of time be safely applied without causing the material to break down. Higher voltages cause the insulation to rapidly heat up until a breakdown occurs. Owing to the nature of the material used for these tests, the heating conditions were very much more

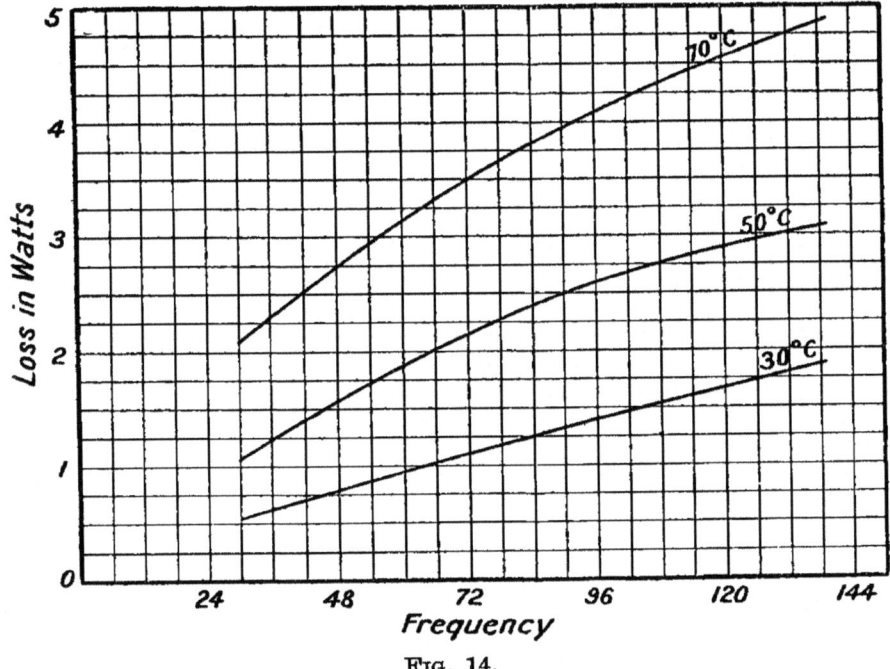

FIG. 14.

marked than with most insulating materials similarly tested. The results, however, afford a very good general idea of the nature of the heating effects produced in most dielectrics when subjected to alternating electrostatic stresses corresponding approximately to the voltage required to break them down.

Seeing how complex are the conditions governing the internal heating of dielectrics, and the difficulties met with in practice in obtaining efficient ventilation, it is impossible to lay down any rules for determining what loss is allowable before danger from internal over-heating is to be feared, and in dealing with insulation from a commercial standpoint, each material must be taken on its own merits and tested as far as possible for failure under the conditions which occur in practice. Probably no solid dielectric when subjected to electrostatic stress has ever been found to break down due to heating without there being also some tendency for mechanical disruption. With many dielectrics the change from the practically non-conducting state to that where breakdown occurs is a

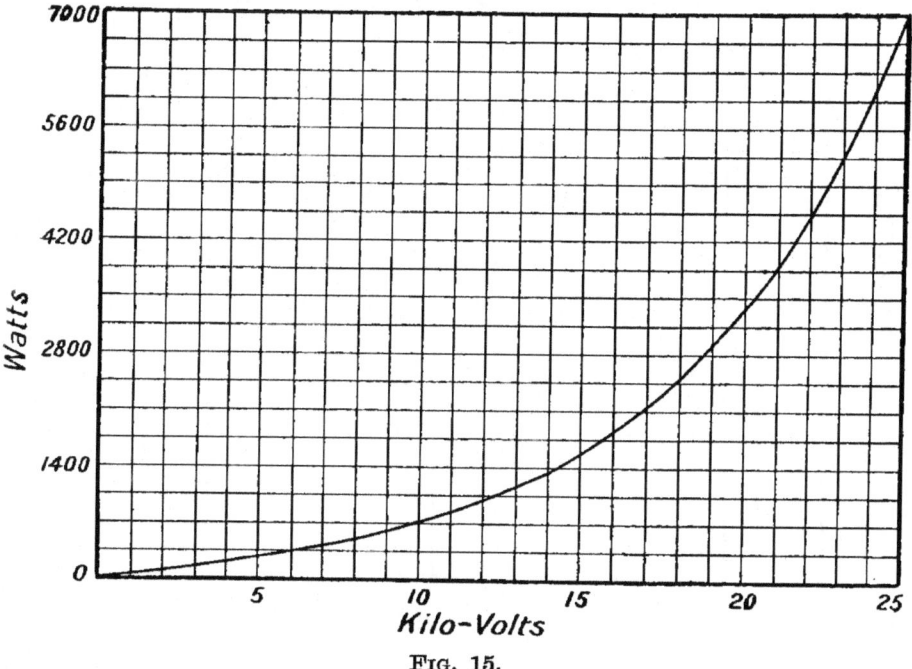

FIG. 15.

very abrupt one and points to something of the nature of a mechanical disruption of the material.

Chemical change.—The effect of an intense electrostatic field on many dielectrics is to cause a chemical change which is usually accompanied by internal heating. In cases where gases are formed during this process, these may become ionised if the field is strong enough, and a discharge through the dielectric similar to that in any ordinary ionised gas takes place.

Practical evidence of breakdown due to chemical change

produced by intense electrostatic stresses will be dealt with in connection with insulation design in Chapter IV.

Absorption of moisture.—When a dielectric which has absorbed moisture is subjected to electrostatic stresses, heating usually results due to the conduction current. This may be sufficient to cause carbonisation, in which case the material breaks down, or the heating may serve to dry out the moisture, after which the conductivity is reduced, and the material cools down. An instance

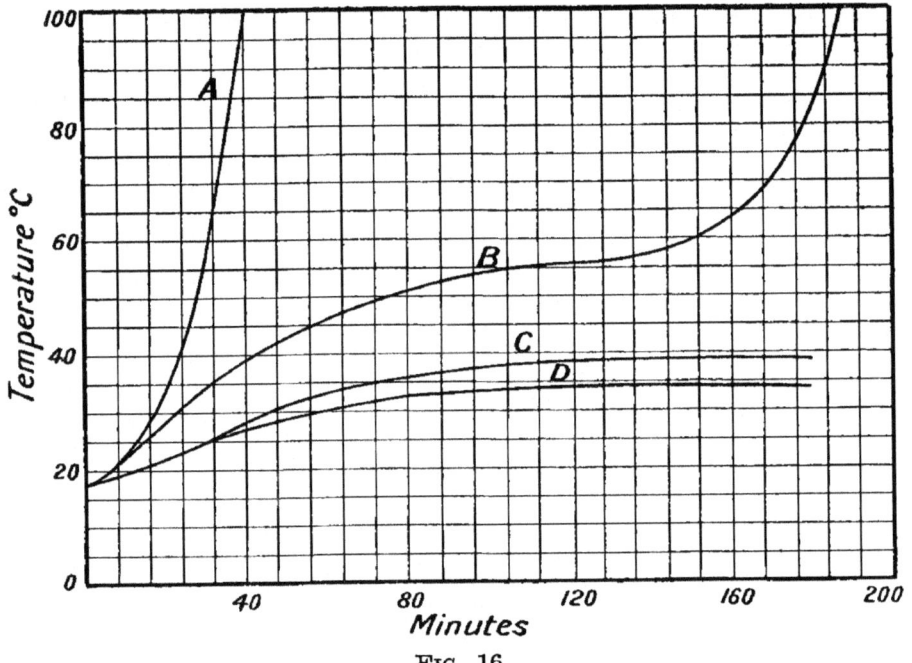

Fig. 16.

A, 10,000 volts.   B, 9500 volts.   C, 9000 volts.   D, 8000 volts.

of this is given in Fig. 17, and shows the results of tests on a sample of fibrous insulation. The curves indicate that when the material is in a normal state a certain voltage causes the temperature to rise sufficiently for the moisture to be evaporated, the material then cooling down. This was checked by repeating the tests on samples which had been well dried, when no serious heating was observed. In these tests the temperatures were measured on the surface of the material, and were consequently much lower than those attained in the interior of the test pieces. If the insulation is such that moisture cannot readily escape, this may reach a gaseous state and become ionised, and for this reason all solids that are to be impregnated or varnished should first be very thoroughly dried, otherwise when heated their dielectric strength will be very much reduced.

Nature of surrounding medium.—In testing solid dielectrics, the

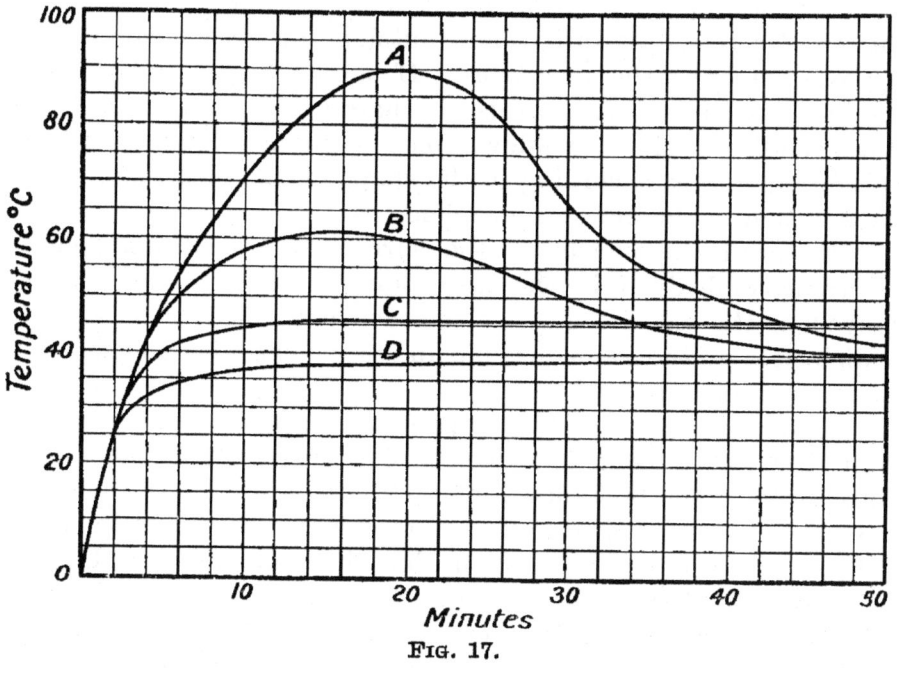

FIG. 17.

A, 15,000 volts before drying.   C, 15,000 volts after drying.
B, 14,000   ,,   ,,   D, 14,000   ,,   ,,

nature of the medium surrounding the test piece may have con siderable influence on the voltage required to produce disruption Taking for example the case of a sheet of insulating materia tested between two flat electrodes. If, as is almost invariably th case with well-dried solid insulation, the voltage required to pro duce disruption is greater than that which would break down th same thickness of air between similar electrodes, a brush discharg forming a conducting envelope around the opposing faces of th electrodes will occur as soon as the electrostatic field set u between the electrodes reaches a certain value, and as the voltage is raised further, the discharge spreads out over a larger area until either the two conducting envelopes thus formed on opposite sides of the test piece extend so near to the edge of the sheet that a breakdown occurs over the surface, or the solid insulation becomes punctured. The effect of this discharge is to tend to heat up the insulation, and thereby reduce its disruptive value, and in a considerable proportion of the tests carried out under these conditions the actual failure occurs outside the area covered by the opposing faces of the electrodes. If the test piece and electrodes are immersed in oil the surface discharge is prevented, and under these conditions the breakdown may occur at a lower or a higher value than in air, according to the shape of the electrodes and the distribution of the electrostatic field.

To annul the effects of the surrounding medium, spherical electrodes embedded in the insulation under test should be employed, or the test piece and electrodes immersed or embedded in a dielectric of the same specific inductive capacity as that of the material under test.

Time element required to produce disruption.—It is evident from the above considerations that a certain time element is introduced in the breakdown of solid dielectrics. If the applied voltage is very much in excess of that which would ultimately be sufficient to produce disruption, this time element, or "lag," will be short, possibly of the order of a small fraction of a second, depending to a large extent on the nature and thickness of the material. The lag will also be influenced by the shape and size of the electrodes, being less as the area of the electrodes in contact with the dielectric increases. This is due chiefly to the fact that with small electrodes the facility for heat and moisture to escape is greater. On the other hand, the cooling effect of the electrodes is less.

When the applied voltage is intermittent and of a very high frequency, such as that due to a condenser discharge, a solid dielectric will withstand many times the voltage ordinarily sufficient to break it down. This, of course, only holds good for occasional discharges, as otherwise the material would quickly heat up due to the energy loss caused by the high frequency.

This property of solid dielectrics of being able to resist momentarily very high pressures is of the utmost importance in commercial working, since it enables electrical apparatus to withstand the high pressure surges liable to occur in practice without requiring abnormal thicknesses of insulation.

The cases occurring in practice where this condition mainly applies are in connection with the surges and high-frequency oscillations at abnormally high potentials. The behaviour of dielectrics under such conditions has been investigated by Hayden and Steinmetz.[1]

Among other conclusions, these investigators determined that the disruptive discharge through dielectrics requires not merely a sufficiency high voltage, but also a definite minimum amount of energy. Prior to failure of the dielectric, where the potential impulse is momentary, the disruptive energy is applied to and absorbed by the dielectric. The disruptive energy required in the case of oil is apparently about thirty times greater than that with air, and for solid dielectrics greater still.

In selecting materials for insulating windings liable to be subjected to momentarily applied impulses, those are most suitable in which a relatively large amount of energy can be absorbed before failure occurs, and in this respect, for instance, certain varnish-treated fabrics are preferable to very well-dried papers.

The power factors of various dielectrics have been fully investigated by Dr. J. A. Fleming and G. B. Dyke, at frequencies of the order employed in telephone service, *i.e.* 900 to 5000 periods per second.[2]

The curves given in Fig. 18 indicate the time required to break down various thicknesses of fibrous insulation at certain voltages, and are representatives of the ordinary run of commercial fibrous insulating materials.

As the thickness of insulation increases, the heat due to the dielectric loss cannot escape readily, hence it follows that the shorter the period of time necessary to produce breakdown, the

[1] See *Proceedings of the American Institute of Electrical Engineers*, Vol. xxix., No. 5, "Disruptive Strength with Transient Voltages."

[2] See *Proceedings of the Institution of Electrical Engineers*, Vol. xlix., No. 215.

more nearly will the voltage be proportional to the thickness of dielectric.

For a given thickness of material the breakdown voltage depends to some extent on the size of electrodes; since, where the electrodes are small, the field between them will not be uniform, and the stress across certain portions of the dielectric may in consequence be much more severe than in the case of a more uniform field produced between larger electrodes; also, as already noted, if there is much discharge around the electrodes, this will virtually

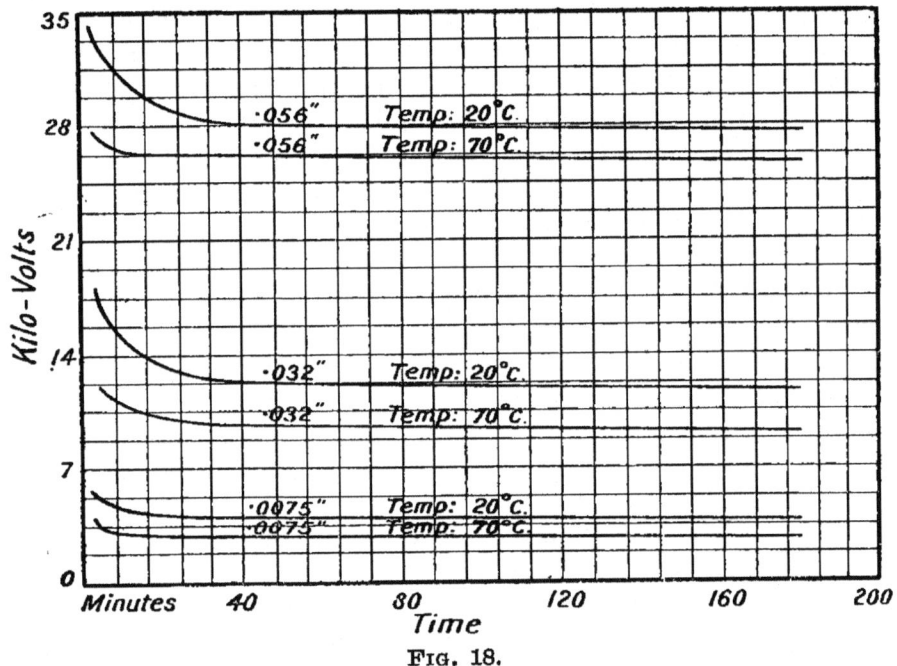

Fig. 18.

increase their effective areas, heat up the surface of the material, and tend to localise the field at the weakest point.

The curves in Fig. 19 show the relation between breakdown voltage and dielectric thickness when breakdown is produced in a definite time at different external temperatures, and can be considered representative for the bulk of fibrous insulating materials when tested under commercial conditions.

Effect of direct and alternating current pressures.—In comparing the electrostatic effects produced by alternating and direct

D

current voltages, as may be expected, dielectrics break down at a lower voltage in the former than in the latter case, since, if the alternating voltage during its periodic cycle varies according to a sine law, its maximum value is about 40 per cent. higher, corresponding to the same R.M.S. value, than that of the direct current voltage. Results of tests on a large number of various materials show that with solid dielectrics a constant voltage, about one and a half to two times the alternating voltage, is required to break down the same thickness of similar materials. This is largely due

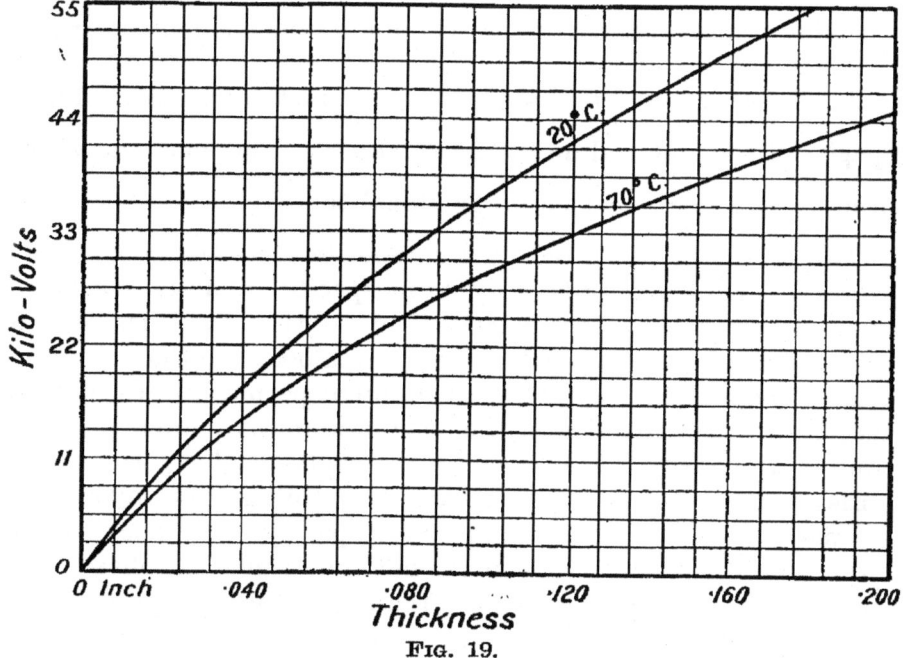

Fig. 19.

to there being no internal heating, owing to the absence of the energy loss which occurs with all solid dielectrics when subjected to alternating electrostatic stress. In gaseous dielectrics the constant voltage requires to be about 40 per cent. higher than the alternating, since in this case the dielectric loss and the effect of heating is very much less marked than in solids.

Behaviour of composite dielectrics.—In the construction of electrical apparatus it is usually impossible to employ entirely homogeneous insulation. For instance, the insulation of a high voltage armature coil may consist of layers of such materials as cotton, paper, mica, and air, and in such a case it is important to consider whether under working conditions the voltage is distributed in such a manner that each material has only to bear that stress which it can safely withstand. In a case of this kind each of the materials may be considered to represent the dielectric of a condenser, so that the total thickness of insulation may be conceived as consisting of so many condensers in series. The potential difference between the surfaces of a condenser into which current is flowing is proportional to $\frac{1}{K}$, where K is the condenser capacity.

Again, K is proportional to $\frac{k}{t}$, where k is the specific inductive capacity of the material and t the thickness. Therefore the voltage borne by any layer will be proportional to $\frac{t}{k}$.

The condition presented by a composite dielectric consisting of several layers of materials of different specific inductive capacities, when placed in an electrostatic field so that the lines of force penetrate the layers at right angles, is analogous to that of several layers of magnetic material having different permeabilities similarly placed. In the latter case the magnetic-motive force per layer required to convey the flux varies inversely as the permeability; similarly in the case of insulation the voltage per layer varies inversely as the specific inductive capacity. As the voltages across the different layers may not be quite in phase, their arithmetical sum may be greater than the voltage applied across the entire dielectric.

The relation $V \propto \frac{t}{k}$ will only hold good when the area of each layer is the same, and also when the electrostatic field is uniform throughout the entire dielectric, which, owing to the irregular shape of the conductors, seldom occurs in practice. This question of voltage distribution across a dielectric made up of several different materials in series is very important when dealing with high tension apparatus, and will be more fully considered in Chapter IV. in connection with the design and insulation of windings.

It will be necessary subsequently to frequently use the term "dielectric strength," which, as already pointed out, refers to that inherent property of an insulating material which tends to enable it to resist breakdown. The term "dielectric strength" is often used where the expression "breakdown voltage" would be more correctly applied, since only the latter refers to certain specific conditions. From the considerations already dealt with in this chapter, it is obvious that the voltage required to produce a breakdown varies with the conditions under which the breakdown occurs, such as temperature, size and shape of electrodes, time during which voltage is applied, and total thickness of material. For this reason, whenever necessary, the controlling conditions will be stated in referring to breakdown voltage.

CHAPTER II

ELECTROSTATIC CONDITIONS IN PRACTICAL WORKING

THE electrostatic stresses produced in the insulation of electrical apparatus under working conditions may be grouped under two heads, viz. (*a*) those due to the internal distribution of potential, *i.e.* the voltage between various parts of the apparatus; and (*b*) those due to the potential difference between these parts and ground.

The internal potential distribution is determined by the electrical design and disposition of the various conducting parts, and, except under abnormal conditions, which will be considered later, to the voltage applied across the terminals of the apparatus.

It must be remembered that in alternating current circuits the voltage as read on a voltmeter is the square root of mean square (R.M.S.) value, and that the maximum voltage attained during each half-cycle is 40 per cent. higher than this when the periodic voltage variation follows a sine law.

In some instances the E.M.F. wave may be considerably distorted and the difference between the maximum and R.M.S. values much more than 40 per cent., but for practical purposes it is sufficient to assume that the voltage curve follows a sine law.

The potential distribution between various portions of a circuit and ground is discussed in the following for the principal conditions met with in practice.

Single-phase circuit, ungrounded.—Fig. 20 (*a*) shows a single-phase circuit comprising a generator, transmission lines marked A and B, and some windings such as those of a motor or transformer connected across the lines at the points C and D.

If the insulation of the line A is the same as that of B as regards capacity and resistance, and the insulation of the generator and windings CD is symmetrical about their centre points, the difference of potential of the points C and D from ground will be the same, one being at some instant above, and the other a similar amount below the ground or zero potential.

The potential of any part of the winding relative to ground potential will lie somewhere between that of the points C and D, and can be ascertained by means of the construction shown in Fig. 20 (*b*). The lengths of the ordinates *ac* and *bd* drawn on opposite sides of the zero potential line *ab* represent the potential difference between the points C and D and ground. As these two points are of equal and opposite potential, it is obvious that at some point between them the potential of the winding will be

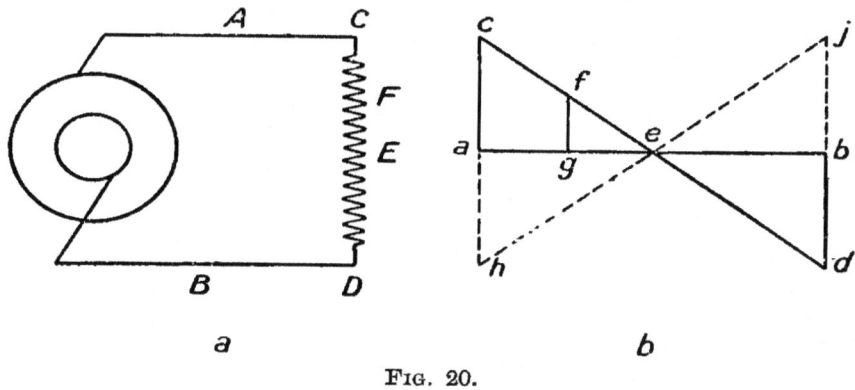

Fig. 20.

zero. On the assumption that the insulation resistance and capacity are symmetrical about the centre points of the generator and windings CD, this point of zero potential will be at E, and may be shown where the line joining the points *c* and *d* cuts the zero potential line at *e*.

The potential at any other point along the winding CD may be represented by the length of the ordinate from a corresponding point on the line *cd* to the zero line *ab*. For instance, the potential of the point F midway between C and E is represented by the length of the ordinate *fg*.

From this it is seen that the potential of the windings is a maximum at C, decreases to zero at the middle point E, and again increases to a maximum at D.

It is therefore evident that, without reducing the margin of safety of the insulation as a whole, the thickness can be graded towards the centre of the winding in proportion to lengths of the ordinates drawn from the line *cd* to *ab*. During a complete cycle the position of the line *cd* will oscillate about the centre *e*, the point *c* occupying various positions along *ch* as the voltage falls to zero and again increases. The maximum value of the ordinates *ac* or *bd* will correspond to half the amplitude of the E.M.F. curve.

Conditions similar to the above hold good for direct current circuits except that the electrostatic capacity of the windings and

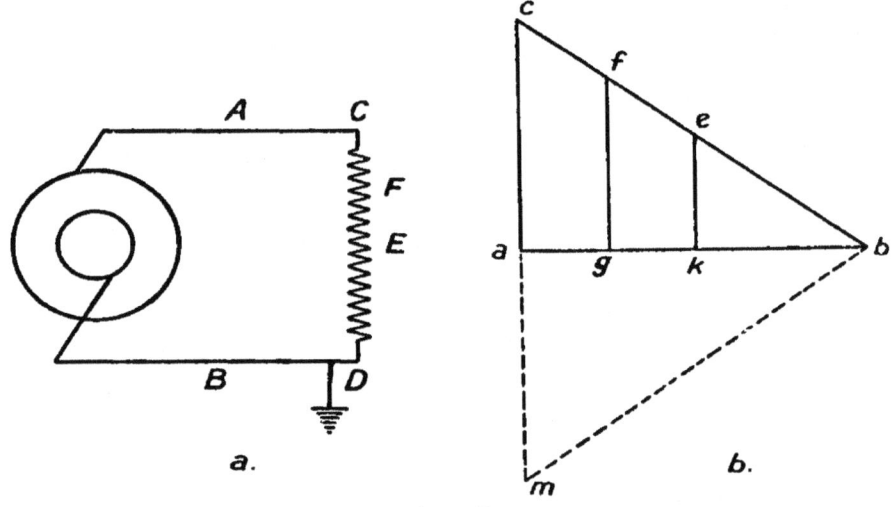

FIG. 21.

lines can be left out of consideration, the insulation resistance only having to be taken into account. The line *cd*, however, in Fig. 20 (*b*) will occupy one definite position, the ordinates *ac* or *bd* corresponding to half the voltage of the circuit.

Single-phase circuit, one side grounded.—Fig. 21 (*a*) represents a circuit similar to that shown in Fig. 20, except that one side of the circuit is grounded at the point D. In this case the distribution of potential between the various points of the winding may be readily seen from the construction shown in Fig. 21 (*b*).

In this case the length of the ordinate *ac* represents the voltage at some instant across the terminals of the winding CD, and, since one terminal is grounded, the potential of the other must be equivalent to the voltage across the circuit.

The length of the ordinate *ac*, drawn above or below the zero potential line *ab*, therefore, represents at some instant the potential difference between the ungrounded terminal and ground. As in the previous case, the potential of any other point of the winding may be determined by drawing an ordinate from a corresponding point on the line *cb* to the zero line *ab*. It will be noted that the middle point of the winding E attains a maximum potential equivalent to half that of the ungrounded terminal and the point F midway between C and E, three-fourths of the potential of the point C.

During a complete cycle the position of the line *cb* will oscillate about the line *ab*, the point *c* occupying various positions along *cm* as the voltage falls to zero and again increases, the potential attaining alternately its maximum value above or below zero.

In a direct current circuit the conditions will in general be the same except that the position of the line *cb* will be fixed. In the case considered the insulation between windings and ground could with safety be gradually reduced in proportion to the potential from a maximum at C to nothing at D.

Considering these two examples from a practical point of view, it is rarely feasible on machines to grade the insulation, as this entails the use of different sizes of slot or unsymmetrical windings. In arranging the insulation of transformer windings, however, advantage can frequently be gained by grading, especially in the case of very high voltages. In no case, however, should the insulation on the centre portion of a winding, unless this point is grounded, be reduced below half the maximum amount, since, should one terminal become accidentally grounded, the stress at the centre portion is increased at once to that originally obtained at the terminals, and on the ungrounded side to double the original amount.

It might here be mentioned that if a single phase transformer is operating with one side of its high tension winding grounded, some part of the low tension winding should also be connected to ground, unless there is a grounded metallic shield between the two windings. If this is not done the two windings act as the plates of a condenser and the potential of the low tension winding will be raised as a whole to the mean potential of the high tension, that is, equivalent to half the voltage applied across the high tension terminals, thereby constituting a source of danger to any one handling any portion of the low tension circuit.

These conditions do not exist when neither side of the high tension is grounded, since the mean potential of the winding is zero, one half being at some instant above and the other an equivalent amount below zero.

Two-phase systems.—In two-phase apparatus there are the following normal conditions to consider :—

If the apparatus contains two distinct windings, as in Fig. 22, and no portion of the system is grounded, the potential distribution

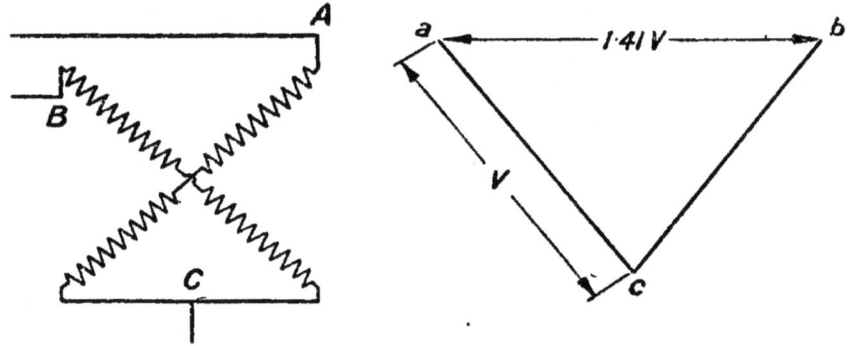

FIG. 22.

is the same as for two ordinary single-phase circuits. If the windings are connected at the middle point this will not alter the electrostatic conditions, and if this point is grounded the case will be the same as for a single-phase circuit with the middle point grounded.

It should be noted that the potential difference between the terminals of different phases is $\sqrt{2}$ of half of that of either phase. If the apparatus is part of a two-phase three-wire system as shown in Fig. 22, the common point being grounded, the conditions will be similar to that of a single-phase circuit with one side grounded. In this case the voltage between the ungrounded terminals is double that in the first case, *i.e.* $\sqrt{2}$ times the phase voltage.

Three-phase systems, delta connected.—Fig. 23 (*a*) represents a three-phase delta connected winding symmetrically insulated and connected to an ungrounded three-phase circuit.

The electrostatic conditions of such an arrangement may be represented by means of a triangle revolving about its centre as shown in Fig. 23 (*b*). The windings represented by the portion of the triangle on one side of the zero potential line passing through

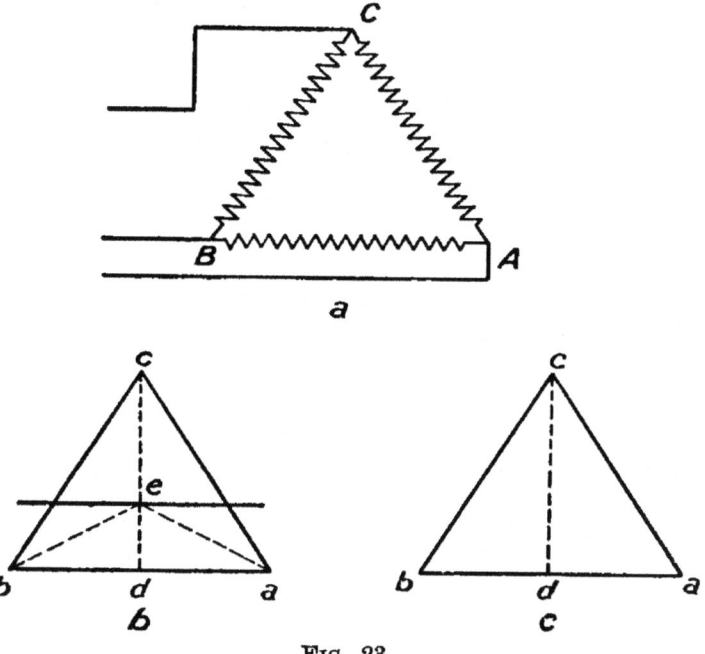

Fig. 23.

the centre will be of opposite potential to those on the other side, the sum of the potentials on either side being equal.

The potential difference between any point of the winding and ground will at any instant be represented by its distance from the zero line, from which it is seen that the maximum potential attained during each half period by the middle point of each phase is $\dfrac{1}{2\sqrt{3}}$ and that of the terminals $\dfrac{1}{\sqrt{3}}$.

If now one terminal of the winding is grounded, for instance, at C, the electrostatic conditions may be represented by considering the triangle *abc* in Fig. 23 (*c*) to revolve about the point *c* which is now at zero potential, from which it will be noted that the maximum potential attained by the middle point of the phase AB and represented by the line *cd* is now $\frac{\sqrt{3}}{2}$ times the line voltage, while the terminals attain a potential equivalent to the full-line voltage. The potential of various points of phases AC and CB will vary from zero at *c* to a maximum at *a* and *b*.

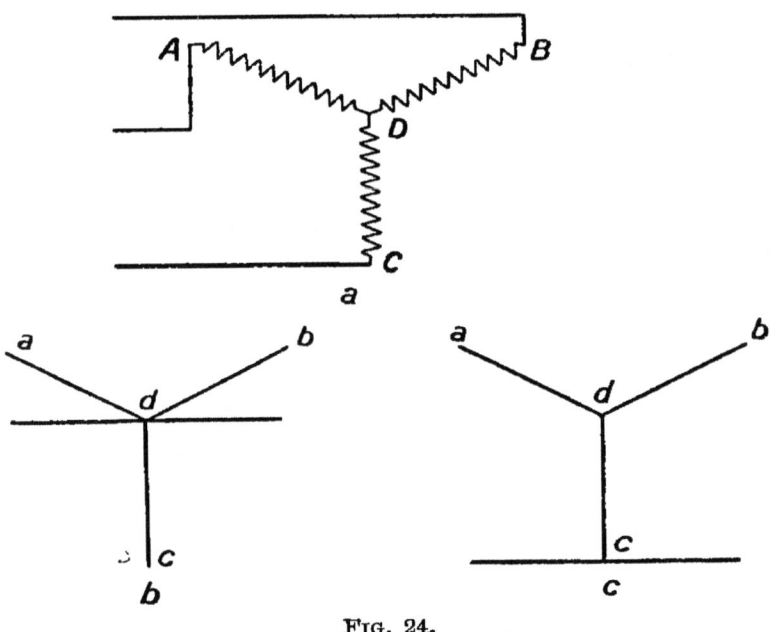

Fɪɢ. 24.

Three-phase systems, star connected.—Fig. 24 (*a*) represents a three-phase star connected winding on an ungrounded system. If the system is symmetrical, the star point D will be at zero potential, and may be grounded without disturbing the electrostatic conditions of the rest of the system.

The potential of the terminals A, B and C will be equivalent to $\frac{1}{\sqrt{3}}$ times the line voltage, and that of any other point on the winding will be proportional to its distance from the zero potential point *d*, see Fig. 24 (*b*). If one phase is grounded, say, at C, see Fig. 24 (*c*), the terminals A and B attain a maximum potential during each half period equivalent to full line voltage, and the maximum potential of any other point will be proportional to the length of the line drawn from that point to C. It will be noted that the star point D, which was previously at ground potential, now attains a maximum potential equivalent to $\dfrac{1}{\sqrt{3}}$ times the line voltage.

Other normal conditions of potential distribution occurring in practice.—Since in practice it is essential to insulate three-phase apparatus so as to provide against the accidental grounding of one of the phases, it follows from the above considerations that very little economy is to be effected by grading the insulation on the various parts of the windings, except in star-connected apparatus with the neutral point grounded. Some advantage may occasionally be gained in this way in designing transformers for three-phase working, but for the reasons already given it is rarely feasible in machines.

Grading of insulation must, in any case, be carried out only after very careful consideration of all the conditions involved. Particularly it must be noted that in the event of an open circuit the distribution of potential will be completely altered. Thus, if one terminal of any single-phase apparatus is disconnected from a circuit, the whole winding—if not grounded at some point—attains the same potential as the line to which it is connected.

In cases where the grounding of apparatus does not occur at the line terminals, or at the neutral point, the general distribution of potential relative to ground can be determined in the manner already considered for certain normal conditions.[1]

In practice very many cases other than those already discussed may arise and increase the stresses on the insulation. For instance, if three single-phase step-up transformers are connected in star and one phase becomes short circuited, this virtually leaves two transformers connected in V with full line voltage across each

[1] For a consideration of the conditions arising on circuits unsymmetrical as regards resistance and capacity, see *Journal of the Institution of Electrical Engineers*, No. 190, Vol. xli., " The Potential of partially insulated systems in relation to the Potential of Earth," M. B. Field.

phase, so that the voltage between lines on the secondary side becomes $\sqrt{3}$ times its original value. Or, under certain conditions, the phase relationship on polyphase systems may become distorted so that the vector sum of the phase voltages is increased possibly to two or three times the normal amount.[1]

Many other conditions of abnormal potential distribution occur in practice and are of considerable importance in comparing the safety of various systems, but, except in a general sense, they do not demand attention from an insulation point of view, since such conditions should be taken care of by suitable protective apparatus rather than by abnormal design of insulation.

Abnormal electrostatic conditions.—In addition to the stresses already considered, the magnitude of which for given conditions may be approximately determined, abnormal rises of potential may occur which originate either internally on the system, or are produced by some external means such as lightning or other atmospheric effects.

The internal disturbances may be due to irregularities in the generator, to critical circuit conditions producing reasonance, to sudden switching or changes of potential resulting in the transference of high potential charges from one point of the system to another.

These conditions are confined mainly to alternate current systems and usually become of practical importance only in the case of high voltage circuits.

Irregularities in the generator in alternate current systems may be merely wave distortion causing a peaked E.M.F. curve, or this curve may contain harmonics of a high frequency.

Resonance.—Pressure rises due to resonance will occur when the self-induction on an alternate current system is balanced by a capacity, *i.e.* when $2\pi n L = \dfrac{1}{2\pi n K}$. To satisfy this condition the frequency must be equal to $\dfrac{1}{2\pi\sqrt{LK}}$. If voltage at this frequency is impressed on such a circuit the current flowing is limited only by the resistance of the circuit and may be many times greater

---

[1] See *Proceedings of the American Institute of Electrical Engineers*, Vol. xxii., Nos. 8 and 9, 1903. J. S. Peck.

than it would be if this balanced condition of self-induction and capacity did not exist. Since the voltage drop across the terminals of a capacity or self-induction is $\dfrac{C}{2\pi n K}$ and $C2\pi n L$ respectively, it will readily be seen that with this excessive current flowing the potential across certain portions of the system may rise to many times the normal. In practice the magnitude of capacity and self-induction are ordinarily such that the natural frequency of the circuit $\dfrac{1}{2\pi\sqrt{LK}}$ is very much higher than that of the generator, so that resonance does not occur, although it may be partially produced if the generator E.M.F. curve contains harmonics of a very high frequency.

Electrostatic disturbances produced by switching.—The line or network and apparatus comprising an alternate current system may be considered to represent a large condenser, there being a certain electrostatic capacity between the various portions of the circuit and between these portions and ground. This condenser is charged up to a certain potential depending on the capacity of the condenser, by current derived from the generating source.

When voltage is suddenly switched on from the generator, a certain time elapses before all portions of the system attain the same potential, and during this period a charge or potential wave travels to the far end of the line, ramifies into the network, and is reflected back, the super-imposition of the return wave tending to raise the potential at the ends of the system or network to nearly double the amplitude of the original wave. During this process a certain amount of energy is absorbed by the system and ultimately the wave motion settles down until a uniform potential is attained at all parts of the system, this uniformity being maintained until disturbed by the switching on, grounding, or short circuiting of some apparatus on the system, or by some external cause tending to suddenly raise or lower the potential at some point.

The effect of switching on a dead circuit or piece of apparatus on to a live alternating current line is equivalent to adding an uncharged condenser to the system, the result being for a charge to flow into the circuit, thereby momentarily reducing the potential of the line at that point. A corresponding charge is applied to the system from the generating source, thereby causing undulations or surges of pressure until a uniform potential is again established. It is conceivable that under favourable conditions the wave motion produced by these static disturbances may result in the formation of " nodes " at various parts of the system where the potential will be very considerably raised above its normal value. Particularly are pressure rises likely to occur at the end of the lines or network where the reflection of waves takes place.

The effects producing during the switching off or the short-circuiting of an alternate current system may be compared with those following the discharge of a condenser. If such a discharge occurs through a non-inductive resistance R, the time taken for the potential difference between. the condenser terminals to fall to zero will be proportional to KR.

During this period the whole of the energy stored in the condenser will be dissipated in the form of heat in the resistance, and

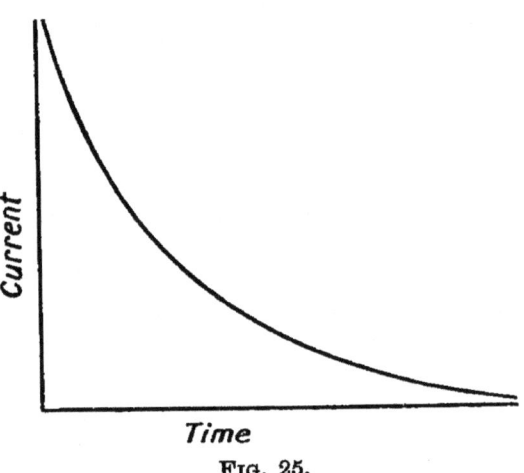

FIG. 25.

the rate of discharge will take the form shown in Fig. 25. If the discharge takes place through an inductive resistance the energy lost by the condenser is absorbed in building up the magnetic field around the inductive circuit and returned again to the condenser, the charge oscillating backwards and forwards until all the energy originally stored in the condenser has been dissipated in heating the resistance of the circuit. The discharge takes the form shown in curve, Fig. 26, the amplitude of each successive oscillation becoming less and less until the potential difference across the condenser terminals becomes zero. The time taken for each complete oscillation is the same, and if the resistance is negligible compared with the reactance, this will be numerically equal to $2\pi\sqrt{LK}$, *i.e.* the number of oscillations per second will be equal to $\dfrac{1}{2\pi\sqrt{LK}}$, this being termed the natural frequency of oscillation of the circuit.

The frequency of these oscillatory discharges will usually be of a very high order, *i.e.* many thousands per second, and often too rapid to be detected by an ordinary oscillograph. If there are windings in the circuit in which the discharge takes place, the impedance offered by a single turn, due to the high frequency, may be so high as to cause the discharge to take place through the insulation or more likely over the air gap separating the turns. This is a contingency which must be carefully guarded against in designing the insulation of high voltage windings.

Electrostatic disturbances produced by atmospheric and similar conditions.—With regard to the static disturbances produced by atmospheric effects, the potential of the apparatus or overhead lines of a system may be raised directly due to a lightning discharge; or a charge on a portion of the lines may be induced by an oppositely charged cloud, which, by discharging to ground, liberates the line charge, which consequently spreads to all parts of the system, the sudden changes of potential occasioned thereby producing waves or surges of the nature already considered.

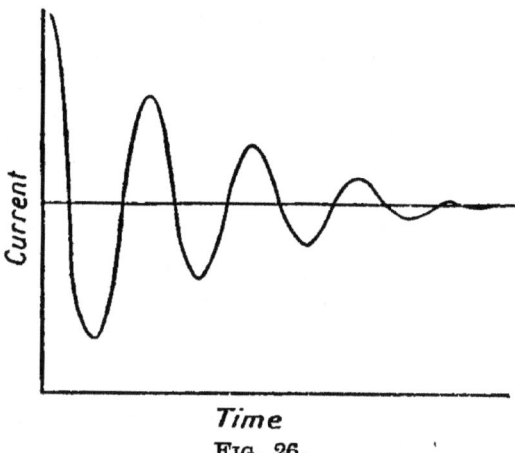

Time

Fig. 26.

High potential charges are also apparently produced on overhead lines by the influence of the wind, and also when the lines are carried over undulating country of considerably varying altitude.

Where transmission lines pass near waterfalls they are liable to be charged from the spray blowing across them; similarly, when steam from an engine condenses and is blown across the lines, the electrical charges in the globules of water have been known to raise the potential of the lines abnormally. These and many other forms of static disturbance have been very fully discussed in many of the papers read in recent years before the American Institute of Electrical Engineers, and need no further reference here.

Effect of external electrostatic disturbances on the internal distribution of potential of windings.—Considering the case of a high potential surge on a transmission line encountering a choke coil or the windings of a transformer connected to the circuit, the progress of the wave is momentarily retarded by the impedance, and a rise of potential occurs at the first turn until sufficient time has elapsed for the charge to pass round or across the coil and thereby release the pressure of the charge which has accumulated. During this momentary retardation the first turn assumes the full potential of the wave, while the rest of the coil is still at its original potential, so that for an instant a very considerable difference of potential may be concentrated across a few turns near the first terminal.

Similar static conditions occur when an uncharged coil is switched on to a live circuit, and momentarily the full voltage of the system may be concentrated across the terminal portions of the winding.

A number of interesting experimental investigations have been carried out by E. J. Berg [1] regarding the potential distribution on alternating current systems when one portion of the system is grounded through an arcing contact, which demonstrate that under such conditions abnormal pressure rises may be produced.

In the foregoing only a few of the very many electrostatic conditions which may occur in practice have been considered. Sufficient has been shown, however, to indicate the lines which must be followed in the insulation design of electrical apparatus.

In regard to the abnormal potential rises which may occur on high tension systems, it is for economic reasons impracticable to

---

[1] See *Proceedings of the American Institute of Electrical Engineers*, Vol. xxvii., No. 5.

insulate apparatus so as to guard against every contingency and abnormal conditions should be taken care of by suitable protective apparatus. In practice, however, there is always the liability of the static disturbance being passed on in a modified degree to the apparatus which is intended to be protected, and the effects of this will be dealt with fully in Chapter IV., in connection with insulation design.

CHAPTER III

INSULATING MATERIALS

THE materials most widely used for insulating purposes are of an organic nature, originating mainly from living vegetable organisms. While such materials alter in character to some extent during the various processes of manufacture, they never become physically inert, but are subject to continual change tending ultimately to disintegration. The rapidity of the change depends on the nature of the materials and the conditions to which they are subjected. For instance, many insulating materials remain fairly stable for almost indefinite periods at ordinary temperatures, whereas others, especially those which readily oxidise, deteriorate rapidly. In all cases physical and chemical changes are hastened as the temperature increases.

The few inorganic materials, such as mica, suitable for the insulation of windings, require for their application the use of organic compounds, and their ultimate insulation value depends largely on the permanence of these latter materials.

The effect of heating on insulation is generally to produce brittleness and eventually carbonisation, which may cause a failure, especially in the case of running machinery where the windings are subjected to vibration and to other mechanical stresses set up under operating conditions.

As already pointed out in Chapter I, heating, in the case of solid insulating materials, produces a considerable reduction in dielectric strength. While, in this way, the margin of safety may be reduced, the insulation value does not usually become permanently impaired—except when definite chemical changes take place—until the temperature is high enough to render the materials useless from a mechanical point of view.

The rating of electrical machinery is to a large extent dependent on the temperature to which it may be safely subjected without deterioration of the insulation taking place, and the advent of a material, otherwise suitable, which would permanently withstand a temperature very much higher than that at present considered permissible, would materially cheapen the production of many types of electrical apparatus. On the other hand, increased temperature limits would tend to produce trouble due to increased expansion and contraction, and these factors would have to be taken into consideration.

The commercial insulating materials at present available differ so considerably in insulating, moisture and heat-resisting properties, that in the insulation of a single piece of apparatus many different materials must be used, each of which is required to fulfil some particular operating requirements. While it is desirable, however, to use, as far as possible, the very best insulation for each particular shop requirement, it must be borne in mind that the multiplication of materials should be kept as low as possible to avoid tying up too much capital in stock as well as to avoid the extra clerical labour in recording stocks, and further to diminish the loss due to deterioration. Having once determined, as the result of experience, the suitability of a particular material for some one class of work, that material should be considered as standard, and possible substitutes compared with it from time to time.

In dealing with the properties of various materials consideration will be given only to those characteristics which render them specially suitable for particular uses, and in general they will be discussed in the order of their widest range of utility.

PAPER.

Paper is one of the materials most widely used in insulation work on account of its general adaptability and cheapness. In all cases where a thin sheet insulation is required that is both flexible and hard, paper is the most suitable, being preferable to other sheet materials such as thin fibres or fabrics, the former of these being of unreliable composition, insufficiently flexible, and too expensive, while the latter are unsuitable for mechanical reasons.

Preparation of paper.—The insulating papers most generally used are prepared from the fibres of various grasses and plants or from wood pulp, while the more expensive qualtities made from cotton and linen fibre are also sometimes used. The essential constituent of paper is cellulose, which has the same chemical composition for all papers, but which differs in structure according to the characteristics of the fibre from which it is produced. Plant fibre is converted into cellulose by the action of strong alkalies, and the toughness and flexibility of the paper produced depends largely on the length and nature of the fibre, which differs with each kind of plant or wood. For instance, the paper produced from short wood pulp fibre is brittle and easily torn, whereas the long rough manilla fibre yields a tough and flexible paper. A microscopic examination of paper shows its fibrous structure, and serves to indicate the nature of the fibre from which the paper is made. Such an examination is of particular value in distinguishing papers prepared from fibre such as manilla from the cheaper wood-pulp productions.

In the manufacture of most papers a considerable percentage of loading, such as china clay, calcium sulphate, and other inert mineral matter is used, and to further improve the surface and render the paper less porous, a sizing of vegetable or mineral solution is sometimes applied.

Papers tend to deteriorate with age, as can be noted for instance from the brittleness and discoloured appearance of old documents. This ageing tendency is much more marked in some cases than in others, and is more rapid the higher the temperature to which the paper is subjected. The durability of a paper is, to a large extent, dependent on the amount of the various chemicals used in reducing the plant fibre, which remains in the paper after treatment; on the activity of the vegetable acids inherent in the fibre, and on the chemical action of the bleaching, loading and colouring matter used. Provided that it is chemically inert, a certain amount of loading matter is not deleterious, and may even prove an advantage in rendering the paper less springy and easier of application.

With some papers a good surface may be obtained by compressing the sheets, and very heavily rolling or calendering them, although this tends to stiffen and render them somewhat brittle.

Limitations to the use of paper for insulating purposes.—The flexibility of paper, to a very large extent, depends on the amount of moisture it contains. Normally, papers contain from about 7 per cent. to 12 per cent. of moisture, and as this is dried off, the fibres which all lie lengthwise in the sheet parallel to its surfaces, tend to contract, thereby being put into a state of tension, and causing the paper to become very brittle. A paper heated to a little over 100° C., almost entirely loses its flexibility, but recovers it as moisture is reabsorbed on cooling down, provided no appreciable oxidation has taking place during the heating process.

When paper is heated it contracts, due to the drying out of the fibres, and continues to do so until all moisture is expelled. If the temperature is carried much above the boiling point of water, carbonisation commences, and at a temperature of from 125° to 140° C., if freely exposed to air, the material quickly becomes so brittle as to be useless for insulating purposes. Until entirely carbonised, however, the dielectric strength is maintained, and, if anything, somewhat increased after all moisture has been driven off.

It will thus be seen that the use of paper as an insulator is limited in two ways, *i.e.* by moisture and carbonisation. Normally its insulating value is comparatively low owing to the inherent moisture, whereas if this is removed by drying the material loses to a large extent its flexibility, and its usefulness is thereby impaired from a mechanical point of view. For ordinary conditions of service, however, as in machine insulation, it is possible to dry the material and obtain a fair insulation value, and at the same time retain sufficient flexibility to enable it to withstand the vibration and mechanical stresses due to operation. Since papers carbonise at temperatures above about 125° C. their use as insulators must be seriously restricted in the future if higher working temperature limits become general.

When high insulating value is required papers must be impregnated with an insulating varnish or compound. The methods of treating papers and the materials used for this purpose will be separately dealt with.

Practical applications.—Papers are largely used in insulation work to afford mechanical protection to other insulations, as, for instance, in the form of slot linings, as backings for mica, and for such purposes as core disk insulation. In such cases they do not require any special treatment to improve their insulating properties.

For the more mechanical functions, the cheaper wood-pulp papers are quite suitable, and a fair amount of inert loading matter is not objectionable.

For general insulating purposes papers are required in thicknesses varying from about 0·001 inch to 0·125 inch. The thinnest paper is used for the insulation of armature and transformer punchings, and the cheapest paper obtainable in the thickness required is generally suitable, provided it is strong enough to be applied satisfactorily. For thicknesses up to about 0·010 inch a fair degree of flexibility and toughness is desired, as such papers are usually required for wrapping round windings, and are liable to a considerable amount of handling. In the heavier kinds, where flexibility is not so essential, a heavily calendered paper may be employed to advantage.

Storage of papers.—In storing papers the storeroom should be kept at a comparatively low temperature so as to avoid embrittling due to drying out and to oxidation, and the paper should be protected from the chemical effects liable to be produced by strong sunlight.

Selection and testing of papers.—Whenever possible it is desirable to investigate new papers chemically and by means of a microscopic examination, and further, a measurement of the dielectric loss when built up in the form of a condenser of certain standard dimensions affords valuable information as to the quality of the material. In connection with cable work, where the quality of paper used may be an all-important consideration, facilities for such investigations are usually available. In more general electrical manufacturing work, however, where paper does not fulfil such an important function, such means are not usually at hand, and materials are tested by submitting them to close scrutiny, and by observing their behaviour when subjected for a period of time to conditions similar to, but more exacting than, those occurring in practice. That is to say, an endeavour is made to employ those means which produce in a few days or weeks the effects likely to occur after years of service. Such tests can be made to yield satisfactory results if carried out with reasonable care and close observation.

As already noted, the actual insulation value of paper itself is of comparatively little importance, and in cases where high insulating properties are required, paper is employed merely to absorb and support the film of the oil or varnish which constitutes the real insulating medium. When, therefore, papers are to be selected for this purpose, test samples should be treated with the oil or varnish according to the usual manufacturing process, and then subjected to breakdown voltage, to the effects of prolonged heating, and to tests for mechanical strength.

Similarly with plain untreated materials, drying tests afford a good guide as to the behaviour of the insulation when subjected to the temperatures met with in practice. Tests of this kind might be carried out to advantage at a temperature of, say, 80° C., which may be taken as approximately the average operating temperature of windings. On the other hand, the period of testing under those conditions would be unduly prolonged, and for comparative purposes, therefore, it is convenient to employ a temperature of about 100° C. At this temperature most papers when freely exposed to the air become brittle enough to break when bent through 180° in about 250 to 500 hours.

For such tests a convenient form of heater is one having a capacity of about six cubic feet, which is either steam or electrically heated. The top and bottom of the heater should be perforated so as to allow the maximum amount of air to circulate through it. In order to obtain a uniform temperature the source of heating must be kept constant, and by screening or plugging some of the perforations, the temperature required can be experimentally fixed. The test pieces must be supported vertically, and the resistance or steam coil should be placed near the bottom of the heater.

As already noted, paper that has become embrittled due to being dried excessively may recover its flexibility if allowed to reabsorb moisture from the air. The drying, however, may be carried to a point beyond which no such recovery will take place.

For most purposes the amount of loading matter used in papers is not of very great importance, provided this does not seriously interfere with the absorption of the treating oil or varnish, with the flexibility, rate of deterioration with temperature, or with the breakdown voltage the material will withstand. A certain amount of loading material may even be advantageous in these respects. In any event the deleterious effects, if any, can be readily ascertained from the ageing and other practical tests already referred to, and for the purpose of comparison an ash test should be made by burning a known weight of paper and determining the percentage of mineral residue obtained. Since papers are purchased by weight, the amount of loading may have some bearing on cost.

With a little experience, a close inspection and handling of paper is sufficient to give a very good idea as to toughness and freedom from flaws, although more accurate comparisons can be made by measuring the tension along and across the fibre and by bending the material around pins of various diameters.

Impurities and foreign matter in paper may often be readily detected by rendering the material semi-transparent by moistening with light machine oil.

In the case of thin sheets of paper minute pin holes are often found, and can be readily detected in a strong light. Such faults, however, are not usually of much importance, especially where the material is to be employed in a treated condition.

In connection with paper of the manilla class, a serious trouble may be introduced by the presence of small metallic particles. Such papers are frequently prepared from ropes that have been used for slings and rope drives, and in which fine particles of iron have become embedded. Such faults can best be detected by breakdown voltage tests. For this purpose it is convenient to lay the sheet on a flat metal plate connected to one terminal of a testing transformer, the other terminal being joined to a metal feeler which can be passed over the sheet on the end of an insulating handle. By raising the voltage of the testing transformer in small steps, any weaknesses are readily detected. Papers tested in this way in their normal undried condition should stand from 200 to 400 volts per mil of thickness, and when dried, at least 50 per cent. higher than this.

The percentage of moisture can be readily ascertained from the loss in weight that occurs in drying; or the hygroscopic nature may be investigated by exposing the paper to moisture vapour until the maximum amount of absorption has taken place. It will usually be found that in a material free from deliquescent salts, the better the quality mechanically, the more moisture it is liable to absorb. Such tests are mainly of use in affording a comparison between the properties of a sample and that of a paper known by experience to be satisfactory.

Under normal service conditions paper is liable to dry out considerably and shrink, and this may be an important consideration in the case of rotating windings particularly for high-speed work. Due also to the centrifugal force in running machinery, and in some instances on account of the weight of conducting portions on stationary parts, the insulation may be subjected to considerable mechanical pressure. The behaviour of insulating materials under these conditions is dealt with at the end of this chapter.

Specification of tests.—In addition to the tests made on new samples of material, it is highly desirable to test from time to time the quality of the regular consignments, and for this purpose the necessary observations and tests are summarised as follows :—

General characteristics.

(*a*) Colour.

(*b*) Surface—matt or glossy.

(*c*) Thickness taken over as large an area as possible. On materials of 0·010 thick and under, gauge two thicknesses and halve the result.

(*d*) Maximum variation in thickness over an area of not less than 1 square foot expressed as a percentage of the average thickness.

Breakdown voltage.—Make a number of careful tests on the voltage required to produce breakdown between flat circular electrodes of one square inch having slightly rounded edges and weighing about 8 ozs. The voltage should be raised slowly at a rate of about 250 volts per second until breakdown occurs. Wherever possible tests should be made on a number of test samples cut from different parts of the sheet.

Percentage of moisture.—Weigh a convenient sized sample and place in a heater maintained at a temperature of 100° C. for four hours. Reweigh and dry for two hours longer, repeating the drying and weighing until a steady value is obtained. Express the loss in weight as a percentage of the original weight.

Shop tests.—Have sample sheets used in the shop under the same commercial conditions as the material which it is intended to replace, and note whether it can be handled with the same facility, amount of waste, etc.

Commercial insulating papers.—The following table gives particulars of some of the trade papers used for insulating purposes :—

Kind.	Thickness.	Approximate price per lb.	Approximate weight per sq. ft.	Remarks.
Core Disc .	0·0015″–0·002″	2·5d.	0·07 oz.	Cheap paper for insulating laminations.
Bond . .	0·004″	2·0d.	0·182 ,,	Used as a support for mica for coil wrappings.
Red-rope .	0·005″	2·5d.	0·356 ,,	Used as a support for mica for coil wrappings where a tougher paper than bond is required. Also when varnished for transformer insulation.
Manilla .	0·006″	6·0d.	0·4 ,,	Used for armature coil wrappings when good quality tough paper is required.
Presspahn .	0·007″–0·125″	3·75d.	0·7–13·5 ozs.	Used treated for slot linings and whenever a strong sheet insulation is required.
Pressboard	0·020″	4·0d.	2·25 ozs.	Tougher than presspahn. Used for slot linings where a strong and fairly good insulation is required. Also as a mechanical protection for thinner sheet insulating materials.
Leatheroid and Fish-paper.	—	—	—	See Fibres.

TAPES.

The tapes ordinarily used for insulating purposes may be classified under three heads, comprising those woven from cotton or silk and untreated, those woven from cotton and treated with an insulating varnish or cut from treated fabrics, and those cut from rolls of fabric which have been loaded with a rubber compound.

Untreated tape.—The first variety is employed largely where the tape can eventually be impregnated with an insulating varnish or compound, such as on armature and field windings, and requires to be fairly strong, closely woven, uniform in thickness, free from

FIG. 27.   FIG. 28.

starch or glaze, and, where used as a finishing tape, as free from nap as possible.

There are two types of tapes belonging to this class which may be termed "straight" and "webbed." The former has the longitudinal threads (filler) and the threads running the width of the tape (warp) crossing at right angles as shown diagrammatically in Fig. 27. In the case of webbed tapes the threads cross on the bias as shown in Fig. 28. The webbed tapes are much stronger, do not stretch readily, and also retain their strength to a greater extent after treating with varnish than is the case with straight tapes.

These tapes often contain bleaching and chemical matter, such as chlorine, which may, in conjunction with the insulating varnish or compound with which they are eventually impregnated, attack the copper. In the case of very fine wire windings this action may be sufficient to cause open circuits, but, ordinarily, while the insulating material becomes discoloured, its insulating value is not seriously impaired.

The presence of harmful chemical matter can best be ascertained by the application of the tape and insulating varnish or compound to test samples of windings, and any action carefully noted after the materials have been submitted to a temperature of about 80° C. for from one to ten days.

The adaptability of the tape can be ascertained by applying it to an irregularly shaped coil and noting the "lay" at sharp bends. A suitable tape should yield somewhat in both length and breadth so to give a smooth surface. This test will also indicate whether the tape has the requisite strength for handling. The exact determination of the stretch and tensile strength is useful in comparing in these respects the quality of a sample with that of a standard tape, and while a light tension testing machine is useful for this purpose, it is quite sufficient to employ a windlass arrangement and spring balance.

Untreated tapes are very hygroscopic, and the test for absorption of moisture can be made as in the case of papers. It might be noted, however, that all the moisture may be removed from a good quality of tape without seriously impairing its mechanical properties owing to the more thorough interweaving of the fibres.

In a general way all the tests already referred to in connection with papers apply to untreated tapes.

Varnish-treated tapes.—The second variety of tapes mainly comprises those cut from Empire Cloth or similarly treated insulating material. Such tapes are chiefly employed on windings which cannot economically or conveniently be taped with plain tape and impregnated. These tapes, however, are not very elastic and do not lie very well on an irregular surface, although this property can be improved somewhat by cutting the tape on the bias, *i.e.* so that the threads run diagonally across the strip, as shown diagrammatically in Fig. 29. Too much tension must not be applied to tape cut in this way, as otherwise the fabric will stretch more than the varnish film, causing the latter to break, thus seriously reducing the insulating value. Such material can best be tested by taping an irregularly shaped coil, noting the lay of the surface and testing for insulation value by applying voltage.

Attempts have been made to impregnate ordinary plain tape with an air-drying varnish or compound, but the results have not been very satisfactory, the tape usually being very poorly filled or having a poor finish.

Rubber-impregnated tapes.—The third class, known as "friction" tape, is used mainly for jointing purposes, or as an outside protection for treated tapes. While having a high insulation value, it is not very suitable for general insulating purposes, as it quickly perishes owing to the deterioration of the rubber compound, especially when subjected to temperatures such as occur on machines under normal conditions, and when freely exposed to air and sunlight. Such tapes should not be used in contact with copper, as the sulphur contained in the rubber compound sets up harmful chemical action.

Fig. 29.

Specification of tests.

General Characteristics.

Colour.

Straight, bias or webbed.

Whether evenly woven.

Threads per inch in the warp and in the filler.

Treated or untreated. If treated, the nature of the treatment.

Thickness—a number of measurements being made. It is best to gauge two thicknesses together and take half the result.

Maximum variation in thickness from the average of not less than five measurements.

Breakdown and mechanical tests.—In the case of treated tapes, apply a layer, overlapping each turn one-half the width of the tape, to a round metal rod of about 1 inch diameter and test for breakdown voltage. Repeat tests at intervals of twenty-four hours after exposing test piece to a temperature of 100° C. in a well-ventilated heater, continuing this ageing for ten days.

In the case of untreated tapes, these should be applied in
a similar manner to a metal rod and dried and treated
with varnish or compound in the same way as will be
employed in practice. Breakdown and ageing tests
should then be made as in the case of treated tapes.

Tests for tensile strength and stretch should be made.

In all these tests comparison should be made with standard
materials, and during the ageing tests the brittleness
of the materials should be tested by handling.

Moisture.—A weighed sample of not less than 6 yards in
length should be dried in a heater for four hours at
100° C. and reweighed. Drying to be continued and the
weight taken every two hours until all the moisture
is expelled, the difference between initial and final
weights being expressed as a percentage of the former.

Shop tests.—Working samples should be applied as in the
ordinary manufacturing processes, and adaptability, waste,
variation in quality, etc., noted.

Commercial insulating tapes.—The following table gives some
particulars of ordinary commercial insulating tapes :—

Kind.	Thickness.	Width.	Approximate price per gross yds.	Remarks.
			s. *d.*	
Taffeta . .	0·003″–0·005″	{ ¼″ ⅜″	1 6 3 6	} Used for taping small fine wire windings.
Cotton . .	0·006″–0·008″	{ ¾″ 1½″	1 4 2 5	} Used for taping heavy coils.
Webbings. .	0·017″–0·020″	{ 1¼″ 2″	3 4 5 0	} Used for heavy coils for mechanical protection.
Empire . .	—	—	—	See Fabrics.
Para . . .	0·030″–0·040″	¾″	7 9 per lb.	Used for insulating joints.
Friction . .	0·010″	1″	1 9 per lb.	—

VARNISHES AND IMPREGNATING COMPOUNDS.

Insulating varnishes may be classified as follows :—

A. Varnishes for impregnating windings.

B.   „   „ treating papers and fabrics.

C.   „   „ cementing purposes.

D. Finishing varnishes.

Under Class A will also be considered impregnating compounds which, while differing very much in their nature from varnishes, fulfil in many respects the same functions.

Class A. Varnishes for impregnating windings.—These varnishes are used to fill the coverings of windings, thereby increasing their insulating value and rendering them moisture resisting. Such varnishes should also withstand the action of hot oil, this being of course essential for oil-immersed windings. They should give a smooth finish and uniform thickness of coating. The varnish film should be sufficiently flexible to withstand the mechanical stresses and expansion and contraction of the windings when in service and should retain its flexibility with age.

It is very important that these varnishes should have no corrosive effect on copper, or destroy the fibrous nature of insulating coverings, that is to say, they should be as free as possible from inherent vegetable and fatty acids, such acids often becoming active during the process of oxidation of the varnish especially at high temperatures.

Oxidising varnishes.—Of the various varnishes of class A, those most largely used are composed of linseed oil with a resinous base of copal or other fossil gum. Such varnishes possess high dielectric strength and are, when thoroughly oxidised, very nearly impervious to moisture and oil. They contain inherent vegetable acids which cannot be eliminated without impairing some desirable feature, but as a rule the corrosive effect of such varnishes is not serious, except perhaps on very fine wire windings, wire of, say, 0·02 inch diameter and smaller. Further, this corrosive action appears to cease almost entirely when the varnish becomes dry.

The green discoloration often noticed on windings impregnated with these varnishes occurs during the drying process, and once the varnish has hardened no further action takes place. In practice this discoloration is not found to be in any way harmful.

Linseed oil varnishes are dried, first by the expulsion of the volatile solvent, then by the oxidation of the oil and gum. During the latter process a film is formed on the surface which renders the complete oxidation of the varnish beneath a very slow process, so that as a whole its flexibility is retained for a very long time.

To hasten the oxidation a certain amount of mineral drier is used in manufacture, the amount depending on whether an air drying or baking varnish is required. The former usually is made to dry in from ten to fifteen hours and the latter when baked at a temperature of about 100° C. in from twelve to twenty-four hours. As a general proposition it may be considered that the longer these varnishes take to dry the more permanent they will be.

The fact that it is impossible to absolutely arrest the oxidising process, and that as this proceeds the varnish covering tends to become brittle, has been held by makers of competitive varnishes to be a very serious defect. In practice, however, if judgment is used in application, no great trouble need be anticipated in this respect. A further criticism has been made that the inherent acids in these varnishes constitute a source of danger, but here again experience has shown that insulation failures traceable to this cause are negligible. Some danger, however, may exist in high voltage apparatus if varnish is present that has been very improperly dried, an intense electrostatic field tending to produce under such conditions destructive heating and chemical action.

Another type of oxidising varnish contains linseed oil and an asphaltum base. It has in general the same characteristics as the clear linseed oil-gum base varnishes, but takes about twice as long to dry. It retains, however, its flexibility for a longer period, but is somewhat less oil resisting and is of lower dielectric strength.

Non-oxidising varnishes.—There are a number of non-oxidising varnishes which are prepared by reducing an asphaltum or gum base with a suitable spirit solvent. The advantage of such varnishes is that windings impregnated with them can be dried throughout their mass, whereas with the oxidising varnishes, only the outside film is readily dried.

Shellac varnish, which is the most widely used of the non-oxidising varnishes, is particularly suitable for the insulation of small low voltage windings, such as instrument coils, where the temperature variation is small and there are no mechanical stresses to be considered. This varnish, while possessing very many inherent defects and while quite useless where flexibility is required, is convenient inasmuch as it dries quickly, has good binding properties, and can be baked so as to yield a very satisfactory finish.

Heat dissipating varnishes.—Many attempts have been made to produce a varnish having good heat radiating and conducting properties, and while certain preparations appear to possess these characteristics in a more or less marked degree, the advantages they offer are comparatively small, and much more satisfactory results are obtained by filling the interspaces in windings with a solid compound. Further, most of the so-called heat radiating varnishes are comparatively poor insulators, due to the amount of mineral matter employed in their manufacture.

Tests for comparative heat dissipation of varnishes can only be determined satisfactorily by observing the temperature rise under working conditions of a number of similar windings insulated with various varnishes.

Application.—Before applying varnish to insulated windings care must be taken to remove all moisture. Cotton coverings and fibrous materials often contain as much as 10 per cent. of moisture which, if not removed before varnish is applied, cannot afterwards escape until the windings are heated and the moisture vaporised. It will be particularly noticeable that the insulation resistance of windings, which have been impregnated before all moisture has been removed from the insulation, decreases in a most marked manner as the temperature is raised, and in the case of high voltage windings the insulation may break down due to the ionisation of the gaseous medium thus formed. The drying out of the windings prior to varnishing is preferably done in a vacuum chamber, since, as the atmospheric pressure is reduced, moisture evaporates more readily, and drying in this way can be done more effectively and rapidly than by any other method. Preferably, also, the varnish should be applied prior to removing the windings from the vacuum chamber, thereby preventing any absorption of moisture from the air and ensuring much greater penetration of the varnish, this being assisted where necessary by additional air pressure.

During storage and handling, varnishes require to be thinned down from time to time as, owing to the evaporation of solvent, their density would otherwise become too great and the penetration and finish of the varnish consequently suffer. Benzine is the thinner ordinarily employed for this purpose, and the best working density of the varnish depends on the absorbing nature of the insulation on the windings. This can best be ascertained by a few experiments with the varnish at different densities on the actual materials with which it will be used, noting the time taken to dry and the dielectric strength and finish.

A few experiments will enable a suitable density to be decided on, and it must be remembered that extremely high dielectric strength is not the most essential feature of this class of varnish.

Where more than one coating of varnish is used special care must be taken to ensure that the first one is thoroughly dried, otherwise considerable trouble will be found in drying the second coating. Where two or more coatings are used, the windings should be drained from opposite ends so as to render the coating as uniform as possible. When vacuum impregnation is not feasible, coils may be dipped in batches; they should be drained thoroughly, however, before heat is applied to dry them.

Solid impregnating compounds.—During the past few years solid impregnating compounds of an asphaltum or paraffin nature have, to quite a considerable extent, superseded varnishes in the insulation of windings. These compounds are superior to varnishes in so far as they are chemically more inert, afford better protection against moisture, fill up the interstices in the windings, and thereby provide better means of heat dissipation. Further, the cost and time of production is reduced, since impregnation is completed in one operation, whereas to produce equivalent results with varnish, several coatings are required with intermediate handling and drying. On the other hand, impregnating compounds are limited in application by their temperature characteristics.

To be suitable for impregnation the compound should not soften sufficiently to ooze or flow at a temperature much below 100° C. and preferably should be quite fluid enough to permeate windings when heated to about 125° C., and, further, at atmospheric temperature should not be brittle. Unfortunately it does not seem possible to produce a compound otherwise suitable which meets all these requirements, and the kinds most widely used, while having a softening temperature of about 105° to 115° C., do not become sufficiently fluid for impregnating purposes below about 150° C.

The necessity for a high softening temperature in compounds is obvious on account of the working temperature of the apparatus on which they are used, and the danger of the compound when heated, oozing, or being thrown out. On the other hand, too high a melting point means that the temperature at which the compound is sufficiently fluid for impregnating purposes is so high as to carbonise, or at least damage, the insulating covering of the windings. To avoid such trouble with the compounds at present available, and which have to be used at temperatures as high as 150° C., the time of impregnation is kept as short as possible.

Uses.—The compounds at present available are utilised mainly on field coils and stationary windings of considerable cross section. Generally they cannot be used for impregnating the windings of revolving parts, since there is a tendency for them to be thrown out by centrifugal force. They are not employed much in transformer work, since for dry types there is some danger of the compound oozing and blocking the ventilating spaces unless considerable care is taken in designing the apparatus so that the interior portions do not get too hot. For the oil immersed types there is too much risk of the compound being dissolved, although perfectly oil-resisting compounds are claimed by some makers. Other makers claim that no harm results from a slight solubility of the compound.

Method of application.—To use the compounds it is necessary to employ a vacuum impregnating plant, consisting of an ordinary steam-heated vacuum chamber, suitable for withstanding high internal pressures, with steam melting-tank attached and coupled up to the vacuum chamber by piping provided with a valve. The general arrangement of vacuum impregnating plant is shown in Fig. 30.

The windings to be impregnated are dried out in the vacuum chamber in the usual way. The compound is reduced to a fluid state and then introduced into the vacuum chamber by opening the valve in the coupling pipe, atmospheric pressure forcing the compound out of the melting tank. The vacuum is then let down and air pressure at about 50 lbs. per square inch applied in the vacuum chamber so as to force the compound into the windings. The surplus fluid is then run off. In this way the insulating coverings of windings several square inches in cross section may be thoroughly impregnated.

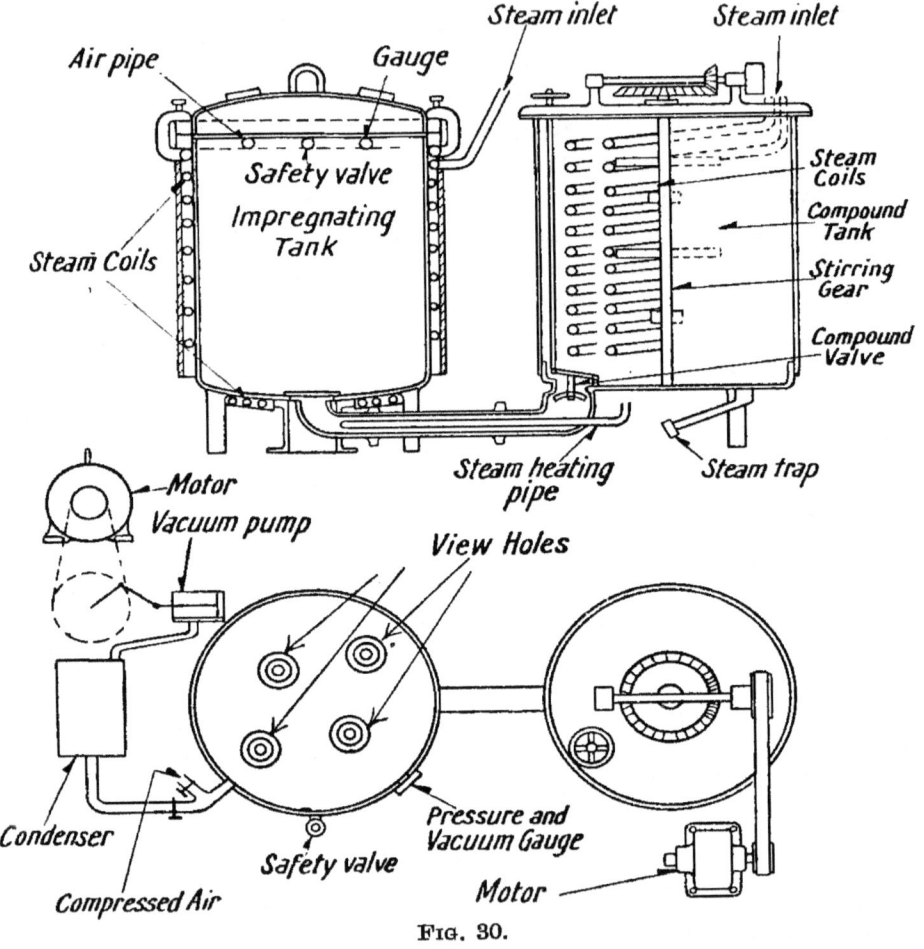

FIG. 30.

Windings impregnated in this way have a very poor finish, and to improve this a covering of open tape is usually put on the windings before impregnation, this being subsequently removed with the outer rough coating of compound.

Impregnating compounds can usually be thinned satisfactorily by means of a small amount of gum of a lighter nature, which is added from time to time to replace the volatile matter lost in heating, thereby keeping the softening temperature within specified limits. The testing of new compounds can only be satisfactorily done by impregnating under working conditions a coil of wire of not less than 5 square inches cross section and noting the amount of penetration and the finish.

Class B. Varnishes for impregnating papers and fabrics.— Varnishes of this class should in general have the same characteristics as those of Class A, and should be tested in a similar way. The insulating materials prepared with this class of varnish must be as flexible as possible, and permanence of physical properties under working conditions is most essential. The varnish should yield a smooth finish and flow so as to produce a uniform thickness of film. It is important that the varnish be moisture resisting and not attacked by hot oil, the latter feature being of course essential when the finished insulation is employed in oil-immersed apparatus. With varnishes of this class it is not so important to preclude the inherent vegetable acids, provided the papers and fabrics on which the varnishes are used do not contain any matter with which these acids will set up chemical action.

Gum base varnishes.—A varnish which fulfils fairly well these requirements is composed of linseed oil with a gum base, and contains a borate of manganese or litharge drier to facilitate oxidation. Such a varnish can be dried in about 8 to 10 hours at a temperature of 100° C., and yields a very good surface on a smooth plain fabric or paper. As the oxidising action by which such varnishes harden goes on continuously, the film eventually becomes brittle. The process, however, can, by suitably proportioning the driers iu the varnish, be made so slow that unless continuously heated and freely exposed to the air at a temperature above that ordinarily attained by electrical apparatus under normal working conditions, the material treated will retain permanently sufficient flexibility for all practical purposes.

Turpentine or benzine are generally used as thinners for varnishes of this class, the former being preferable as it tends to yield a better surface. The best working density for these varnishes depends mainly on the absorbing properties of the materials on which they are used, and can only be ascertained by a series of trials. The insulating value of a varnished material depends on the penetration and density of the varnish. Too thin a varnish penetrates well but gives poor dielectric strength, due to lack of body. Too thick a varnish yields poor dielectric strength due to lack of penetration. The most economical density is that at which the dielectric strength of finished material is a maximum for a minimum increase in thickness, *i.e.* when the breakdown voltage per unit thickness is a maximum.

Method of application.—Papers or fabrics are usually treated in sheets by immersing them in the varnish and baking in suitable heaters, or they may be treated in long strips which are slowly passed through the varnish bath and then through a steam heated chamber. In the latter way the waste which occurs around the edges of sheets due to handling is avoided.

It is usual to apply two coatings of varnish to sheet material, and in order to produce as even a coating as possible, the sheets are drained alternately from opposite ends. The thickness of coating usually applied is about 0·002 inch.

Other types.—Linseed oil alone to some extent has been used successfully in the treatment of fabrics and papers. Other fluids, such as heavy mineral oils and molten paraffin wax, have been used under special circumstances for impregnating fibrous materials, and in some instances, a combination of paraffin wax and linseed oil, but such materials have not had any very general application.

In all cases, before impregnating, papers and fabrics should be dried out somewhat, and while this tends to reduce the flexibility of the finished materials, if moisture is not removed the dielectric strength, especially when the insulation is heated, will be considerably reduced.

Class C. Varnishes used for cementing purposes.—*Kinds.*—The varnishes of this class comprise those suitable for cementing purposes which require, in addition, to have good insulating properties. Such varnishes are largely used in the preparation of mica compositions, as, for instance, in the building up of mica sheets from the natural laminæ, and in the preparation of mica cloth.

Shellac varnish, prepared by dissolving shellac gum in methylated spirits to a density of from 0·84 to 0·89 is the most widely used of this class of varnish, although in the preparation of mica cloth and sheet mica used for slot linings, a spirit varnish having a flexible gum base, such as copal, is frequently used. For general purposes, such as for cementing together the wires of coils, shellac varnish is very satisfactory. The ordinary adhesive properties of this varnish may be improved by boiling it carefully after the gum has been reduced by the methylated spirits. This tends to thicken up the mixture and to raise its melting point by driving off some of the more volatile of its constituents. Various other gums have been used as substitutes for shellac, such as gum-lac, stick-lac, and garnet-lac, and are all of very similar nature.

Uses.—Varnishes of this class are employed in the preparation of insulating tubes and cylinders formed of paper, or paper and mica, very heavily compressed. For such purposes shellac varnish is generally employed and acts both as an insulating filler and as a cement for the paper.

Varnishes of Class C are by no means chemically inert. They have fair insulating properties, but their tendency to soften when heated determines very largely the temperature limitations of the insulating materials with which they are employed.

Varnishes and compositions for cementing purposes can only be satisfactorily tested on a practical scale in connection with the materials with which they are used.

Class D. Varnishes for finishing purposes.—Varnishes of this class are used mainly to give a finishing coating to the windings of completed apparatus, and, apart from appearance, their most essential function is to provide a hard smooth finish, which, as far as possible, will prevent the lodgment of dirt or dust. They should also dry quickly in air, resist the action of lubricating oil, and have no deleterious action on the insulation of windings or contain matter which will tend to facilitate surface leakage or discharge.

Kinds.—A fairly suitable varnish for finishing purposes is prepared from shellac with or without a black pigment. This dries quickly and yields a hard glossy coat. It resists lubricating oil fairly well, but tends to crack somewhat under service conditions. A number of Japans are on the market containing an asphaltum base and spirit solvent, which give a very good finish when first applied, but tend to disintegrate under working conditions. Clear air-drying and sometimes baking varnishes are used for finishing purposes, but the application of the latter is mainly limited to small machines which can be varnished bodily.

In many instances better results are obtained by relying on the varnish used for impregnating the windings, which must subsequently be very carefully handled to preserve the finish. This, however, generally entails the use of a very smooth tape on the windings and hand brushing the surface instead of dipping, thereby adding somewhat to the cost of production.

Method of application.—Finishing varnishes are usually applied by means of an air-spraying machine. The spraying should

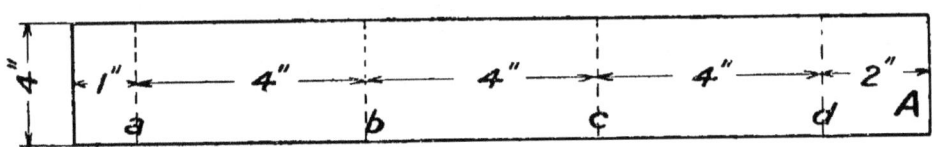

FIG. 31.

preferably be done immediately before the final temperature test, so that the solvent is quickly driven off, otherwise a certain amount of moisture may be absorbed.

Specification of tests.

General characteristics.—Note carefully the following :—

Colour and general appearance.

The surface and finish obtained when test pieces of cotton covered conductor, taped coils, and paper, are treated with the varnish and dried until a hard coat is obtained.

Specific gravity at 15° C. measured by ordinary hydrometer.

Drying tests.—Take strips of bond paper about 0·003 inch thick, cut to the dimensions shown in Fig. 31, and dry for three hours at 100° C. Dip some of these samples in neat varnish and others in varnish thinned with benzine to a suitable working density, which will be of the order of 0·85. Drain test pieces for half an hour and dry out at a temperature of 100° C., noting the time required to obtain a hard coat when the test sample has been allowed to cool down.

Breakdown voltage.—Dip test strips of bond paper, cut to the dimensions shown in Fig. 31 in varnish thinned to a suitable working density and dry at 100° C. until a hard coat is obtained, the test sample being suspended from one end during the draining and drying process. The voltage required to break down the test piece at the points *a*, *b*, *c*, and *d* should be ascertained and the thickness of sheet measured at these points. The voltage required to produce a breakdown should be of the order of 1000 volts per mil. in a thickness of say 0·006 inch.

Effect of hot oil.—Similarly prepared strips should be immersed in mineral oil of a density of about 0·89, and heated to a temperature of 100° C. for 100 hours. The test pieces should then be removed, dried, and the surface examined to ascertain whether the oil has had any soluble effect on the varnish.

Effect of brittleness.—Similarly prepared test pieces should be dried at 100° C. for from 10 to 600 hours and tested by bending around pins of various diameters until the varnished surface shows signs of fracture.

Economy test.—For varnishes of Class B thin down samples of the varnish with benzine and prepare a number of test pieces, as shown in Fig. 31, for each density. Ascertain the voltage per mil. of thickness required to produce breakdown. Plot a curve similar to that shown in Fig. 32 which will indicate at what density the breakdown voltage per mil. is a maximum, and then calculate the quantity of thinner (benzine) required per unit volume of neat varnish at this density. From the cost of benzine and varnish the working cost per gallon of the product is obtained. It should be noted that the bond paper used for this test must be in texture comparable with that used in practice.

For varnishes of Class A the best density is governed mainly by the time required to dry. As a rough guide, however, the test noted above can be applied so as to approximately determine the point of greatest breakdown voltage per mil. of thickness, this point being reached when the effect of the penetrating property together with density is a maximum.

Shop tests.—Careful observations are required of varnish in bulk to confirm the results of tests on samples, and

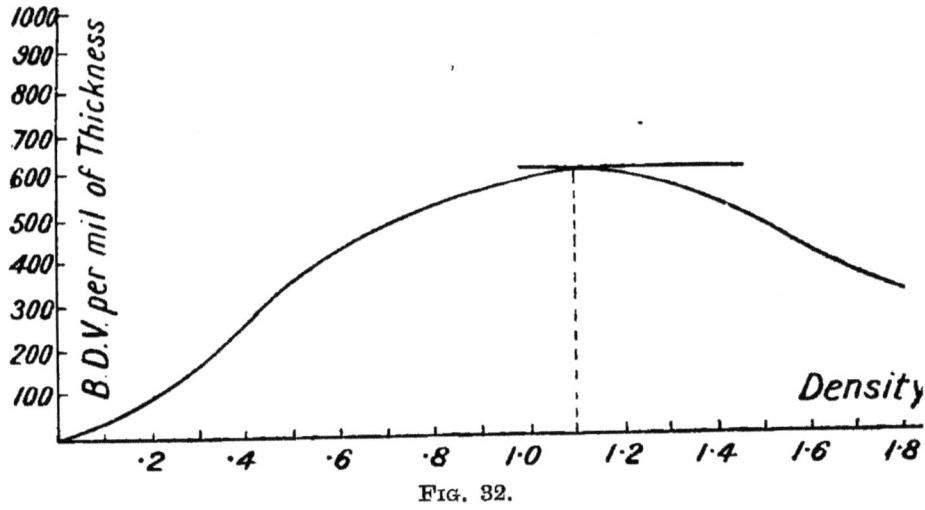

Fig. 32.

a frequent check is necessary on the density and insulating properties to ensure that a consistent quality of material is being supplied.

Specification of test of compounds.—The comparative melting points of compounds can be conveniently ascertained by placing a small pellet of the material on the bulb of a thermometer which is suspended in a test-tube heated in a bath of sulphuric acid or clear high-flash point oil, and noting the temperature at which the compound commences to drip off.

The penetration of a compound at various temperatures may be obtained relatively by noting how far it will penetrate a thickness of absorbent material, such as cotton or linen, made up in a number of layers. The rate of moisture absorption of compounds may be ascertained by thoroughly impregnating a coil, immersing it in water for several days and measuring the insulation resistance at frequent intervals between the copper and water. The test should be repeated at various temperatures.

TREATED MATERIALS.

Nature.—These materials comprise sheet insulation prepared by impregnating fabrics and papers with certain insulating varnishes, oils, and compounds.

Treated fabrics are largely used in the insulation of windings, and, in tape form, are particularly useful for insulating joints and awkwardly shaped coils to which ordinary sheet insulation cannot be applied conveniently.

Treated papers are very largely used in the insulation of transformers, especially of the oil-cooled types.

The essential features of these materials are high dielectric strength, flexibility, permanence and non-absorption of moisture. It is also desirable that they should be unaffected by hot oil, this being, of course, essential in the materials used in oil-cooled transformers.

Preparation.—The varnishes, oils, compounds, papers, and fabrics used in the preparation of treated materials should be free from all chemical matter likely to produce deterioration. Tests should be made to determine the changes in physical and insulating properties of the prepared materials, after prolonged heating at a temperature of about 100° C.

Treated materials for use in oil-immersed apparatus and when likely to be exposed to lubricating oil, should be tested by immersion in mineral oil at a temperature of about 100° C., and the solubility of the varnish or compound noted. A hygroscopic test similar to that described for papers should also be made. The most widely used of the treated fabrics is known as Empire Cloth, and a number of similar materials are sold under various trade names. These materials are prepared by impregnating cambric with linseed oil or linseed oil gum base varnish and thoroughly drying. The cambric merely acts as a base for supporting the varnish film, and is usually treated in long strips some four feet wide and fifty feet or so long, which are slowly passed through the varnish vat and through a drying oven. The drying of a single coating of varnish requires some eight to ten hours at a temperature of about 100° C.

The finished material is ordinarily supplied in thicknesses varying from about 0·005 to 0·015 inch, and has a smooth surface.

While the dielectric strength and, to some extent, the flexibility of the material depends on the varnish, its durability and ultimate value as an insulating medium depends very largely on the quality of cambric. This should be closely woven, undressed and without nap, and about 0·004 inch thick or upwards, according to the thickness of insulation required. A four mil. cambric will build up to about six mils. in a single treatment, and nine mils. with a double coating of varnish.

All fabrics tear and are liable to split very much more easily after being treated, since the fibres are cemented together by the varnish and cannot stretch, whereas before treatment the fibres stretch and can bunch together, forming thereby a strong strand.

Papers are, in general, treated in the same way as fabrics, and for this purpose qualities like manilla, having a very tough, fibrous nature are most suitable, although the finish of the treated material is not so good as in the case of the smoother wood pulp papers. These latter papers, however, lose their toughness to a very large extent when treated, and there is on this account some difficulty in preparing them in long strips.

Well treated papers in thicknesses of 0·007 to 0·125 inch have a breakdown value of 500 to 750 volts per mil.

Very satisfactory results have been obtained by treating presspahn in hot mineral oil—such as used for transformers—this method of treatment being specially adapted for the insulating cylinders employed on core type transformers.

Other materials have been used for the treatment of papers, such as resin oil, molten paraffin wax, and mixtures of these two. Their use, however, except in the insulation of cables, is very limited.

Limitations.—The varnishes used for treating fabrics are of an oxidisable nature, and, consequently, tend eventually to cause the insulation to become brittle, according to the rapidity of the oxidising process, this being determined in the case of linseed oil gum varnishes mainly by the amount of drier used in their preparation. This embrittling tendency increases with the temperature, but, unless exposed to excessively high temperatures, the treated fabrics retain their flexibility sufficiently to withstand the handling and mechanical stresses occurring in practice.

The dielectric strength of treated materials, with a few exceptions, falls off considerably as temperature increases, due largely to the presence of occluded moisture, which cannot be dried out thoroughly before treatment without embrittling the fibres, and to some extent to the presence of only partially oxidised varnishes.

The actual disruption of treated materials appears to take place when the cohesion between the treating material and the fibres is overcome by the repulsion due to the intensity of the electrostatic field, which tends to expel the varnish or oil from the meshes of the paper or fabric.

The effect of temperature on the dielectric strength of treated fibrous insulation is shown by the curves in Fig. 18, Ch. I.

FIBRES.

Materials of this class are used in all cases where hardness and mechanical strength are required, rather than high insulating properties.

Kinds.—The most widely used of the fibres is known as "vulcanised fibre" and is composed of cellulose, chemically treated and very heavily compressed into sheets. In the preparation of this material certain deliquescent salts, such as zinc chloride, are used, all traces of which are not entirely removed during the manufacturing process, with the result that the finished product is more or less hygroscopic.

Other materials of similar nature, known by the trade names of leatheroid, fishpaper, horn fibre, etc., are somewhat more flexible due to their being more fibrous, have better insulating properties and are more reliable.

Limitations.—All these chemically prepared fibres are of the same general nature, but while much stronger and tougher than papers are subject to the same temperature limitations. Further, they are more hygroscopic than papers, and cannot be satisfactorily treated so as to render them moisture proof.

A hygroscopic test similar to that described for papers indicates in a general way to what extent the curing, and the removal of the deliquescent chemical matter, has been carried out. Owing to their hygroscopic nature and comparatively poor insulating properties, materials of the fibre class should not be relied upon entirely for insulation purposes, except for very low voltages, and whenever possible should be reinforced by materials of higher insulation value, which do not necessarily possess such good mechanical features.

Vulcanised fibre is prepared in sheets of thicknesses varying from $\frac{1}{32}$ inch upwards, and can also be supplied in rods or tubes. Leatheroid and fish-paper are usually supplied in sheets varying from a few mils. up to about $\frac{1}{16}$ inch thickness. Vulcanised fibre is particularly useful mechanically, as it can be turned, drilled, and tapped satisfactorily. It is, however, very liable to warp, and unless very thoroughly cured shrinks considerably on drying out. It is also liable to contain conducting impurities. In addition to the troubles arising from residual chemical matter, fibres are in general liable to the same defects as papers.

An important use of fibre is for wedges of armature windings. For this purpose, and especially in connection with high-speed rotating parts, specially selected material should be used. This is best done by arranging a standard form of wedge-groove and periodically testing samples under mechanical pressure, as described at the end of this chapter.

Trade fibres.—The following table gives particulars of the various trade materials belonging to the fibre class of insulation.

Name.	Thickness.	Approximate price per lb.	Lbs. per sq. ft.
		s. *d.*	
Vulcanised fibre (red or grey) . . .	$\frac{1}{8}''$ $\frac{1}{4}''$	0 8 0 8	0·85 1·7
Leatheroid or fish-paper	0·007'' 0·030''	1 8 1 0	0·73 ozs. 3·0 ,,

MICA AND MICA PRODUCTS.[1]

Mica is one of the best known and most widely used of all solid insulating materials. It is found as a constituent of granite, gneiss, and mica schist. The larger crystallisations occur in granite veins intersecting these rocks. There are a great number of micas. That most commonly used for electrical purposes is known to mineralogists as muscovite. Chemically it is a double silicate of aluminium and potassium, with varying proportions of impurities. An analysis of one sample gave—

Silica	46·3
Alumina	36·8
Potash	9·2
Iron sesquioxide	4·5
Fluorine	0·7
Water	1·8
	99·3

There are many valuable deposits of muscovite in the United States and in Canada. In New England plates 2 to 3 feet across have been obtained. Large quantities of mica are now obtained from India. A specially soft kind, commercially known as amber mica, is obtained from Canada. Much of the amber mica consists of the mineral phlogopite, and one analysis gave—

Silica	43·00
Alumina	12·37
Potash	10·32
Magnesia	27·70
Soda	0·30
Iron sesquioxide	1·71
Fluorine	5·67
Water	0·38
	101·45

The colour is mainly a yellowish-brown, with a copper-like reflection. This amber mica is quite distinct from the other qualities, not only on account of its colour, but its crystalline

[1] The information under this heading is included in an article by the authors, entitled " Use of Mica in the Insulation of Electrical Apparatus," published in the *Electrical Review*, Vol. lxxi., Nos. 1817 and 1818. The acknowledgment of the permission of the Editors to reproduce this matter is hereby gratefully tendered.

structure is different, and also such physical characteristics as cleavage, hardness, flexibility, and insulating properties. It is of particular value on account of its softness, and this characteristic will be specially dealt with later in connection with mica for commutator work.

In general, the hardness of mica lies between two and three in the standard scale—that is to say, two to three times the hardness of talc, while the specific gravity ranges from about 2·7 to 3·1.

The qualities of mica most extensively used are the harder and cheaper varieties known commercially as white, ruby, and soft green, mined mainly in India. A very hard form, also of a greenish tint, mined in the United States, is seldom used for electrical work.

In addition to these qualities, there are varieties of each, mottled or stained with flecks of green, ruby, brown, and black colour.

As regards insulating properties, amber mica has about half the dielectric strength of the other varieties used. When tested in sheets of 0·002 inch or 0·003 inch thickness, the voltage required to puncture amber mica is about 2000 volts per mil. With the white, ruby, and soft green varieties, the voltage per mil. to produce breakdown is about the same for each, and runs from 3000 to 4000 volts. Compared with other insulating materials, even the lowest of these values is so high that, as a general rule, it may be said that any kind of mica may be used for any insulating purpose to which its other characteristics render it adaptable.

The principal features to be considered in selecting mica for any particular insulating purpose are cleavage, flexibility, softness, and cost. As regards the latter, amber mica is by far the most expensive. It is also more difficult to cleave into thin laminæ; there is considerable waste in cleavage and a marked tendency for the laminæ to split so as to form " heels "—*i.e.* there is considerable difference in the thickness of opposite edges of the same sheet.

The harder varieties are cheaper, and cleave more readily; in fact, in general, the harder the mica the cheaper the cost of cleavage and the less the waste. These varieties can be split economically as

G

thin as 0·0005 inch, or about half the thickness of the usual amber splittings.

As regards hardness, the micas can be classified as follows, commencing with the softest : .Amber, green (the variety known as " soft Madras green ") ; ruby, white, Indian ; green (U.S.A.). In addition to this classification, various trade terms are sometimes introduced by suppliers to mark special consignments..

It should be noted that while the amber mica is consistently softer than the other varieties, the difference in hardness between it and the softest of the green micas is not great. Further, samples of white mica, quite as soft as Madras green, can sometimes be obtained, and *vice versâ*. But while experts are able to judge this by merely handling the material, the above classification is, in general, a fairly good guide to a purchaser.

Regarding the mottled mica noted above, this is frequently avoided by purchasers under the mistaken idea that the insulating properties must necessarily be poor. In the vast majority of cases, however, this is by no means the case, and very rarely is there found to be any appreciable difference in insulating value between the clear and mottled portions of the same sheet. The discoloration in some cases has been caused by the action of radio-active substances, in others it is due to the presence of microscopic quantities of organic material enclosed between laminæ, and in others, again, to slight traces of inorganic deposit.

Mica is obtained from the mines in rough flakes encrusted in schist, the latter being trimmed away with the fingers or by knife or machine on the spot. The sheets are graded into sizes varying from a few square inches to 100 square inches and upwards in area, and in thicknesses varying from about $\frac{1}{16}$ inch to $\frac{1}{4}$ inch. They are further graded and shipped as " knife " or "thumb " trimmed, as the case may be, the former best lending itself to further cleavage.

The cost of raw mica of any variety varies enormously with size, e.g. soft green mica of approximately 3 square inches of superficial area can be bought as cheaply as 5*d*. per lb., whereas pieces of 30 square inches will cost as much as 6*s*. per lb.

It will be readily seen that the most economical size of raw mica to purchase depends on the use to which it is to be put.

When the laminæ are to be built into sheets, as is usually the case, it becomes a compromise between the cost of splitting and building and the initial cost of the raw mica. The cost of raw amber mica runs approximately from three to four times that of soft green.

For the bulk of work where the harder varieties of mica are used, two sizes have become practically universal, and are known as No. 5 and No. 6 respectively. These sizes are of irregular shape, and are of such an area that from No. 5 mica a circle having a diameter of about 2 inches, and from No. 6 a circle of about 1½ inches, may be cut.

Large sizes are used for special purposes, as will be noted later. Amber mica is ordinarily sold in sizes varying from 6 to 10 square inches.

Many users purchase their mica already split into laminæ of a thickness suitable for building into sheets, others prefer to split it themselves. Sometimes this is done by machine, but more usually by knife in the hands of girl workers.

It is not generally appreciated that mica is capable of absorbing considerable quantities of water, oil, etc.; in fact, nearly all raw mica contains considerable moisture absorbed between its laminæ. Similarly it will readily absorb oil by capillary action along the surfaces of the laminæ.

The effect of moisture between the laminæ is apparently to increase the flexibility—a characteristic that is liable to be mistaken for softness; the resilience is destroyed, and the mica assumes a talc-like nature. As regards softness, while a comparison of different qualities of mica can be obtained by testing with a hardened " scraper," an expert can form a good idea by the mere feel of the material.

Mica is unaffected by heat until a temperature of several hundred degrees centigrade is reached. The harder varieties then undergo a remarkable change. The laminæ separate, giving a very flexible and soft character to the mica, which tends to disintegrate into very small scales or flakes. Some attempts have been made to utilise this softening effect produced by " annealing " mica, as will be noted later. Amber mica is much less affected than the other varieties, possibly because it contains less water in its composition.

Mica is generally employed built up into large sheets from small splittings in the manner described later. Block mica and splittings without any adhesive cement have only a restricted application on account of the limited area of the sheets. For small insulating washers, and, to some extent, for commutator work, mica in its pure form is used, and this will be considered at greater length in dealing with commutator insulation.

Mica products.—For most purposes where mica is employed as an insulator, it is first necessary to build it up into one of the following forms :—

Stiff, flat plates of various thicknesses.

Flexible sheets.

Sheets made up of a combination of mica with paper or cloth.

In each of these forms the process of manufacture is similar, in that small splittings are cemented together in layers by means of suitable insulating varnish.

The mica splittings vary from 0·0005 to 0·0025 inch in thickness, and are usually of the No. 5 or No. 6 size.

When specially uniform sheets are required, mica of rectangular shape is employed, otherwise quite irregular pieces are used on account of cheapness. The splittings are overlapped when irregular-shaped pieces are used. Each layer as it is built up is sprayed or brushed with varnish, and the layers are so arranged that the joints are broken.

For stiff, flat plates the sheets are usually built up with a varnish made by dissolving shellac, or one of the many similar gums, in wood alcohol or methylated spirits. When a sufficient number of layers have been thus prepared, the sheets are heavily compressed in a steam-heated press to expel the solvent and excess varnish. When cold they are usually milled to a uniform thickness. Except for commutator work, where amber mica is sometimes employed, the cheaper green or white mica is used for these sheets. The trade term " Micanite " is generally applied to mica built up in this form.

Flexible sheets are built up in a similar manner, except that a non-drying varnish is employed for cementing the laminæ together, and the hot pressing is omitted. Greater care has, therefore, to be exercised in the building, so as to obtain uniformity in the thickness of the sheet. For this work also the splittings should be the thinnest possible.

Insulating sheets composed of mica and paper or cloth are prepared by cementing one or more layers on to the paper or cloth with either shellac or a flexible sticking varnish, according to the use to which the product is to be applied.

Great care must be exercised in the choice of flexible varnish to be used, as there are a number of preparations on the market that are chemically active and liable to attack any copper with which they may come into contact. For mica sheets backed in this manner with paper or cloth, the thinnest soft green splittings are best employed, so as to give the most flexible product. Scrap and powdered mica are used to some extent in the preparation of many of the fire-proof insulating compositions sold in the form of bushings, strain insulators, arc shields, etc.

Application of mica to commutator insulation.—For the insulating of commutator segments from one another, mica is almost invariably used, and also, with few exceptions, for the insulating bushings between the segments and supporting frame.

Considering first the insulating of the segments, the mica sheets employed are usually from 0·020 inch to 0·035 inch thick. Unless the mica is milled out between the copper segments on the wearing face in the manner referred to later, it is necessary to use a quality of mica that will be as soft as, or softer than the copper itself, otherwise there will be uneven wearing of the commutator, ultimately resulting in high mica and destructive sparking under the brushes. The safest plan is to use amber mica, but this entails high cost, and the softer green micas are now very largely employed with, on the whole, satisfactory results. In the case of large machines, it becomes possible to make up the insulating sheets with the wearing surface only of amber mica, and the remainder of green or white mica, the increase in expense over sheets made up entirely with hard mica not then being very great.

Considerable difference of opinion exists as to the relative merits of "pure" mica and built up mica for the insulating of commutator segments. Many engineers maintain that in cases where oil has crept on to the commutator, pitting of the insulation between bars has resulted rapidly when the insulation has consisted of built-up mica, whereas pure mica has withstood such deterioration fairly well. It is the experience of the authors, however, that in this respect there is very little to choose between built-up mica, when well made, and pure mica. Deterioration is bound to occur in either case when oil is present on the surface of the commutator, and the prevention of this class of trouble can only be effected by keeping oil off the commutator by means of properly designed bearings and oil throwers.

Another objection put forward to the use of built-up mica is that the small pieces composing it are liable to work loose and creep up from between the bars. While this may happen with poorly manufactured material, experience does not show it to be the case where the insulation has been properly prepared.

In the case of large machines the question resolves itself, as it then becomes impossible to obtain pure mica in sheets sufficiently large for the purpose, and there is no alternative to the use of built-up sheets.

As a commercial proposition, where the segments are longer than about 12 inches, a pure mica insulation is impossible. When the segments are small, say not longer than about 4 inches, economy favours the use of pure mica, the strips being sawn or punched out of the raw block. When this is done the increase in cost due to the large mica is more than compensated for by the saving in the building, pressing, and milling.

The one great advantage that well-built-up mica possesses over the pure sheet, is that it ensures uniformity of wear, the splittings being thoroughly well mixed.

With pure mica it is impossible to ensure that all the segments will be of equal softness, and even in the same sheet hard spots will often occur.

The principal feature in the manufacture of the hard sheets of built-up mica for commutator segments is the pressing. The pressure employed should be as great as possible, and the temperature sufficiently high to expel all traces of solvent. The amount of shellac or other insulating cement left in the finished segment should not exceed 10 per cent. by weight ; 5 per cent. is sometimes attained.

Where pure mica segments are used, improved wearing is

obtained by dividing the sheets, after these are cut to size, into as many thin laminæ as possible, and reassembling to the thicknesses required before placing into position between the copper bars.

"High mica" will occasionally occur in practice whatever kind and quality is used, and it is now common practice to mill down the mica from $\frac{1}{32}$ to $\frac{1}{16}$ inch below the wearing surface of the copper of the finished commutator. This may appear to involve some risk of trouble due to the lodgment of dirt in the channels thus made. In actual practice, however, trouble of this kind is scarcely ever experienced, and the only drawbacks to the practice are some slight tendency to cause "chattering" of the brushes and the necessity of remilling the ducts from time to time.

For very high-speed commutators rectangular strips of considerable size have frequently to be employed in the building up of the mica sheet, the strips being arranged so that their ends are held in place under the shrink rings or bands around the commutator. If this is not done the cement and the friction of the surfaces may not be sufficient to prevent the mica being forced out from between the bars.

Some attempts have been made to use annealed mica for commutator segment insulation, but, as already stated, there is very considerable tendency for this material to disintegrate, and thus far such experiments have not met with much success.

With regard to the bushings insulating the commutator from the supporting frame, some manufacturers prefer to use paper instead of mica, partly on the score of cheapness, and partly because an even thickness, and consequently better bearing surface, is more readily obtainable.

Unless a very good fit is effected, so that the commutator remains rigid when running, "high bars," "flats," "high mica," and other troubles will be experienced. Moreover, with very high speeds where the stresses are great, an actual grinding action may take place on the insulating bushings, and these, if of mica, will be readily reduced to powder at the places where the grinding takes effect.

It is, however, only a matter of careful manufacture to make mica bushings as uniform in thickness as paper, and undoubtedly mica insulation possesses great advantages over paper for this work. Even when the commutator never attains a very high temperature, paper rapidly dries to extreme brittleness. Paper, moreover, loses its insulating value when subject to deposits of moisture, as may occur when the conditions are such as to favour " sweating " of the commutator.

Mica bushings for commutators are moulded from stiff built-up sheet. Thin sheets are used for this purpose, and a considerable number employed to make up the total thickness required. These sheets are softened by heating them in an oven or on a steam plate. They are pressed by hand into the hot mould, the heated core then being inserted and screwed down.

Mica bushings are made in thicknesses from $\frac{1}{32}$ inch to $\frac{3}{32}$ inch, according to the size of the commutator for which they are intended. When these bushings have been arranged in position, it is the general practice to heat the whole commutator up in order again to soften the insulating cement, and thus allow the various parts to be tightly screwed up, and in this way properly bedded. For this reason a much larger percentage of cement is allowed to remain in the bushings than in the mica for the segment insulation.

Other applications of mica.—In addition to commutator work, mica is extensively used in the insulation of armature windings, especially those for high voltages, and also for moulded work of various kinds, insulating bushings, tubes, washers, etc.

For the insulation of oil-cooled transformers mica is not generally used, since the oil is liable to attack the binding cement.

For bushings and washers the principal value of mica lies in its permanence and heat-resisting nature, and in this connection it is well to remember that the insulating value of such bushings and washers depends mainly on the amount of creepage surface it is possible to provide, this often being entirely out of proportion to the breakdown value of the materials employed.

For mica tubes, particularly when of small diameter, a turn or two of paper both inside and outside should be used as a protection, otherwise there is a tendency for the mica to flake and to be easily damaged. It is still better to make the tubes of paper and mica throughout, this improving their mechanical strength considerably. With this method, the insulating value is not seriously reduced, and if the tubes are well made by rolling the material on to mandrels under heavy pressure and heat, they are as fire-resisting as the all-mica tubes.

Specially constructed machines are now used for the manufacture of these tubes. The paper used for backing the mica usually amounts to from 40 to 50 per cent. of the total weight of the finished tubes. These tubes can be made circular, and afterwards re-softened by heat and blocked out to rectangular shape for the lining of armature slots, or they can be made directly to the shape required on suitable split steel mandrels.

For low voltage armature coils, owing to the necessity for keeping the thickness of insulation in the slots down to the minimum possible, it is much more difficult to apply mica satisfactorily than the other kinds of insulation more commonly employed. Except for railway motor work, where the temperature conditions are severe, it is very doubtful whether its use is justified. Insulations of prepared paper or cloth have proved perfectly satisfactory for low-voltage work, and are, of course, much cheaper.

For the insulation of low-voltage armature coils, the most satisfactory plan is to build the mica on to a backing of thin tough paper with flexible sticking varnish, and to wrap the sheets thus formed around the slot portions of the coils, holding the wrapping in place with a layer of tape.

A second method is to avoid the use of the paper by moulding hard troughs of mica to fit the slots and to push the coils down into these. There are two disadvantages in this method, the first being that since the troughs are open there is only a very short creepage path from the coils to the teeth of the armature, and the second, that in winding the coils into the troughs it is easy to fracture the insulation at the immediate ends of the slots. A similar method, designed to overcome the first of these weaknesses, is to mould the troughs with lips at the top. These troughs are sprung on to the slot portions of the formed coil, the lips overlapping, and in this way effecting a completely closed insulation. This is bound tightly in place with a layer of tape, and the coil thus insulated is then placed in the slots.

For high voltage armatures the radial thicknesses of insulation necessary around the slot portions of the coils are sufficient to render it possible to make a sound mechanical job with a mica insulation, and there is no question as to the utility of the material for this class of work.

The mica is used with a backing of either treated cloth or paper, made up with flexible varnish and wrapped on by hand, or made up on a thin paper with shellac varnish and hot ironed on to the coils by machine. Coils insulated in either of these two ways can, of course, only be used in machines with open slots, or in closed slots when one end of the coil is left open so that the coil can be pushed into position, and the open end afterwards jointed up. When the coils are formed directly in the machine by threading the wires singly through the slots, the latter are lined with tubes made up of mica or paper and mica, as referred to earlier.

The most satisfactory insulation is that obtained by ironing the mica directly on to the coils, as in this way a solid thickness of material free from air pockets can be obtained. When applied to coils where the individual turns are separated from one another by mica strips or troughs, and the interspaces between conductors filled solid by impregnating with insulating compound, these coils are rendered best capable of resisting deterioration due to electro-chemical action.[1]

Where severe mechanical stresses may be expected on the end connections of armature coils, as is sometimes the case in turbo-generators, the flexible cloth and mica insulation is preferable, unless the projecting portions of the coils are so heavily clamped as to prevent any movement.

The end connections of armature coils are generally insulated with treated cloth strips or cotton tapings. Mica tape has also been used for this work, such tape consisting of one or two layers of thin mica splittings built up with a flexible varnish on paper or cloth. Such a tape, however, is expensive to apply, and its use is limited to that class of work where resistance to high temperature is essential.

The proportions of mica and paper or cloth in the wrappings

---

[1] See paper on "Chemical Action in High-Voltage Armature Windings," by Fleming and Johnson, *Journal of the Institution of Electrical Engineers*, Vol. lxvii. No. 209.

used on high-voltage armature coils are usually such as to give about 40 per cent. by weight of mica in the finished insulation. Where very thin paper is used, as much as 70 per cent. of mica is sometimes obtained, but the insulation is usually not so good mechanically.

OILS.

Practically all oils, whether of mineral, vegetable, or animal origin, have normally very high insulating properties. The use of insulating oils is mainly confined to such apparatus as switches, transformers, and rheostats. Mineral oil is generally employed, although resin oil is also occasionally used. For switch work the oil, although acting as an insulator, is used primarily to prevent arcing when the switch is operated. For transformers and rheostat work, the main function of the oil is cooling, the oil absorbing heat when in contact with the active materials, and transferring it by convection to the containing case from which it is radiated. The high specific heat of oil, which is about 0·35, is an invaluable feature in retarding the temperature rise of the apparatus with which it is used. At the same time the insulating properties are very important, especially for high-voltage apparatus ; so much so that it is commercially impracticable to construct transformers for working pressures much higher than 30,000 volts unless they are oil-immersed.

In general, an insulating oil should possess high dielectric strength, low viscosity, and high flash point ; it should be neutral in its action on metals and the insulating materials that will be immersed in it, be free from moisture, sediment, and impurities, and—especially for switch work—it should not readily decompose under the effects of high local temperatures.

The neutrality of an oil may be tested roughly by boiling a small quantity with distilled water, decanting the oil, and testing the water for acid and alkali. High flash point is essential in view of fire risk, and should not be less than about 160° C. when tested in a closed oil vessel.

The apparatus for ascertaining flash points consists of a small metal vessel, with removable cover, containing the oil under test. This is surrounded by a metal shell containing a very high flash-point oil. This outer bath is heated and constantly stirred, while the cover of the inner vessel is removed from time to time so that a torch can be applied to the vapour coming off. The temperature at which the vapour flashes is read on a thermometer immersed in the oil itself, this being checked by a reading on a thermometer immersed in the outer bath. The "Abel" tester is that very largely used for flash point testing, although many modifications of the same type of apparatus exist.

The amount of evaporation of the oil should be tested by heating a weighed quantity for six hours at 100° C., and noting the loss of weight. This should not exceed 0·3 per cent.

Low viscosity is essential in transformer and rheostat work, since the rapidity of the circulation, and consequently the heat-dissipating properties, depends on the fluidity; and in oil switches, if the oil is too viscous, there is a tendency for a vacuum to be formed when the switch contacts are rapidly opened, which may enable the arc to hold over. Further, under these conditions, vapour and inflammable gas may be formed which accumulate in the containing vessel, and on becoming ignited explode with violence. For the same reason it is important that the oil used for switches in cold climates should not thicken up too much at the normal working temperature. The viscosity of oil is measured by noting the time taken for a given quantity contained in a vessel to flow through a certain sized orifice. A uniform temperature is maintained by means of a water jacket surrounding the containing vessel. When the viscosity is to be tested at a low temperature, the water is replaced by a freezing mixture. The standard apparatus for viscosity measurements is that known as the Redwood Viscosimeter.

Rape oil is often taken as a standard for the comparison of the viscosity of various oils, and corrections for the effect of varying specific gravities should be made. The curves in Fig. 33 show the effect of temperature on the viscosity of various oils.

From an insulation point of view, freedom from moisture and impurities, especially sulphur or sulphur compounds, are most important factors in an oil, and have a direct bearing on the dielectric strength.

The dielectric strength of oils may conveniently be tested by a spark gap with needle point, or point and plane electrodes placed vertically, all comparative tests being made with approximately the same head of oil above the spark gap.

The tests should be made with the oil thoroughly dried, and again when it is saturated with moisture. The drying can be done very thoroughly by passing the oil through a series of filter papers. The effect of moisture on the dielectric strength is shown in the curve, Fig. 10, Chapter I. All breakdown tests should be repeated

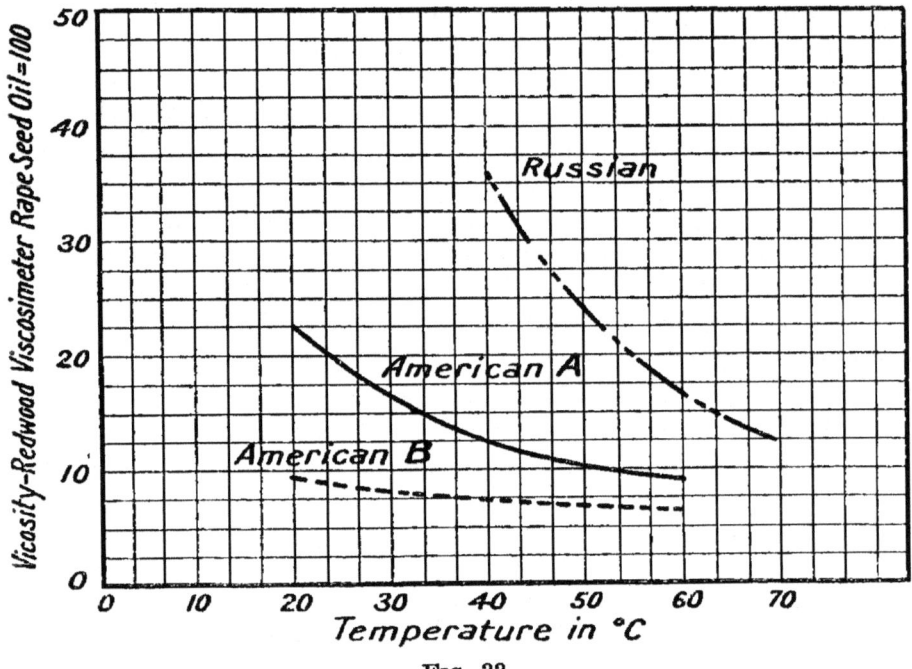

FIG. 33.

a number of times, and, as already noted, it will usually be found that after the first breakdown a higher voltage is required for the succeeding breaks.

The voltage required to break down a gap of $\frac{1}{8}$ inch between a point and plane in the case of a well-dried oil varies from 15,000 to 30,000 volts. The more viscous the oil the lower will be the breakdown voltage.

Practically the only oils employed on a large scale for insulating purposes are of mineral origin and belong to the C_nH_2

series. They are prepared by the distillation and refining of crude petroleum, and, in the sequence of distillation, come after the light burning and lubricating oils. There are two main classes according to the origin of the oil, namely, American and Russian. The former has a paraffin base and the latter a bituminous one. A further distinction is that for the same density and flash point the Russian oil is usually much more viscous than the American, and the dielectric strength lower.

In transformer operation, in connection with which the bulk of this oil is used, it is found that a flocculent deposit of reddish brown colour forms, which in course of time becomes darker and more dense and ultimately fills up ventilating spaces and causes over-heating of the transformer. This deposit is at first of about the same density as the oil and is a pure hydro-carbon. In its final state, however, it is of the nature of an oxidised oil and shows a distinct acid reaction.

There has been much controversy as to the origin and nature of this deposit. It was at first held that it was due to soluble insulating compounds in the transformer windings, and in certain cases this may account for some kind of deposit being formed. Such a deposit, however, is quite distinct from that due to the oil itself. The principal factors governing the formation of the deposit with a given oil are temperature, presence of air, presence of certain metals, impurities and moisture in the oil. Temperature is probably the most important factor. The average commercial transformer oil will form a deposit if maintained continuously at a temperature of 80° C., although the best modern oils will withstand a temperature of 150° C. without showing any formation.

As regards the presence of air it is fairly certain that oxidation plays an important part at certain stages of the deposit formation, since, if the oil is heated in a vacuum, very little deposit is formed compared with that obtained in the open air; moreover, the deposit shows an acid reaction, indicating that a compound with oxygen has been formed. Further, it might be noted that if heat is applied directly to an open beaker containing oil, the deposit forms more rapidly than when it is placed in a heated atmosphere and raised to the same temperature.

When heated in the presence of certain metals the deposit

occurs more readily, although there is no chemical action on the metals. Such metals appear to constitute a link between certain physical changes and enable a so-called "catalytic" action to take place. In this respect copper shows most effect, and after this iron, lead, tin, and zinc in order of activity, the latter having practically negligible effect.

The presence of impurities and moisture tend also to hasten this action.

For oils that are otherwise comparable, those of Russian origin are less likely to form deposits than American oils, although the latter can be obtained suitable for all practical purposes.

Some efforts have been made to utilise other materials of greater specific heat, and it has been suggested that tetra-chloride of carbon and other more volatile fluids should be employed, their function being to absorb heat sufficient to produce evaporation, the vapour being condensed in a cooling chamber and the cool fluid again returned to be heated. No such methods of cooling have, however, been put into any extended practical use.

Specification of tests.

General Characteristics.

Colour and general appearance.

Specific gravity at 15° C.

Flash point.—Test with "Abel" or "Pensky-Martin" apparatus, raising the temperature of the oil very slowly. This test to be made on a sample of oil that has not been dried specially.

Breakdown voltage.—Filter a sample of oil once and test between standard electrodes. These may consist of a point and plane or small sphere and plane separated ⅛ inch. All tests to be made cold, and the oil should not be dried other than by filtering before being tested.

Viscosity.—Test by means of a Redwood viscosimeter at temperatures of 30°, 40°, 50°, 60°, 70°, and 80° C. Set forth results on a curve and take Rape oil as 100 for purpose of comparison.

Deposit test.—Place a strip of bright copper foil about 2 inches by 8 inches, coiled spirally in a beaker together with 200 c.c. of the oil. By means of a glass tube coupled to an air supply, bubble air through the centre of the spiral of copper foil up through the oil. Heat the oil to a temperature of 185° C., and maintain at this temperature for one hour, filter the oil and if no appreciable darkening or evidence of deposit appears on the filter paper, continue the heating for a further period of one hour, and again filter, the heating and filtering process being continued until evidence of deposit is obtained. The time taken for the first sign of deposit to occur affords a measure of the quality of the oil.

Evaporation.—Heat 100 gms. of oil in a water bath for 6 hours at 100° C. and note loss by weight, expressing this as a percentage of the initial weight.

Foreign matter.—Chemical tests should be made to detect the presence of sulphur, resinous matter, acids, and alkalis.

ASBESTOS

While this material is valuable on account of its non-combustible nature, its scope in electrical work is limited by its hygroscopic nature and normally poor insulating properties.

Asbestos is supplied in sheets varying in thickness from about 0·010 inch to upwards of ½ inch, the heavier sheets being often made up by cementing together smaller thicknesses. In sheet form, asbestos is usually mixed with other fibres and loading material to give it the necessary mechanical strength and finish. Tape, however, can be manufactured from pure asbestos which, while of very coarse texture, is strong enough for ordinary handling.

Sheet asbestos has been employed as a backing for built-up mica so as to provide a material of suitable insulating value and at the same time non-combustible, and has been used in railway motors and other apparatus. Asbestos covering in place of cotton on conductors has been used for windings where a non-combustible material was desirable ; but the cost, the additional room taken up, and the poorer mechanical protection afforded, has limited its use in these directions.

In other directions asbestos has been found useful for arc

deflectors in controllers, coverings for fuse blocks, switches, etc., and for such purposes it is usually impregnated by boiling in a solution of silicate of soda and then heavily pressing. This gives a solid durable material which, however, is very hygroscopic and useless for purely insulating purposes. Attempts to impregnate this material in any manner so as to render it non-hygroscopic and improve its insulating nature have not been very successful and usually detract from its non-combustible nature, and whenever asbestos is required to be used in contact with current carrying parts, it should be reinforced by a good insulator.

Asbestos is also largely employed in the manufacture of many moulded compositions where great heat resistance is required.

The following table gives particulars of a few of the commercial asbestos products.

Name.	Thickness.	Approximate price per lb.	Ozs. per sq. ft.
Asbestos paper . . .	0·010″	2¾$d.$	0·5
,, millboard . .	$\frac{1}{16}$″	1½$d.$	6·3
,, ,, . .	$\frac{1}{8}$″	1½$d.$	12·6
,, slate . . .	¼″	2½$d.$	2·4 lbs.

WOOD

The insulating value of wood is determined almost entirely by its condition as regards sap and moisture. Thoroughly well dried and well seasoned wood of almost any variety possesses sufficiently high insulating properties for all practical purposes; moreover, its hard fibrous nature renders it specially suitable for those cases where a material capable of withstanding considerable mechanical stresses, as well as possessing good insulating characteristics, is required. Unfortunately, it is extremely difficult to remove the sap and moisture from wood without causing it to split or warp, and this can only be done satisfactorily by slow drying for several years in a wood kiln. Even then pieces of the same kind of wood similarly treated will often differ considerably in insulating value, owing to the moisture in the one case not being effectually removed.

To prevent the absorption of moisture by dried wood it is

H

advisable to boil it in paraffin wax or linseed oil, or a mixture of these two materials, for 48 hours or more at a temperature of about 70° C., or the wood may be dried under vacuum and impregnated with a wax or gum under high pressure. Wood treated in these ways should previously be dressed to approximately finished dimensions, as the impregnating compound does not usually penetrate very far. It is extremely important that wood shall be thoroughly dried and capable of meeting the required insulation tests before it is impregnated as, not only is it very difficult to remove the moisture after treatment, but also during treatment it may warp and crack badly.

The woods most generally employed for insulation purposes are ash, teak, maple, hornbeam and lignum-vitæ. The best of these is hornbeam when of good quality, for while it is very close texture and extremely tough, it nevertheless can be treated much more thoroughly than the other kinds of wood. Well dried wood should stand a voltage of 10,000 per inch of thickness without signs of burning or heating.

Moulded Compositions

The innumerable moulded insulating materials on the market, sold under various trade names, may be classified under three heads—

(a) Those used for their good appearance and finish and having fair insulating and mechanical properties.

(b) Those having good insulating and mechanical features, capable of withstanding without injury temperatures up to about 100° C., but not necessarily possessing a brilliant finish.

(c) Those materials of essentially fire-resisting nature.

Class (a) comprises materials such as hard rubber and ebonite. These have very high dielectric strength, soften at comparatively low temperatures, are non-hygroscopic, are somewhat brittle and of low tensile strength, but are susceptible of a very high finish and consequently are very suitable for insulating bushings and parts of switchgear and detail apparatus where good appearance is essential.

Class (b) comprises materials of a more or less fibrous nature containing a binder of rubber or other suitable material. Such materials can be moulded into almost any required shape and can be prepared so as to have a high softening temperature. They are usually fairly good mechanically and are non-hygroscopic, but their finish is not generally so good as that of the materials under class (*a*).

Materials of class (*c*) are almost invariably of a hygroscopic nature, of low dielectric strength and poor mechanically. They cannot usually be relied upon exclusively for insulating purposes, but require to be reinforced with a material having the requisite insulating and non-hygroscopic nature. Materials of class (*c*) are used mainly as arc-deflectors, fuse covers, etc., and in such places where good heat-resisting properties are essential.

All moulded compositions should be tested by noting the effect of hot water, alkali, and oil upon their surface and the increase in weight after prolonged immersion. Samples should be heated in air to determine the softening temperature, and the breakdown value and machining properties should also be tested.

Heat-resisting compositions should be tested by an arc, its effect on the surface being noted.

Ageing tests are usually unnecessary.

Specification of tests.

General characteristics.

Colour.

Specific gravity.

Fibrous or non-fibrous.

Hardness—test by cutting and drilling.

Brittleness—test by hammering.

Finish—whether this is due to friction or lacquer.

Inflammability—determine temperature of ignition. If the material is not inflammable, try the effect of an arc between two electrodes placed about $\frac{1}{2}$ inch below it. For comparative purposes the power expended in the arc should be about the same for each test.

Softening temperature.—Heat a small sample in an oven and note the temperature at which it will take a thumb-nail impression.

Breakdown value.—Test a given thickness between electrodes in the usual way. Where possible, hot and cold tests should be made.

Absorption tests.—Immerse weighed samples in known solutions of caustic soda, sulphuric acid, in a mineral oil such as used for transformers, and also in water. Dry and reweigh after 100 hours. Note the amount of absorption, also whether the materials have been affected.

MARBLE.

The various kinds of marble used for electrical purposes are known according to their colouring and from whence they are mined, as White Sicilian, White Italian, Blue Vermont, and Dove.

From an insulation point of view there is little to choose between them, variations in quality being in general independent of colour. Marble is employed largely in switchboard work, and its value for this purpose depends mainly on its non-combustible nature and its "showy" appearance. At the same time it has fair mechanical properties, and can be cut, drilled, and polished satisfactorily.

The most serious defects in marble are due to metallic veins, which are always liable to be present, and which cannot usually be located except by applying a high voltage test between the several parts of a slab. Such veins are most likely to occur in the more heavily marked marbles.

Marble is very hygroscopic, and normally contains so much moisture that for high-tension work it is necessary to bush the holes through which conductors pass. This is all the more necessary because the water, usually employed in drilling, is absorbed by the marble and cannot effectually be removed except by baking for a considerable time. If the marble in such cases is not suitably bushed, local heating will occur which may be sufficient to fracture the material; also there will probably be a surface discharge which in time will ruin the appearance of the polished surface. Where marble is not required to have a good finish, its insulating and moisture-resisting properties may be improved by treatment in molten paraffin wax or linseed oil, after all moisture has been removed from it. This treatment discolours the marble, and for this reason cannot be employed where good appearance is essential. Slabs of marble can be dried in from 12 to 15 hours at about 100° C., but care must be taken to raise and lower the temperature gradually to avoid cracking the material.

To detect the presence of metallic veins, the surfaces should be explored by means of movable electrodes on the opposite sides, and a voltage of from 5000 to 10,000 applied for a thickness of from $\frac{3}{4}$ inch to 1 inch.

SLATE.

In general, the same limitations apply to slate as to marble.

Slate is used for switchboard work, fuse boards, etc., where a non-combustible material having fair insulating properties is required. It is harder and somewhat less hygroscopic than marble, but is much more liable to contain metallic veins, and is, consequently, very unreliable from an insulation point of view. Slate should not be used for voltages higher than a few hundred unless the conductors passing through or supported by it are very thoroughly insulated.

For switchboard work slate is very useful for installations where polished marble would quickly become discoloured. For such purposes it is usual to give the slate a black finish, which is obtained by two or more coats of a black baking varnish polished by hand rubbing.

Where good appearance is not essential, slate should be treated in the way described for marble.

STONE.

Under this class can be placed soap stone, talc, etc., and the manufactured substances, such as lavite and artificial stones. Soap stone is used to some extent for high voltage mountings, and is of high dielectric strength, free from metallic veins, and easily drilled and worked. On account of its high price artificial stones are largely used as substitutes. None of these, however, are as satisfactory, being very porous and hygroscopic. Lavite, steatite, and other similar materials are largely used as small bushings, and while brittle, usually have very high dielectric strength.

PORCELAIN.

Porcelain occupies a unique position among insulating materials on account of its non-combustible and high insulating properties, and because it is hard and very durable.

It is prepared from special clays, which are vitrified by baking at a very high temperature, and the various qualities or grades of porcelain differ mainly according to the kinds, or proportions, of the various clays used, and on the baking temperature.

The porcelain used for high tension insulating purposes consists principally of the best china clay (Kaolin) and the more plastic potter's clay, with an admixture of flint to add toughness and felspar to provide a flux. These ingredients are mixed with water and masticated until a homogeneous mass is obtained. This is partially dried and moulded or spun to the required shape.

The remaining moisture (about 10 per cent.) is then dried out and the articles vitrified by baking for a couple of days at a temperature which is gradually raised to 1200°–1500° C. The porcelain is subsequently glazed with a solution of felspar or other aluminium silicate. During the manufacturing process the porcelain shrinks some 10 to 20 per cent., and in designing special shapes very great care must be exercised to proportion the parts so that no undue stresses will be set up during the baking, which will crack or distort the porcelain. Further, too great a thickness should not be used or poor vitrification will result.

Porcelain of good quality should be translucent, and, when broken, the fracture should have a clean glassy appearance. A fractured sample should absorb no appreciable amount of moisture after 24 hours' immersion in brine.

The inferior qualities of porcelain are porous and readily absorb moisture, and are quite useless for high-tension insulation work. Such grades of porcelain depend mainly for their insulating properties on the glaze, whereas the essential purpose of this is to provide a smooth surface to prevent the accumulation of dust and to give a good appearance.

Good porcelain has a tensile strength of about ten tons and a compressive strength of some twenty-five tons per square inch. Porcelain is used largely for high-tension transmission line insulation and for high-tension bushings, fuseboards, high-tension switch supports, etc. Its use is limited by its brittle nature, and, in high-tension work, its high specific inductive capacity is a drawback as this facilitates the formation of a surface discharge.

MECHANICAL AND PHYSICAL PROPERTIES OF INSULATING MATERIALS OF MOST PRACTICAL IMPORTANCE.

In high-speed rotating windings the insulation between conductors placed at right angles to the radial direction may be subjected to considerable mechanical pressure. In the case of direct current turbo-generators, for instance, the pressure on the wedges holding the coils in the slots may be as high as 1700 lbs. per square inch, while in turbo-alternators this may be of the order of 6000 lbs. per square inch. To study the behaviour of the insulating materials employed on such windings when subjected to compression, a number of sheets of various thicknesses and kinds were tested between two accurately machined steel cubes.

Preliminary tests of sheet insulation compressed between copper faces showed that if the load was taken to a point at which the copper commenced to flow, a grinding and tearing action on the insulation took place, and its mechanical disruption quickly followed. Tests therefore were made first on copper alone to determine the loads at which appreciable flow occurred, and the following results were obtained.

(1) *Hard drawn copper strap.*—A test piece one inch wide flowed $\frac{1}{64}$ inch, *i.e.* increased this amount in width, when compressed between cast steel blocks with a maximum load of 46,000 lbs. per square inch.

(2) *Soft annealed copper.*—A test piece one inch wide tested under similar conditions flowed $\frac{1}{64}$ inch with a maximum load of 10,000 lbs. per square inch.

Since the copper usually employed in electrical windings is very soft, a load of 10,000 lbs. per square inch represents about a maximum that can safely be employed if distortion of the conductor is to be avoided. The effect of compression on the insulation for loads up to this amount is of considerable importance.

Tests on fullerboard, etc.—The curves in Fig. 34 show the results obtained on various thicknesses of fullerboard (a variety of press-pahn), leatheroid, and fibre. Up to a maximum compression of 10,000 lbs. per square inch, the law is a linear one, except in the case of thick fibre, where this relation holds only up to about 6000 lbs. per square inch. For thinner sheet materials than shown on these curves, the same general characteristics are observed except

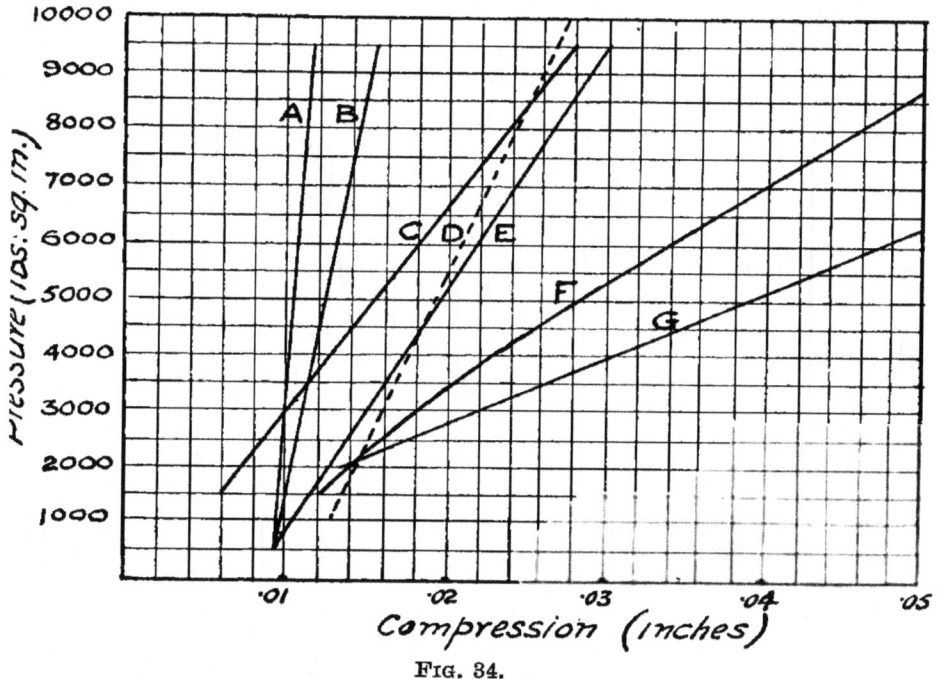

FIG. 34.

A, 0·030″ treated fullerboard.   D, 0·056″ plain fullerboard tested between hot cubes.
B, 0·034″   „   leatheroid.   E, 0·137″ treated fullerboard.
C, 0·056″ plain fullerboard.   F, 0·375″ treated fibre.   G, 0·5″ plain fibre.

that the amount of compression obtained is relatively very much smaller. As noted on the curves, certain of these materials were varnish treated, and the point of intersection with the axes in these cases is different from that of the untreated materials, due apparently to the squeezing out of the varnish film. The plotted curve refers to a sample tested at approximately the temperature likely to occur in practical working. As this temperature could not during the tests be readily controlled, the results can only be taken as generally indicating the effect of heating on the compression of the material.

The curves in Fig. 35 show the effect of thorough drying on the compression of a piece of fullerboard $\frac{3}{8}$ inch thick. It will be seen that the curve departs from the linear law and compresses more at low loads than the undried insulation, due probably to the shrinkage and opening up of the layers of the material. As soon as the "give" is taken up, the dried material resists compres-

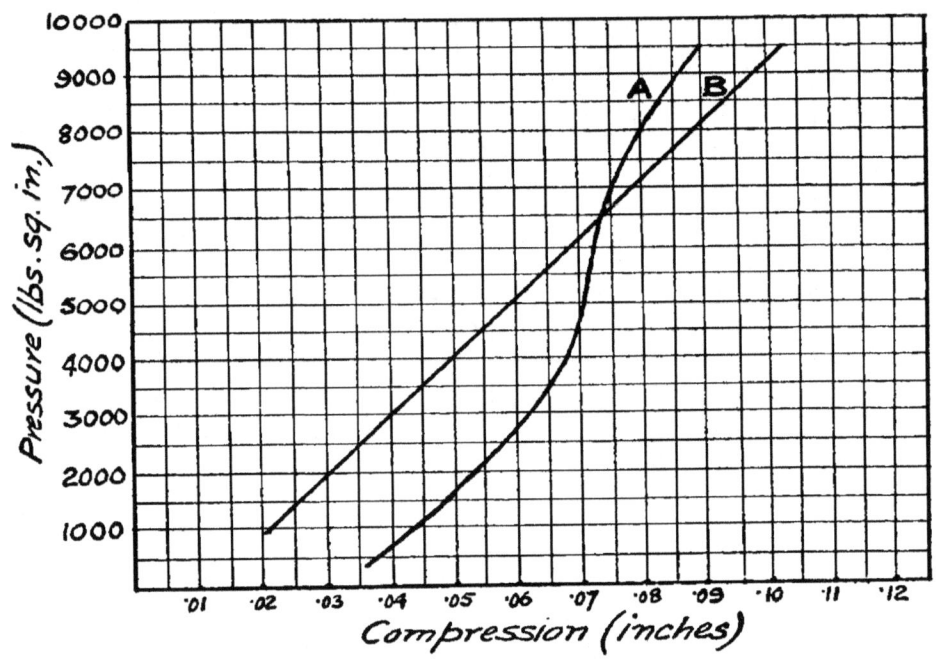

FIG. 35.

A, 0·375″ dried fullerboard.   B, 0·375″ undried fullerboard.

sion better than when undried, as is clearly shown if the load is carried up to the point of mechanical disruption.

When very thin sheets of fullerboard are tested, *i.e.* 0·010 to 0·030, there is very little difference to be noted between the dried and undried conditions.

The curve (*a*) in Fig. 36 shows the results obtained on undried and untreated fullerboard $\frac{1}{2}$ inch thick when compressed beyond the point of mechanical disruption which is indicated by the peak of the curve. This curve appears to be characteristic of all the fibrous insulating materials, but the pressure at which disruption occurs increases considerably as the thickness decreases. The following are the loads at which disruption occurred with various materials.

0·250″ undried, untreated fullerboard	. 41,000 lbs. per square inch
0·250″ dried ,, ,,	. 57,000 ,, ,,
0·134″ undried, treated fullerboard .	. 58,000 ,, ,,
0·130″ ,, ,, fibre . . .	. 58,000 ,, ,,
0·130″ dried ,, ,, . . .	. 80,000 ,, ,,

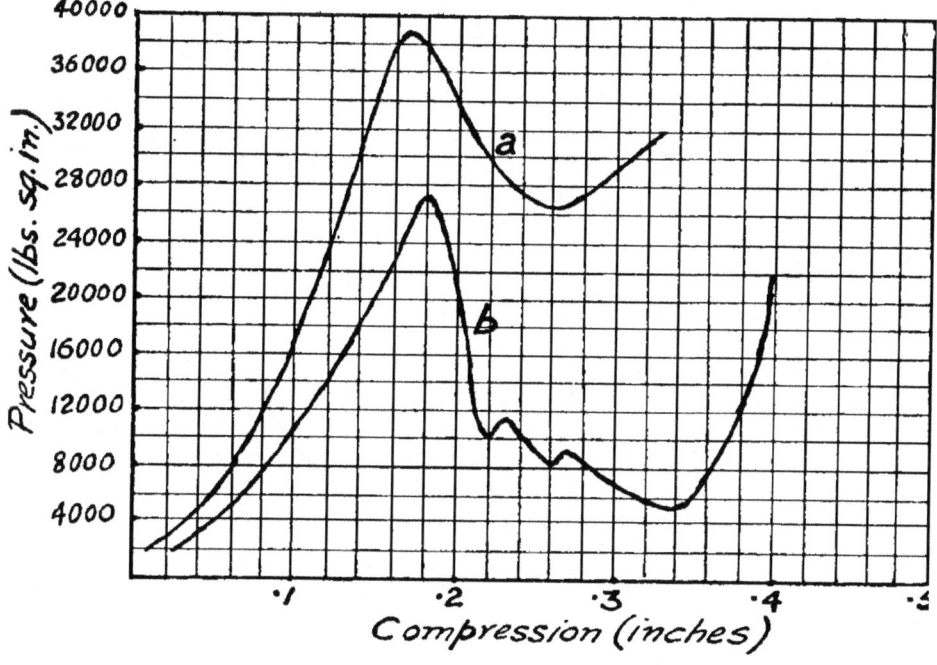

Fɪɢ. 36.

The above tests were made with the insulating material projecting beyond the edges of the test blocks, and consequently the area under compression was to some extent reinforced by the tensile strength of the fibres extending into the uncompressed surrounding portions, and to determine to what extent this affected the load at which disruption took place, tests were made on samples cut to the same area as the testing blocks. The results are shown on the curve (*b*) in Fig. 36.

It will be seen that with the smaller test piece the disruption point was considerably reduced, and after this point was reached the material flowed out until the thickness between the test blocks was reduced to about $\frac{1}{8}$ inch.

In all cases it was found that practically no deterioration of the materials occurred until the point of disruption was very nearly reached. Beyond this point the compressed area tends to disintegrate and the material almost entirely loses its fibrous nature.

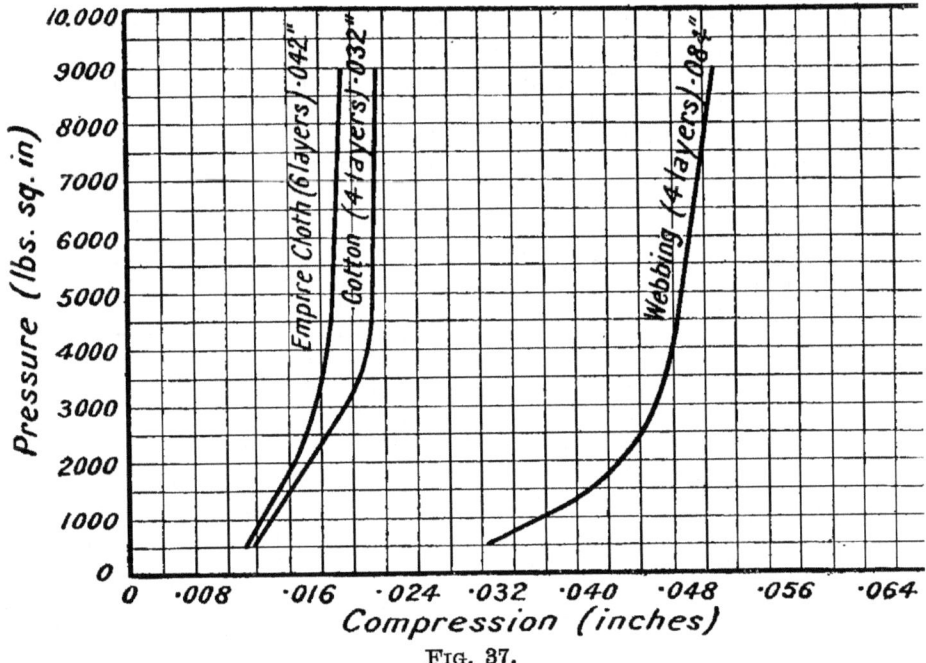

FIG. 37.

Tests on Empire cloth, fabrics, etc.—The curves in Fig. 37 show the effect of compression on Empire cloth, untreated fabrics and untreated cotton tape, from which it will be seen that up to loads of about 4000 lbs. per square inch considerable compression takes place, but comparatively little occurs beyond this point. Except in the case of Empire cloth no appreciable deterioration in the insulation was noted for loads up to 10,000 lbs. per square inch.

In the case of Empire cloth, where a number of layers were pressed together between cast steel cubes, it was found that the internal layers were cracked and torn considerably, due apparently to the varnished surfaces sticking together and preventing the layers from adjusting themselves to the load. The following tests were made to determine the safe working load for Empire cloth with ten layers of material.

(*a*) Between cast steel test blocks a maximum load of 6000 lbs. per square inch produced no deterioration.

(*b*) Between soft copper test blocks at the same load the layers were badly broken.

(*c*) Between soft copper test blocks with a load of 4000 lbs. per square inch a slight deterioration was observed.

(*d*) At lower loads between soft copper test blocks no deterioration occurred.

With a single layer of Empire cloth tested between either soft copper or steel test blocks, no deterioration occurred up to loads of 10,000 lbs. per square inch.

Somewhat similar tests were made with a number of layers of cotton tape treated with varnish, and up to loads of 10,000 lbs. per square inch no mechanical deterioration of the tape itself took place, whether tested between steel or copper test blocks, although with loads above about 6000 lbs. per square inch the varnish was squeezed out and apparently disappeared in some places.

When tested up to loads of about 40,000 lbs. per square inch, the fibrous nature of the tapes, fabrics, etc., was entirely destroyed.

Tests on micanite.—When tested between cast steel test blocks no mechanical injury, and very little compression, was obtained on built-up mica with loads up to 60,000 lbs. per square inch, but when tested between soft copper blocks at the same load the flow of the metal tore and entirely destroyed it. When tested between soft copper blocks up to 10,000 lbs. per square inch the material was uninjured.

Conclusions.—For the materials at present employed in connection with those windings on which the greatest mechanical stresses occur, loads up to 10,000 lbs. per square inch between soft annealed copper are, except in the case of Empire cloth, quite safe whether the insulation is in a well-dried or undried condition, provided of course that the drying has not been carried to a point where the fibrous insulation has become brittle.

In the case of Empire cloth, a load of 4000 lbs. per square inch is about the safe maximum limit between soft copper surfaces.

Materials used for wedges for rotor slots.—An important application of vulcanised fibre and certain kinds of wood is in connection with the wedges used in rotor slots. The stresses to which such wedges are subjected depends on the method of supporting them, and may be of the nature of compression, shearing, or bending, or a combination of all three. In testing materials for such purposes, therefore, the only satisfactory method is to ascertain the force required to displace a wedge radially from its position in the slot. For this purpose it is convenient to prepare testing blocks of the same shape as the actual slot, in which test wedges are placed and forced out by means of pressure applied to the under side, as shown in Fig. 38. By such means comparative tests of different materials can be made, as well as a check obtained upon the various consignments of similar materials.

A number of experiments were carried out with such a testing arrangement to determine the behaviour of fibre and wooden wedges under conditions comparable with those occurring in practice.

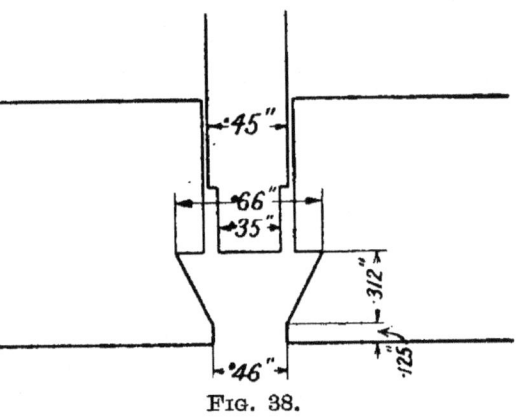

Fig. 38.

Tests to determine the variation in strength of untreated fibre wedges.—Considerable variation is found to occur in the mechanical strength of fibre wedges. In this respect there is very little to choose between the red and grey varieties, excepting perhaps for very thin sheets, say of $\frac{1}{8}$ inch and less, when the red fibre appears to be somewhat superior. Using a testing slot of the shape shown in Fig. 38 the force in lbs. per inch of length, required to displace the wedge, is shown in the following table for sheets supplied by different makers. The load was taken at its maximum value, which occurred about the time the wedge was three-fourths the way through the slot. A characteristic curve showing the relation between load on a 5″ length and compression is as given in Fig. 39 (*a*).

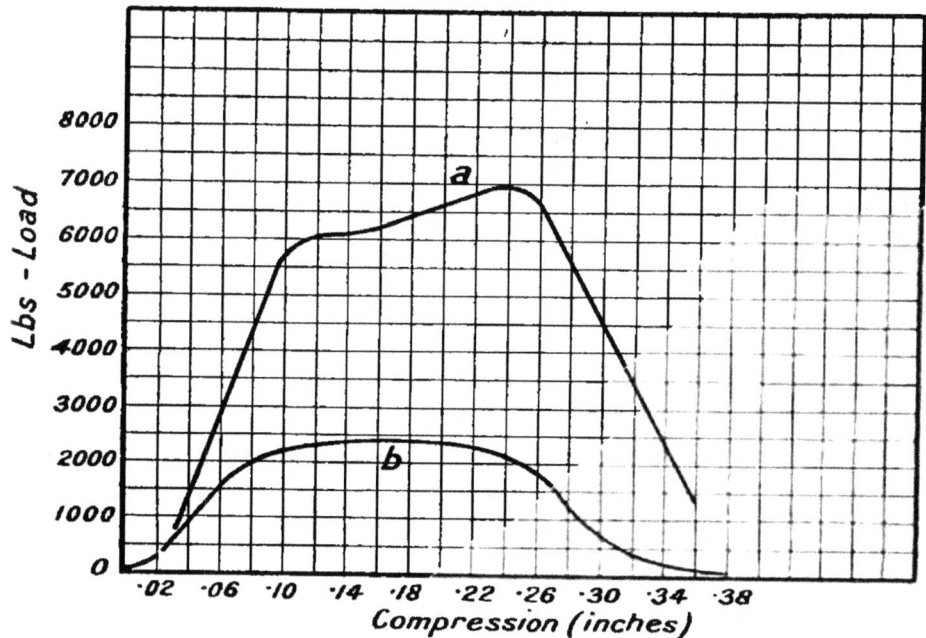

FIG. 39.

Maker.					Thickness.	Load (lbs. per inch of length).	Thickness.	Load (lbs. per inch of length).
A (grey)	.	.	.	.	$\frac{1}{4}''$	1480	$\frac{3}{16}''$	1580
B (red)	.	.	.	.	,,	1270	,,	1630
C (grey)	.	.	.	.	,,	1740	,,	2050
D (red)	.	.	.	.	,,	2410	,,	2100
E (grey)	.	.	.	.	,,	2080	,,	1960
F (red)	.	.	.	.	,,	1100	,,	1220
G (red)	.	.	.	.	,,	2140	,,	1050
H (grey)	.	.	.	.	,,	1770	,,	1330

From these figures it will be noted that a variation of as much as 100 per cent. may be expected in the strength of various makes of this material.

Effect of moisture on mechanical strength.—Fibre absorbs moisture readily, and when damp loses to a considerable extent its mechanical strength. The following table shows the effect of absorption of moisture in test pieces which were dried and then exposed in a cool damp room for from 3 to 15 days.

Sample.	Original strength in lbs. per inch length.	Strength after exposure.	Period of exposure. Days.	Per cent. decrease in strength.
1. Grey untreated .	1840	1420	3	22
2. Red ,, .	2140	1450	5	32
3. ,, ,, .	2410	2000	5	17
4. Grey ,, .	1770	1470	5	17
5. ,, ,, .	1740	1450	9	17
6. ,, ,, .	1480	1310	9	11
7. Red ,, .	1260	1080	9	14
9. ,, * treated . .	1325	1220	7	8
10. Grey ,, .	1480	1270	15	14

* The treatment consists in a slight drying and then the application of a coat of varnish to prevent re-absorption of moisture.

Similar samples were immersed in water for 12 hours and then air-dried at atmospheric temperature for 7 days, after which the following results were obtained.

Sample.	Original strength.	Subsequent to soaking and drying.	Per cent. decrease in strength.
Red untreated . .	2000	810	60
Grey ,, . .	2160	560	74

Effect of moderate drying on the mechanical strength.—The following table shows the effects of moderate drying on the mechanical strength of fibre wedges, from which it will be noted that slight drying is beneficial.

Treatment.	Lbs. per inch length.
None	1840
1 hour drying at 100° C.	2050
2 ,, ,, ,, ...	1900
3 ,, ,, ,, ...	1640
1 hour drying in vacuum at 75° C. . .	1900
2 ,, ,, ,, ,, . .	1680
3 ,, ,, ,, ,, . .	1640
4 ,, ,, ,, ,, . .	1580

Effect of heat on mechanical strength.—Attempts were made to determine the effects of a temperature such as might be expected under operating conditions. As, however, some difficulty was found in controlling the heating, the results can only be taken as a general indication of the effects. For the sake of comparison, figures for teak and hornbeam wedges are also given.

Sample.	Maximum load on 4·75″ length.		Per cent. decrease in strength.
	Cold.	Hot.	
Grey untreated fibre . .	9900	4900	50
Red ,, ,, . .	6060	3630	40
,, treated	6500	3310	49
Hornbeam	3200	2570	20
Teak	2100	1220	42

Mechanical tests on wooden wedges.—The following figures were obtained with the same testing appliances as used for fibre.

Sample.	Thickness.	Lbs. per 1″ of length.
Hornbeam untreated . .	$\frac{1}{4}″$	675
,, treated . . .	$\frac{1}{4}″$	695
Teak untreated	$\frac{1}{4}″$	443
,, treated	$\frac{1}{4}″$	445

The decrease in strength after drying and then exposing to a damp atmosphere for 14 days was as follows :—

Sample.	Before exposure.	After exposure.	Per cent. decrease in strength.
Hornbeam untreated . . .	675	615	9
Teak untreated	443	393	11

From this it will be noted that the effect of moisture is much less with wood than fibre. In general, hornbeam, while—like other kinds of wood—weaker than fibre, is much more reliable under varying conditions of humidity and temperature.

The curve (*b*) in Fig. 39 shows the relation between load and compression for hornbeam.

Shrinkage of fibrous material due to removal of moisture.— As already noted, insulating materials of a fibrous nature tend to shrink considerably when dried out. This is a matter of considerable importance in the case of certain types of windings, and requires some consideration from the point of view of mechanical design.

The following table gives the percentage shrinkage in thickness of various materials after prolonged drying at 100° C. where oxidation also could freely take place.

Material.	Original mean thickness.	Hours of drying.				
		40	60	90	110	230
Pressboard untreated . . .	0·020	0·5	0·5	0·65	1·0	1·2
,, varnish treated .	0·025	6·25	7·0	7·2	8·0	8·3
Fullerboard untreated . . .	0·0082	4·0	4·4	7·2	7·6	9·0
,, varnish treated .	0·01	7·1	7·4	9·8	10·5	10·9
Grey fibre (A) untreated . .	0·130	3·9	4·15	4·4	4·8	4·9
,, ,, (B) ,, .	0·0338	1·0	1·0	1·0	1·0	1·5
Red fibre untreated . . .	0·075	2·5	2·7	3·0	3·1	3·1
Rope paper ,, . . .	0·0053	5·0	5·1	5·7	6·3	6·3
,, ,, varnish treated .	0·0079	6·6	8·0	9·6	9·9	10·9
Bear paper untreated . . .	0·0034	9·9	11·6	14·0	19·0	20·0
Empire cloth	0·0075	4·0	4·3	6·2	6·6	6·6

Voltage required to break down various fibrous insulating materials.—The following table gives the voltage required to break down some of the most commonly used fibrous insulating materials. The tests were made between electrodes of one square inch area with approximately one pound pressure between them, the voltage being raised gradually at the rate of about 250 per second until disruption occurred. These figures are only of value in giving a comparison of the breakdown voltages of various materials, and it must be remembered that in practice the maximum permissible voltage per mil. is governed by the total thickness, ventilation, mechanical stresses, etc. These considerations are dealt with in connection with the design of insulation in Chapter IV.

I

It should be noted that the figures given are the results of a large number of tests, and the minimum values obtained only are given. Further, the samples were taken in an undried state straight from storage, so that the least favourable testing conditions possible were chosen.

Material.	Thickness inches.	Breakdown voltage.		
		Minimum total.	Per mil. approx. Untreated.	Treated.
Parchment paper	0·0018	420	230	—
Jap paper	0·0020	370	190	—
Bond paper	0·0031	600	200	—
Bear ,, ...	0·0032	600	190	—
Rope ,, ...	0·0050	800	160	—
Treated rope paper . . .	0·0075	4200	—	560
Fullerboard	0·0070	850	120	—
Treated fullerboard . . .	0·0090	4000	—	450
Fullerboard	0·010	1200	120	—
Treated fullerboard . . .	0·013	4400	—	340
Fullerboard	0·014	2000	150	—
Treated fullerboard . . .	0·018	5100	—	290
Fullerboard	0·028	3000	110	—
Yellow Empire cloth . . .	0·0078	6400	—	820
Black treated cloth (Grade 1)	0·0075	6500	—	870
,, ,, (Grade 2)	0·0071	5000	—	700

Effect of heating on mechanical strength of fibrous insulation.— As the moisture is dried out of fibrous insulation, the material becomes brittle, as already noted, and if the drying is continued, oxidation takes place, and the fibrous nature of the insulation becomes entirely destroyed. The curves in Fig. 40 show for various materials the time taken at different temperatures for the insulation to become so brittle as to fracture when bent completely back on itself through an angle of 180°. The heating was carried out in a well-ventilated oven maintained at a uniform temperature, and through which a stream of fresh air continually passed so as to give the most favourable conditions for oxidation.

The results show that to arrive at an embrittled condition in which, under the vibration and mechanical stresses occurring on a running machine, failure due to mechanical disruption is liable to occur, a temperature of at least 90° C. is required. In practice it may be somewhat higher than this on account of the

less favourable conditions for oxidation, although tests similar
to the above carried out in a partial vacuum did not indicate any

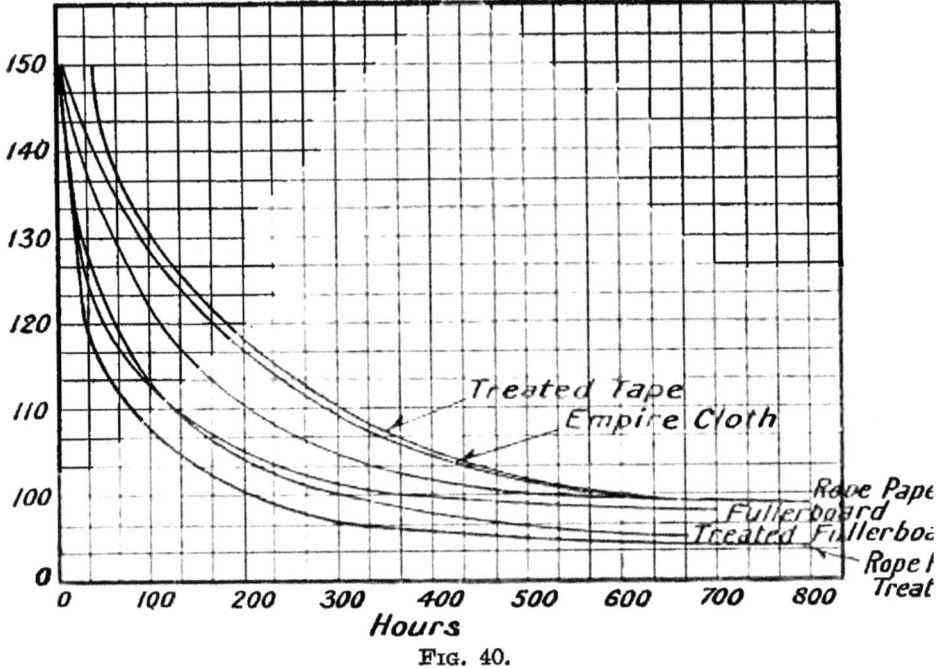

FIG. 40.

marked difference in the time required at any particular temperature to cause the insulation to become brittle.

CHAPTER IV

DESIGN OF INSULATION AND WINDINGS

General considerations.—In designing the insulation of electrical apparatus there are two main considerations to be observed, namely, the limitations imposed by the physical characteristics of the materials available, and the service conditions under which the apparatus will operate.

The insulation designer's knowledge and experience are required mainly in connection with apparatus containing windings, as in practically all other apparatus the current-carrying parts are insulated by air, oil, or surface distances, for which fairly definite rules can be laid down.

The various kinds of windings will be considered later under three heads, namely, those applying to machines, transformers, and detail apparatus.

A knowledge of the service conditions is particularly necessary in designing the insulation of large and costly apparatus. These conditions comprise, firstly, those of the station itself as regards moisture, dirt, chemical fumes, and variations in temperature; secondly, the conditions of the circuit as regards the likelihood of pressure rises.

From the manufacturer's point of view, one of the most important considerations is the bearing that the insulation design has on the total cost of the apparatus. Too liberal allowances in thickness increase the weight and consequently the cost of the apparatus, and reduce the efficiency. On the other hand, reliability must be the first consideration, and sound insulation must not be sacrificed in order to obtain high electrical efficiency or low cost.

As the cost of the insulating materials used bears only a small proportion to the total cost of the apparatus, there is very little room for economy in the materials themselves, the quality of which should consequently be the best obtainable. There is, however, greater scope for economy in the methods and time required in applying the materials.

Limitations in rating of machines.—The limit to the rating of electrical apparatus is governed at the present time almost entirely by the inability of the insulation to withstand high temperatures. It must be remembered that, in all electrical apparatus when in operation, a loss producing heat occurs in every small volume of active materials, both iron and copper, and the actual temperature attained in any portion depends on the facility with which this heat is conducted to a cooler part or to a surface from which it can be dissipated.

In the case of windings, the heat generated in the internal portions is conducted either from layer to layer through the insulation, or along the turns until the surface layers are reached, and then dissipated through any insulating covering there may be on the winding, into the surrounding cooling medium. It will thus be noted that the internal temperature of windings is to a large extent governed by the thermal conductivity of the insulation, which depends not only on the nature of the materials used, but also on the way in which they are applied. The inclusion of air-pockets, for instance, in the covering applied to windings very materially alters the rapidity of heat conduction, and their prevention between the layers of winding and in the insulation on conductors, by impregnating coils with solid insulating compound, is of the utmost importance in facilitating the conduction of heat from the interior portions.

Measurements have been made from time to time to determine the thermal conductivity of insulating materials. Perhaps the most important investigations in this respect have been made by Messrs. Symons and Miles Walker,[1] who found that, of the ordinary insulating materials, pure mica possessed very much higher thermal conductivity than built-up mica and the various fibrous insulations.

Figures obtained on test samples of insulation, while affording an interesting comparison, do not of course take into account the

[1] See *Journal of the Institution of Electrical Engineers*, Vol. xlviii., No. 213.

discrepancies which may be introduced as mentioned above due to the method of application.

There is a considerable difference of opinion as to the actual temperatures permissible for windings, and rules have been laid down both in America and on the Continent defining the temperature limits, and the load conditions to which they apply. In general the Continental practice is to rate apparatus harder and allow higher temperature limits than is considered good practice in this country or in America. The practice in this country closely corresponds to that in America, although no definite rules have as yet been established.

German Standard Specification for the testing of electrical machinery.—The temperature rise of all parts of generators and motors, except field coils excited with continuous current, to be measured by thermometer. The temperature rise of field coils excited by continuous current, and of transformer windings to be measured by increase in resistance.

Where the air temperature does not exceed 35° C. the temperature rise must not be greater than as follows :—

Rotating windings.

With cotton insulation	50° C.
With impregnated cotton and paper insulation	60° C.
With insulation by enamel, mica, asbestos or preparations of these	80° C.

Stationary windings.

The above figures may be increased 10° C.

Tramway motors—stationary and rotating parts—after 1 hour continuous working at normal load—

With cotton insulation	70° C.
With paper insulation	80° C.
With mica, asbestos, etc.	100° C.

Rules of the American Institute of Electrical Engineers. The temperature rise of all generator, motor and transformer windings not to exceed 50° C., referred to a standard room temperature of 25° C. The temperature to be measured by thermometer in the case of machine windings and by resistance in transformers.

Comparison of Continental and American practice.—The lower temperatures recognised by the American Institute of Electrical Engineers afford a bigger margin for overloads, and in general necessitate a more liberal and expensive design. As regards discriminating between the various kinds of insulation, this is logically sound, but in the authors' opinion the marked difference allowed by the German Normalein for cotton and papers is not justified.

With regard to the method of measuring temperature, the increase in the resistance of windings indicates the mean temperature rise, but affords little indication of the maximum temperature reached by the hottest part. The temperature indicated by thermometer depends entirely on how and where the thermometer is placed. If the windings are heavily insulated, there is usually a considerable difference between the temperature of the windings and that of the outer surface of the insulation, so that this method of measurement may be very misleading.

For experimental purposes the hottest portion of coils may be conveniently ascertained by placing thermo-couples in various positions during winding, and connecting these to a galvanometer during test, or small bobbins of high-resistance wire may be substituted, the variation in resistance of which can be ascertained, and a record taken from time to time during the heating test.

The temperature of oil-immersed transformers is often taken at the hottest portion of the oil, *i.e.* a few inches below the upper surface.

MACHINE WINDINGS.

Machine windings may be divided into two classes, namely—

(a) Those consisting of coils wound into radial slots in either the rotor or stator, *i.e.* the armature coils of direct current machines and small alternators, the primary and secondary windings of induction motors, the stationary windings of large alternating current generators, and the field windings of certain types of high-speed turbo-generators.

(*b*) The magnet coils for the stationary fields of direct current machines and small alternators, and for the rotating fields of large alternators and certain types of high-speed turbo-generators.

ARMATURE AND SIMILAR WINDINGS.

To meet certain electrical requirements such as output, voltage, speed, frequency, etc., the designer has usually a choice of several different methods of winding, and it requires very considerable experience to determine the best arrangement by which

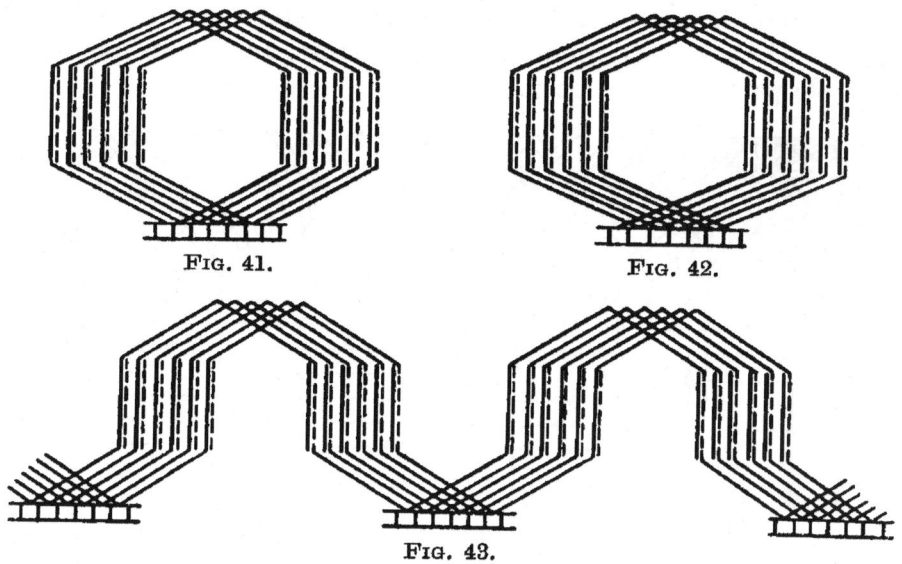

FIG. 41.   FIG. 42.

FIG. 43.

the maximum value can be obtained with the minimum weight of copper, at the same time keeping the labour of winding and the cost of other parts of the machine as low as possible.

Innumerable types of windings have been devised from time to time, but all of these fall into certain general classes, typical examples of which will be considered.

Diagrams of connections for various general types of winding are shown in Figs. 41 to 46.

Lap or multiple winding.—This type of winding is shown in Figs. 41 and 42.

Wave winding.—This type of winding is shown in Fig. 43.

Uses and comparison of lap and wave windings.—These two types cover the usual methods of winding direct current armatures. For two-pole machines both types give the same result, and it is usual to employ the lap method only. For four or more poles it is usual for the wave winding to be arranged to form a *two-circuit winding, i.e.* to give two paths only for the current to flow through the armature, and this, where the voltage permits, is preferable to the lap winding inasmuch that equalising or balancing connections are not required as may be the case when the latter type of winding is used.

Lap windings are employed when the voltage is so low that, on account of the small number of conductors, and their large size, multiple paths have to be provided.

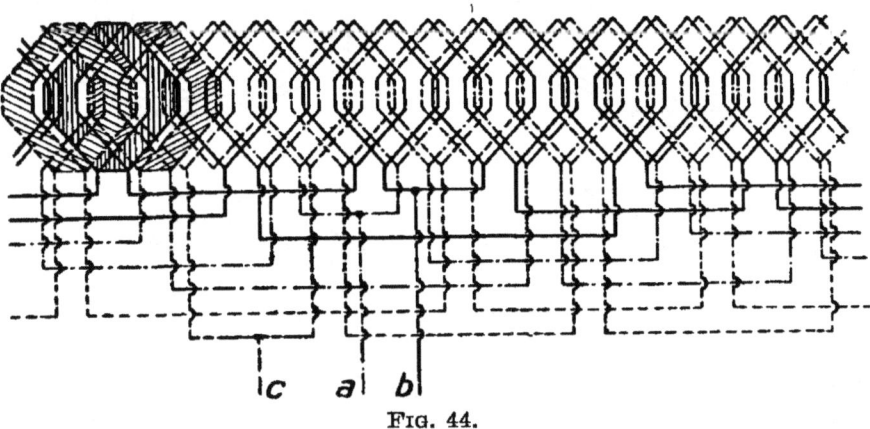

Fig. 44.

Progressive and retrogressive windings.—The difference between these two methods of connecting will be seen by tracing the direction of winding and connection to the commutator shown in Figs. 41 and 42, the former being, as its method of connection indicates, progressive, and the latter retrogressive. Both lap and wave windings may be arranged with either of these methods of connection. A lap retrogressive and a wave progressive give the same direction of current flow around the armature, and in a generator will give a positive brush under a north pole for clockwise rotation.

Typical alternator windings.—Fig. 44 shows a method of winding whereby the coils of various groups are lapped as in the case of direct current machines.)Fig. 45 shows the coils of each group arranged concentrically, this arrangement being usually employed where there is one coil only per slot.

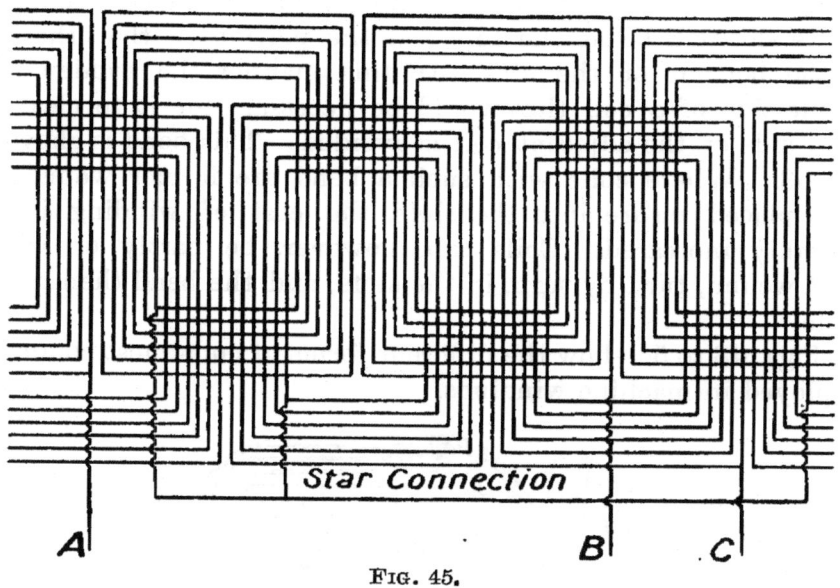

Fig. 45.

Figs. 46 and 47 show a method of winding employed only on small low voltage machines. It is known as the "skein" winding,

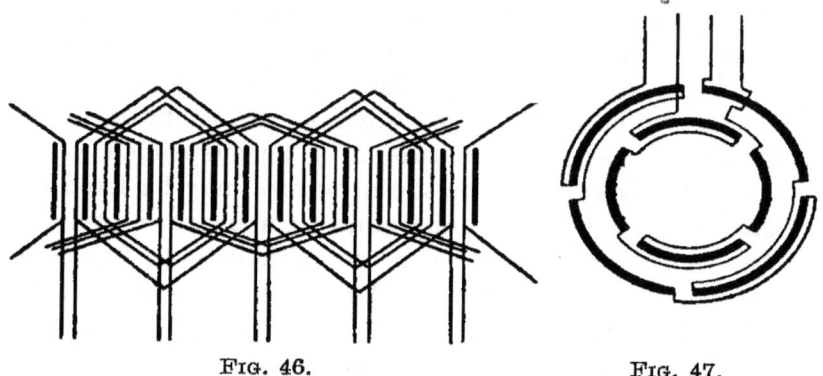

Fig. 46.   Fig. 47.

a skein of wire being taken and looped backwards and forwards into the slots. By this means a number of joints are eliminated, and a cheap and satisfactory winding obtained.

General design of windings.—In windings where the coils are not concentric with each other, the most convenient arrangement is to have two coils in each slot, *i.e.* viewing in section the part of the armature embraced by one coil, the portion of the coil contained in one slot will be at the top, and the portion in the other slot at the bottom of the slot. In this manner the sudden bend on one side of a coil that would be necessary for it to clear the other side of the adjacent coil is avoided. This bend is shown in Fig. 53. Where coils with such a bend are former wound, and then placed entire into the slots, the cost of winding is considerably increased. Coils can, however, be partly or wholly hand wound, turn by turn, in the slots, and the bend then readily made.

Figs. 48 to 54 show the different forms of coils most commonly employed in machine windings.

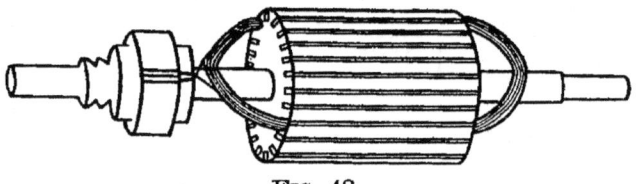

FIG. 48.

Windings for very small machines with semi-enclosed slots.—Where semi-enclosed slots, as in the case of very small direct current armatures, are used, the type of winding employed is one in which the wires are threaded through the opening at the top, into the slots which are lined with insulation, as shown in Fig. 48. During this process the armature may be suspended in a lathe and wound during rotation, or the armature may be fixed and the wire taken from a bobbin, and wound turn by turn by hand into the slots. An alternative to these two methods is to first wind the coil in a loose hank, and thread the turns a few at a time into the slots. This latter method is the most wasteful of copper, but makes all the coils of equal size. With either of these methods the part of the shaft and the end plates on which the portions of winding outside the slots lie must be first carefully insulated.

Diamond winding.—For the general run of direct current armatures and the stator windings of induction motors having open slots, formed coils are usually employed, and the commonest type of winding for this purpose is that of the diamond shape, which is

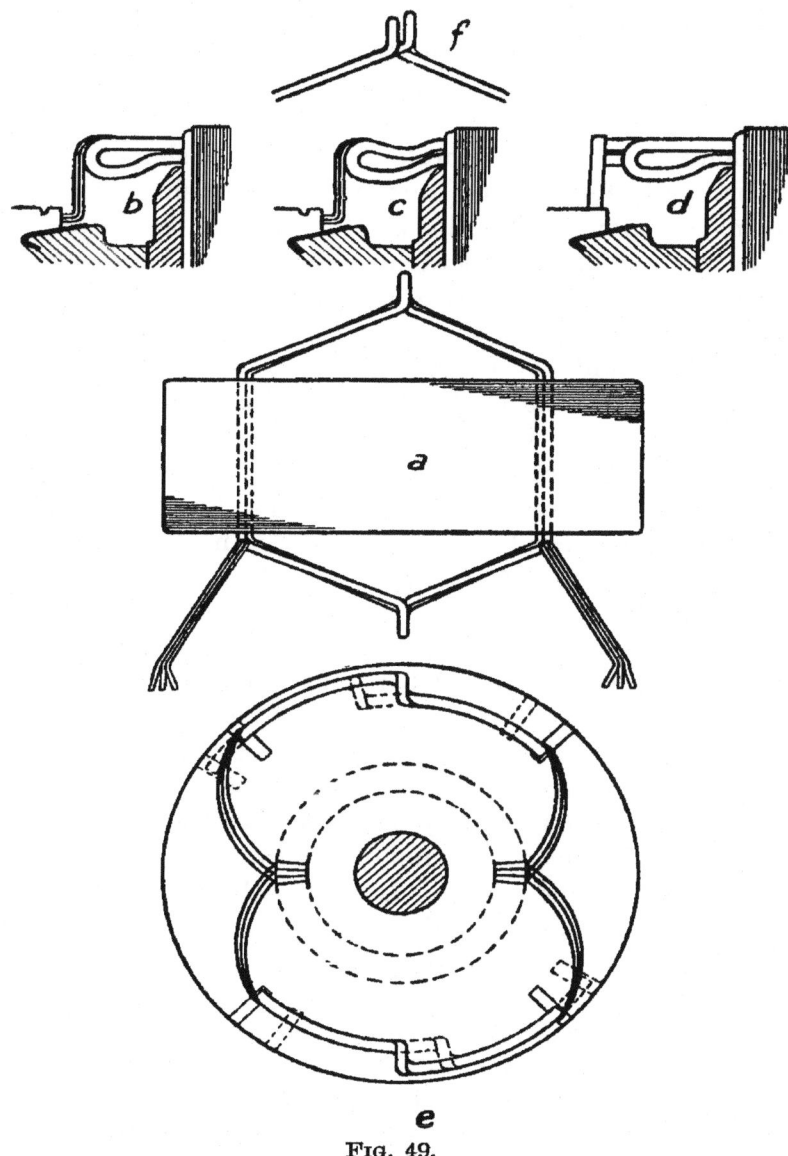

Fig. 49.

shown in Fig. 49 (*a*). It will be seen that with such a coil the starting and finishing leads both leave the coil on the upper edge.

Where the conductors are heavy, this introduces some difficulty in bringing the leads down to the commutator, and, where coils consist of two turns only, it is now common practice to make a double loop at the rear end so as to cause one lead to come out on the upper and the other on the under side of the coil, as shown in Fig. 49 (*f*).

Diamond coils may be completely formed to shape on a wooden mould, or partly formed and then pulled into shape on a special device in the manner described later. With the latter method the coils are usually left straight between the loop and the slot portions, and a sectional view of the ends of the coils as they thus appear in the armature is shown in Fig. 49 (*c*). When the coil is entirely formed and not pulled to shape, the ends are given the curvature corresponding to that of the armature, and the sectional view is then as shown in Fig. 49 (*b*).

In the case of wire coils the leads are flexible enough to be brought down to the commutator, as shown in Figs. 49 (*b*) and 49 (*c*), whereas with strap conductors commutator necks are required, as shown in Fig. 49 (*d*). An end view of this type of winding is shown in Fig. 49 (*e*).

Where there are only two bars per slot a cheap winding is obtained by inserting straight bars into the slots and bending the ends to the diamond shape by means of a suitable tool. The bars are then joined by soldering suitable connecting sleeves over their ends. Such an arrangement can of course be used for four or even six bars per slot, but usually in such cases the complexity of joints renders some other scheme of winding more desirable.

When the diamond winding is used with rectangular insulated wire, the sharp bends around the loops are a source of danger, and such coils can best be wound flat and afterwards pulled into shape.

The diamond type of winding has been employed to some extent for turbo-generator field coils with three or more straps per slot side by side. The diamond shaped coil possesses the advantage of being readily formed, it takes up little room in depth on the ends, and can easily be banded suitable for high speeds. It takes up considerable room in length, however, in an axial direction, and with coils of fairly small conductors a shortened form of coil is sometimes desirable. This can be arranged as shown in Fig. 50, the coil no longer having a loop at

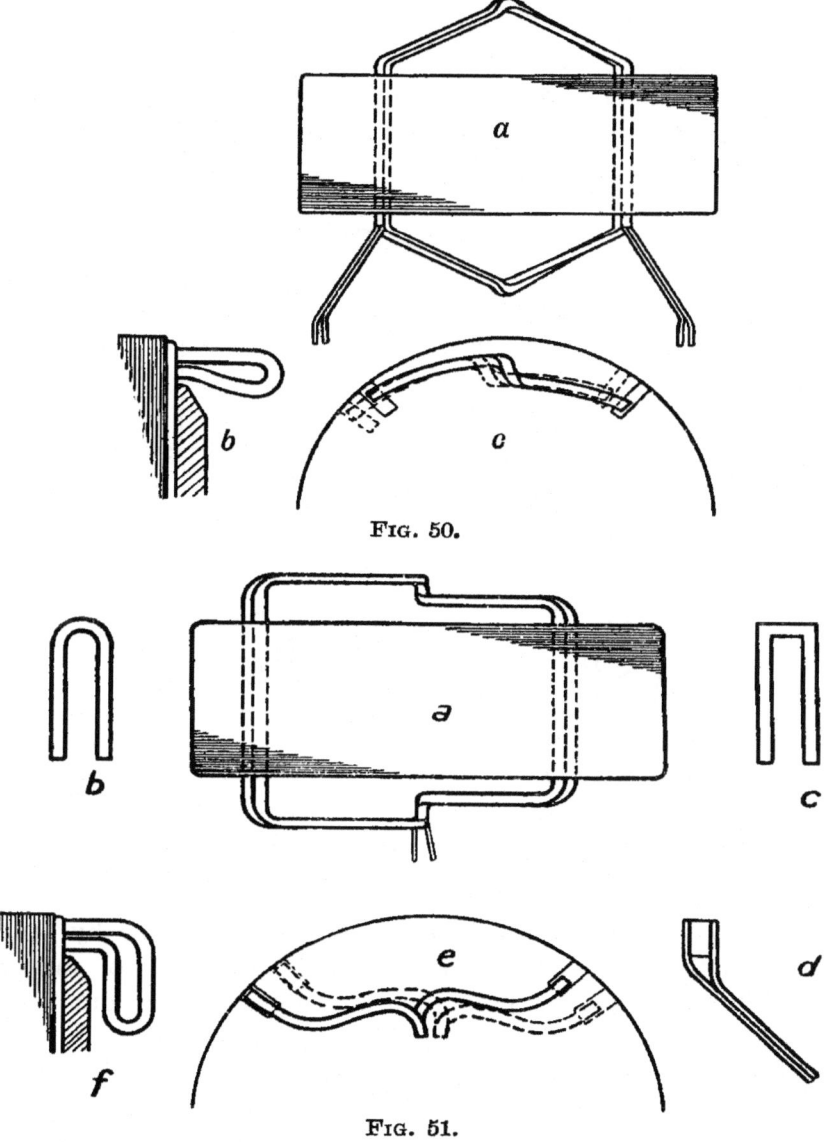

FIG. 50.

FIG. 51.

the ends, but taking a somewhat flattened formation. It will be noticed that such an arrangement brings the leads out on the upper and under sides of the coil, and is advantageous in this respect. The twist at the ends requires plenty of depth, otherwise the coils will not lay nicely.

Involute windings.—When a comparatively short coil is required, the involute type of coil shown in Fig. 51 (*a*) is usually employed. Such coils can be completely wound on a mould to their final shape, or more cheaply wound on a stepped former, as shown in Fig. 56, and then pulled to shape.

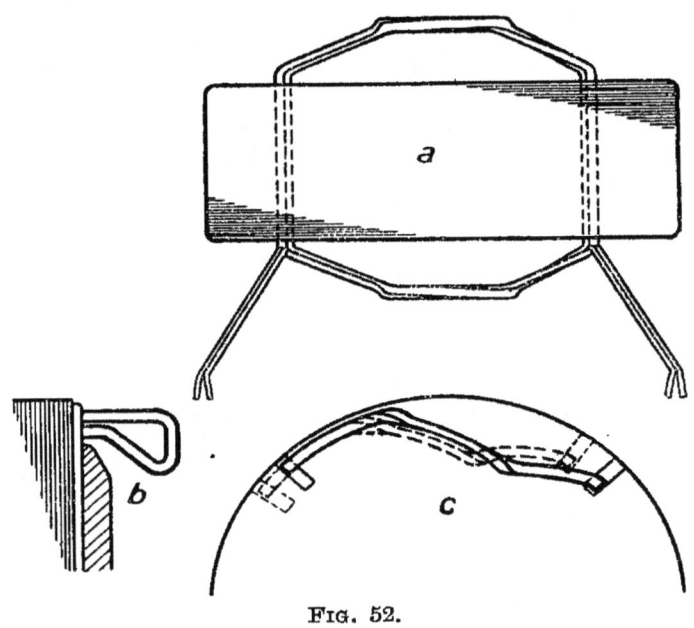

FIG. 52.

Where two bars only per slot are employed, it is usual to make the ends of separate connectors formed either by bending strap on edge around a pin and then pulling to shape, as shown in Fig. 51 (*b*), or by punching the connector out of solid sheet and bending to shape as shown in Fig. 51 (*c*).

Octagonal winding.—This type of coil combines the diamond and involute formations, and is shown in Fig. 52. It gives a very compact winding, and is useful in many cases where there is limited room in both depth and length. Such a coil requires to be wound completely to shape on a suitable mould.

Basket windings.—The stators and rotors of induction motors having semi-enclosed slots can, for low voltages, and where the coils consist of a large number of turns of small round wire, be conveniently wound with the basket type of winding as shown in Fig. 53. The coils are first wound in a hank and the turns

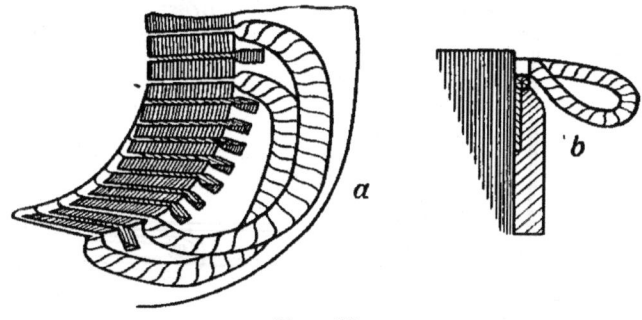

FIG. 53.

threaded a few at a time through the opening at the top of the slot, the latter being first lined with suitable insulation. Such a winding can be used with two coils per slot, but more often is employed where there is only one coil per slot.

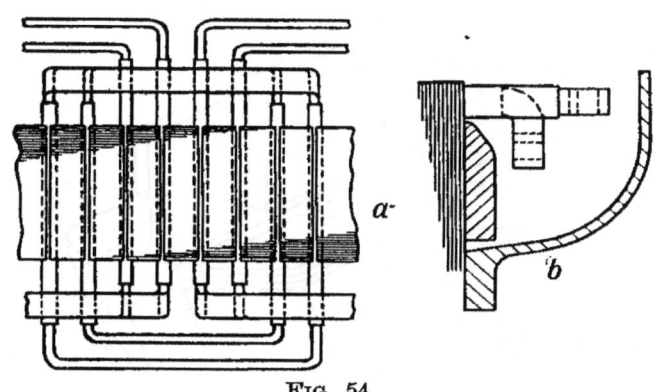

FIG. 54.

Concentric windings.—For large alternators and induction motors, except where the voltage is very low and two conductors only used per slot, the concentric form of winding shown in Fig. 54 is employed. For high voltages this form is particularly suitable as the end portions can readily be insulated.

Coil-forming apparatus.—Fig. 55 shows a standard form of wooden mould used for winding octagonal coils.

Fig. 56 shows a mould for involute winding, where the coil is wound and afterwards pulled to its final shape.   Fig. 57 shows

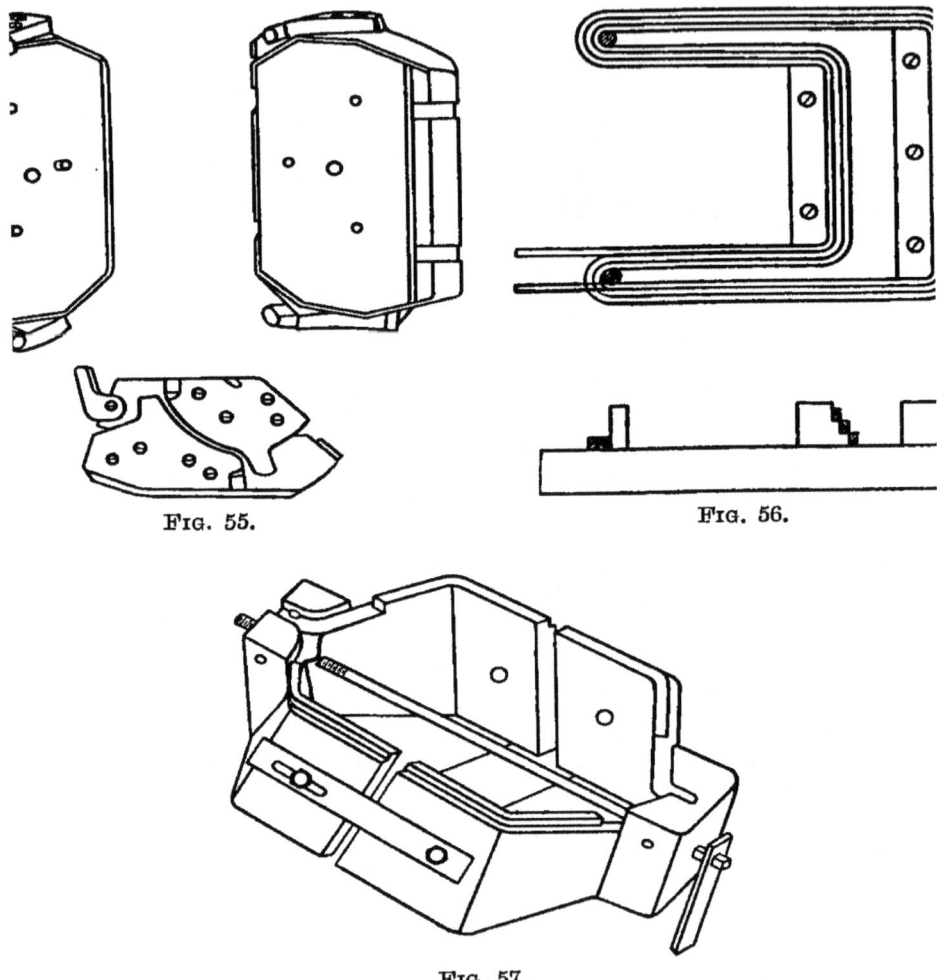

FIG. 55.

FIG. 56.

FIG. 57.

a metal mould of the kind used for forming strap coils of the diamond type.

Fig. 58 shows one of a number of forms of the apparatus employed for shaping the coils of the diamond type that are first

K

wound on a flat mould and then pulled to shape. Where much repetition work has to be done, this method is very much cheaper and requires fewer winding machines than is the case where the coils are wound directly to their final shape.

Insulation of windings.—The insulation of windings falls under two heads, namely, the "internal" and "external" insulation. The former refers to the insulation on individual conductors, between adjacent turns, layers, etc.; and the latter to the insu-

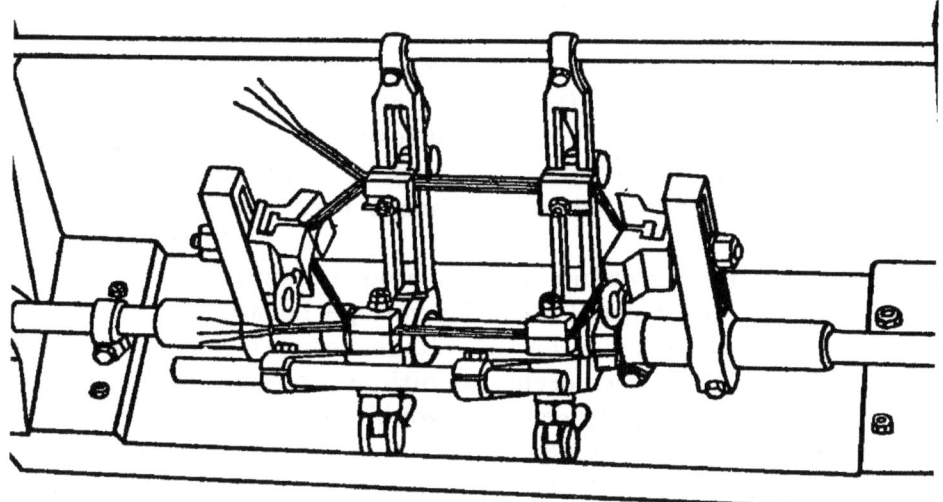

Fig. 58.

lation between complete coils or windings and ground, or adjacent circuits.

Internal insulation.—Except in the case of very high voltage machine windings, the principal consideration in connection with the insulation on conductors is the danger of mechanical damage during winding. This is especially the case where the conductors are large and much tension is required to wind, and the thickness and nature of the insulation is to a large extent governed by these considerations. The operating conditions, especially in regard to temperature and moisture, determine the kind of treatment required on the materials used between turns and layers.

In practice conductors are usually insulated by a covering

of silk, cotton, or tape. In some types of winding effective insulation can be obtained by spacing the bare conductors apart.

Where a cotton or silk covering is used it is spun on to the conductor in one or more layers. Cotton covering is used very largely on wires of sizes ranging from about 0·008 inch diameter round wire up to 0·25 inch square wire. Silk covering is very much more expensive than cotton covering, and for this reason is only used on small wires where the economy effected by the saving in space over cotton covering more than balances its higher price. Double cotton covering is capable of withstanding a considerable amount of hard usage, and for this reason has a very wide range of application. A coil wound with conductors insulated in this way will, when the insulation is quite dry, withstand between turns a voltage of from 1500 to 2000; in practice, however, the voltage between adjacent turns should not exceed about 20.

Triple cotton covering can be used advantageously on conductors where the normal working voltage between turns is more than 20 volts, and, for a lower voltage between turns, when the shape of the coil, or the service conditions, demand for mechanical reasons a covering heavier than double cotton. Whatever the working conditions, it is advisable to treat cotton covering on the wires with some varnish, enamel, or compound so as to render it moisture-resisting, and to improve its power of withstanding deterioration due to high temperatures. Methods of treatment will be dealt with later.

With silk coverings this does not apply so generally. Silk-covered wires are usually very small, and a treatment that may be perfectly satisfactory on a cotton-covered wire of moderate size may corrode a fine wire sufficiently to produce open-circuits. When a fine wire covered either with silk or cotton is treated, the treating material should be dried very quickly so as to safeguard as much as possible against chemical corrosion on the wire.

Cotton braiding is sometimes used, and may be put on in one layer over the bare conductor, or over the conductor when this has already been covered with one or more layers of cotton. This is a stronger covering mechanically than ordinary cotton covering. When used directly over the bare copper it should be very closely woven, as otherwise it will open badly in bending around sharp corners. The remarks made above regarding the treatment of cotton covering apply equally to braiding.

Conductors of considerable section may be insulated by taping either during winding or after the coil has been completely formed. This method is used generally only with heavy wire or strap where a stronger insulation mechanically is required than is obtained with cotton covering. It is, however, also of use where two or more wires are wound in parallel, since economy can be effected both in cost and space by using these bare and taping them together instead of having a cotton covering on each of the wires. If untreated tape is used for this purpose, the coil should be finally treated in such a way as to thoroughly impregnate the tape.

The treatment of the internal materials necessary to render windings moisture-resisting and better able to withstand high temperatures, may be effected in several different ways.

Cotton or silk covered or braided wire may be treated before use with a suitable varnish or compound. The wire should be dried carefully before treatment. The advantages of treating wire in this way are, that the treatment helps to bind the covering to the conductor and thus renders it more capable of resisting abrasion during winding, a stock of wire can be prepared ready for immediate use, and the treated wire is dry when wound into coils. On the other hand, the varnish has to be very thin to keep the turns from sticking together when the wire is being dried after treatment, and also to prevent the insulation from thickening up and wasting space.

Treatment may be effected after winding by drying the coil under vacuum at a temperature of about 100° C., then, while at this temperature and still under vacuum, impregnating it with a compound having a melting point of about 110° C. The molten compound is forced into the interstices of the coil by air pressure of about 50 lbs. per square inch. Coils for treatment in this way are best wound with untreated material between turns and layers, such material becoming thoroughly impregnated. Coils of cross sectional dimensions 6 inches by 6 inches, or even more, can be treated very satisfactorily in this way. This is perhaps the very best treatment, as it cements the conductors into a solid mass, thereby assisting heat dissipation and rendering the winding waterproof. The treatment is, however, only generally applicable to stationary coils, as when used on windings of rotating parts the compound may be thrown out by centrifugal force. Varnish is sometimes used instead of compound, and the treatment can then be carried out at a much lower temperature. The method, however, is not very satisfactory, since if an oxidising varnish is used, it is very difficult to dry it throughout the coil.

In another method the coil is dried out in an ordinary drying oven, or under vacuum, then dipped while hot in varnish, being afterwards dried by baking. This treatment is quite satisfactory for small coils where the varnish can readily reach the parts requiring treatment, and is simpler and cheaper than the other methods given. It is also useful in those cases where little other than a surface coating is required.

External insulation—slot portions.—As regards external insulation, the size and shape of slot should be chosen, and the insulation and conductors so arranged as to give the best "space factor," that is, to allow the maximum amount of copper to be used. The space factor is the percentage of the section of slot occupied by copper. The dimensions of the slot below the wedge or banding wires should be taken as giving the fairest comparisons. It will be readily seen that the smaller the size of conductor, the greater will be the space lost in internal insulation. Similarly, if round wires are used the inter-spaces will be greater than in the case of rectangular conductors. The higher the voltage, the greater will be the thickness of external insulation, and consequently the poorer the space factor. The shape of coil will also have an important bearing, and it will be apparent that whether one or two coils are used in each slot, the most economical section for each coil is a perfect square. If the coils are wound in regular layers they will give a better space factor than when "mush" wound, provided, of course, that the width of the slot is such as to just accommodate a particular number of wires. With small wires and certain types of winding it becomes impossible to wind in regular formation, and a "mush" or irregular arrangement has to be used.

The radial thickness of insulation necessary on the slot portions of the coil depends mainly on the voltage, the size of the coil and the mechanical stresses it will have to withstand when the machine is in operation.

Safe figures for the radial thickness of insulation for various voltages can be obtained from the curve in Fig. 59. It will be noted that for voltages above about 3500 between windings and ground, the radial insulation requires to be not less than about

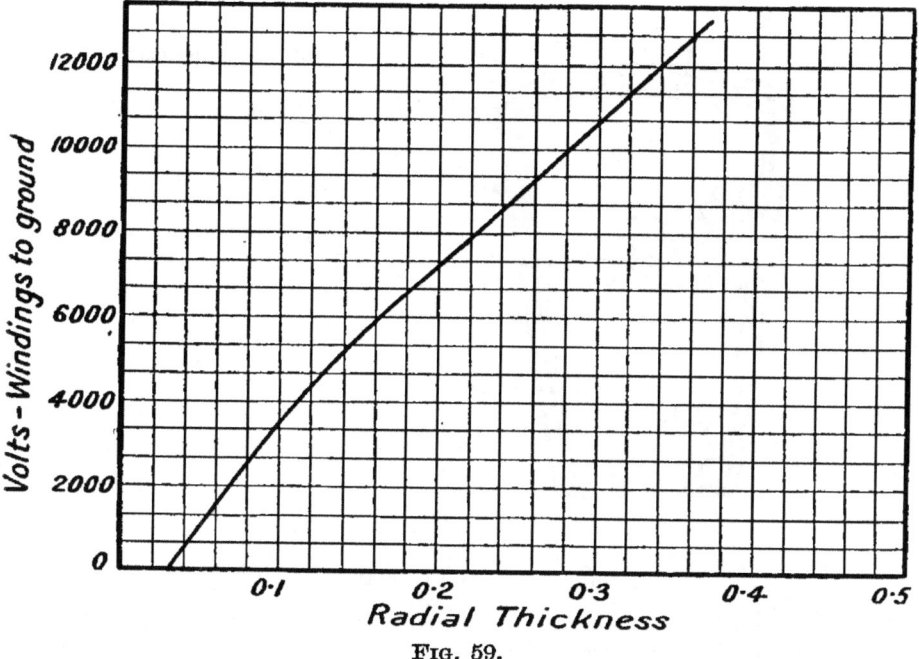

FIG. 59.

0·001 inch per 35 volts. This is necessary on account of the danger of internal chemical action, as will be noted later.

A variety of methods have been employed in the insulation of the slot portions of windings, depending on the voltage, type of coil and shape of slot used. Where coils are hand wound into partially closed slots, all the external insulation has to be used in the form of slot lining and the only variations possible are in the kind and amount of insulation used. In the case of formed coils for low voltages, the external insulation may be placed all on the coils, all in the slots as a lining, or part on the coils and part in the slots. In the case of high voltage coils of the concentric form all the insulation is placed on the coils, excepting where the conductors are threaded turn by turn through insulating tubes. The latter type of winding is now falling into disuse on account of the difficulty of ensuring satisfactory insulation between conductors and the impossibility of eliminating air pockets between the conductors and external insulation.

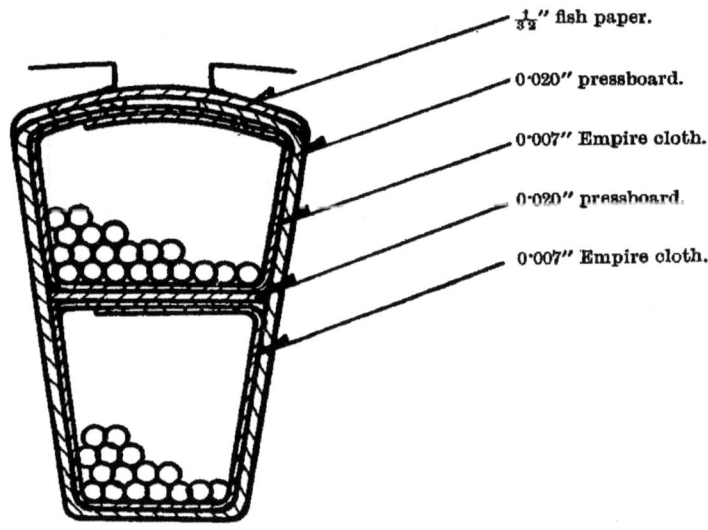

$\frac{1}{32}''$ fish paper.

0·020″ pressboard.

0·007″ Empire cloth.

0·020″ pressboard.

0·007″ Empire cloth.

FIG. 60.

Area of slot under wedge = 0·247 sq. in.
Area of slot after deducting external insulation = 0·195 sq. in.
Each coil = 75 turns of 0·022 d.c.c. wire.
Total area of cotton-covered wire = 0·046 sq. in. × 2 = 0·092 sq. in.
Area of bare wire = 0·057 sq. in.
Space factor = 23·8 per cent.

Figs. 60 to 67 show various methods of insulating the slot portions of coils. In each of these particular cases complete figures and the resulting space factor are given for a typical example.

Small direct current armature coils.—Fig. 60 shows the method of insulating small hand-wound coils enclosed in slots between parallel teeth. The slot lining consists of pressboard and Empire cloth, which in practice gives probably the best form of insulation for such a winding. This insulation is turned over at the top of the slot when the coil is in place, and held down by means of a wedge. A lining of micanite, backed with paper or cloth, is sometimes used, but this cannot be bent over so readily at the top, and further, requires to be supported with considerable care where the insulation projects beyond the ends of the slots, otherwise the insulation may be mechanically strained at these points.

For this and all mush windings—other examples of which are given in Figs. 61 and 65—it will be found that, allowing for twists and crosses in the wires during winding, the maximum

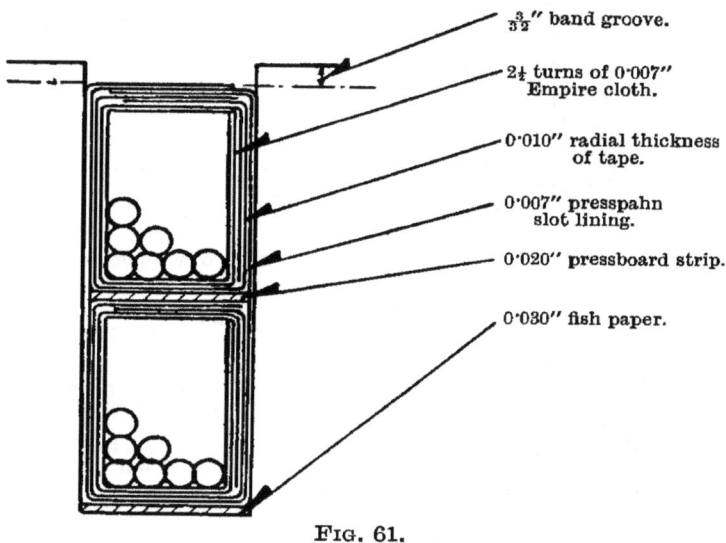

Area of slot under band = 0·284 sq. in. Area of copper = 0·084 sq. in.
Each coil = 16 turns of 0·057″ dia. d.c.c. wire. Space factor = 28·8 per cent.

sectional area of cotton-covered wire that can be used is approximately 66 per cent. of the space available inside the external insulation. For very small slots the percentage is lower.

Formed coils for low voltages.—Figs. 61, 62, and 63 show different methods of insulating the slot portions of formed coils of round or rectanglar section conductors for voltages up to about 600. The coil shown in Fig. 61 is of the mush type, the wires being wound into the space provided on the wooden former without any attempt at a regular formation. Before removing from the mould the coil is tied, and afterwards varnish treated to cement the wires together and thus preserve the shape. The slot portions are then insulated by wrapping with Empire cloth, as shown in

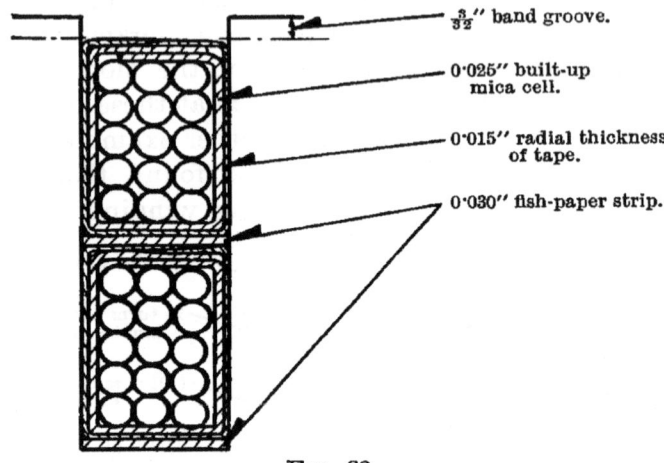

$\frac{3}{32}$" band groove.

0·025" built-up mica cell.

0·015" radial thickness of tape.

0·030" fish-paper strip.

FIG. 62.

Area of slot under band = 0·363 sq. in.   Area of copper = 0·122 sq. in.
Each coil = 15 turns of 0·072" dia. d.c.c. wire.   Space factor = 33·6 per cent.

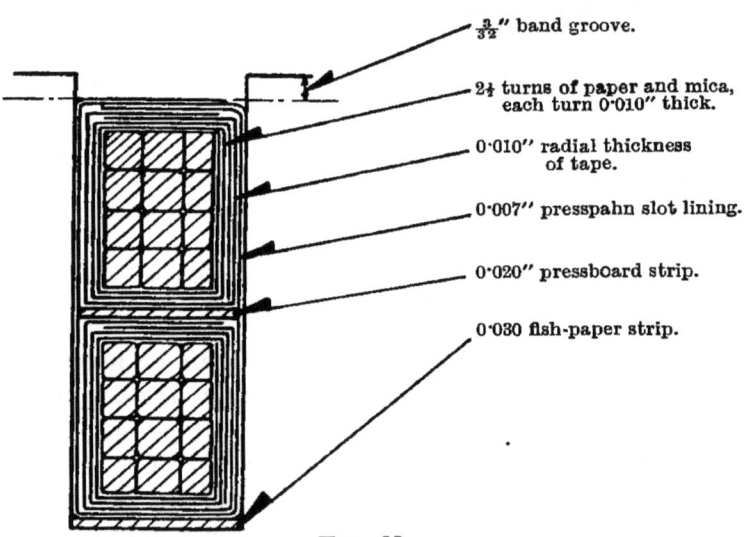

$\frac{3}{32}$" band groove.

2½ turns of paper and mica, each turn 0·010" thick.

0·010" radial thickness of tape.

0·007" presspahn slot lining.

0·020" pressboard strip.

0·030 fish-paper strip.

FIG. 63.

Area of slot under band = 0·375 sq. in.   Area of copper = 0·137 sq. in.
0·055 × 0·11 d.c.c. rectangular copper ribbon.   Space factor = 36·5 per cent.

Fig. 61.   In all three methods shown the coils are completely insulated before placing in the slots, the lining shown being used simply to afford mechanical protection to the tape when the coils are pushed down into the slots.

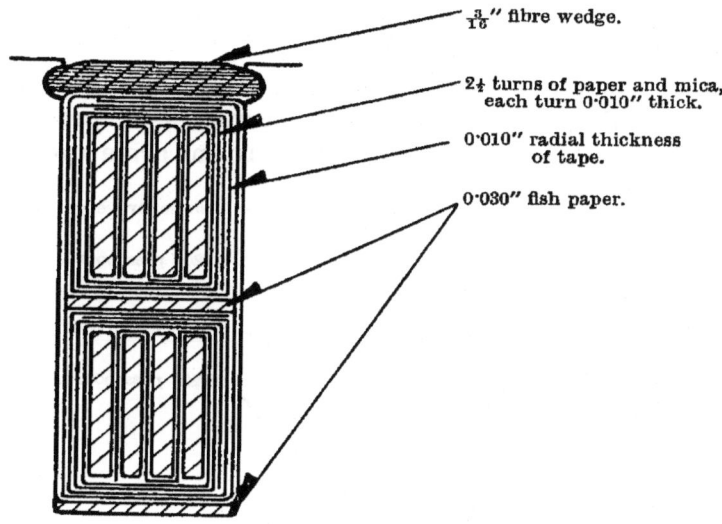

$\frac{3}{16}''$ fibre wedge.

$2\frac{1}{4}$ turns of paper and mica, each turn 0·010″ thick.

0·010″ radial thickness of tape.

0·030″ fish paper.

FIG. 64 (a).

Area of slot under wedge = 0·5 sq. in. Area of copper = 0·28 sq. in.
Each coil = 4 turns of 0·07″ × ½″ copper. Space factor = 56 per cent.

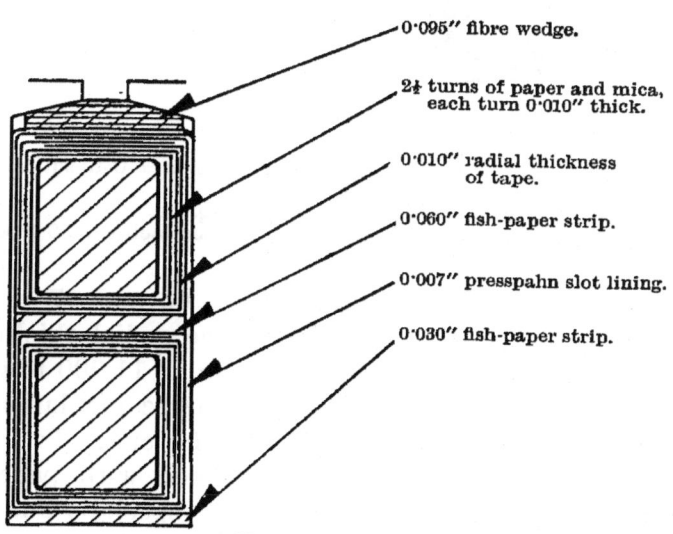

0·095″ fibre wedge.

$2\frac{1}{4}$ turns of paper and mica, each turn 0·010″ thick.

0·010″ radial thickness of tape.

0·060″ fish-paper strip.

0·007″ presspahn slot lining.

0·030″ fish-paper strip.

FIG. 64 (b).

Area of slot under wedge = 0·410 sq. in. Area of copper = 0·242 sq. in.
Each coil = 1 turn of 0·25″ × 0·5″ copper strap. Space factor = 59 per cent.

Where strap conductors are used, as shown in Fig. 64 (*a*), the insulation between these can be made by interleaving the paper and mica in the manner shown. Fig. 64 (*b*) shows a single conductor coil similarly insulated.

Basket winding.—Fig. 65 shows a method of insulating this form of winding. The slot lining consists of pressboard and Empire cloth as used for small direct current armature coils.

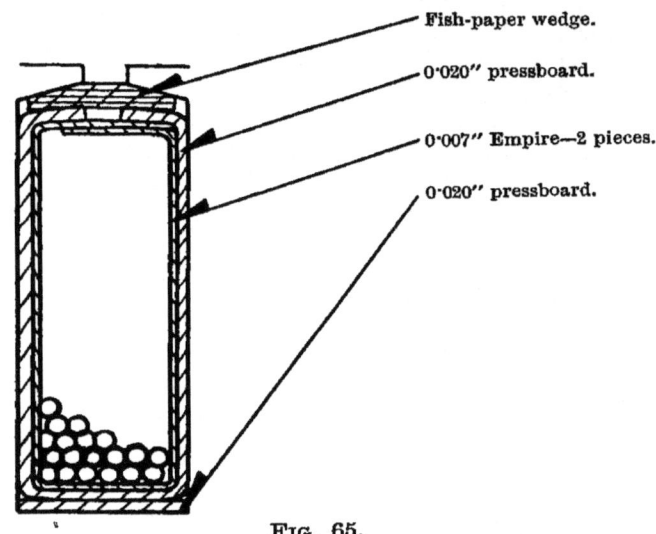

Fish-paper wedge.

0·020″ pressboard.

0·007″ Empire—2 pieces.

0·020″ pressboard.

FIG. 65.

Area of slot under wedge = 0·60 sq. in.
Area of slot after deducting external insulation = 0·49 sq. in.
Each coil = 86 turns of 0·057 d.c.c. wire.
Total area of cotton-covered wire = 0·324 sq. in.
Area of bare wire = 0·22 sq. in.   Space factor = 36·4 per cent.

High voltage concentric coils.—Figs. 66 and 67 give methods of insulating this type of winding. The radial thickness shown in Fig. 66 is that necessary for a voltage of 11,000 to ground, and in Fig. 67 for 6000 volts. In each case the insulation is applied to the coil before this is inserted into the slot. In the first case the insulation is of built-up mica backed with paper, moulded on to the coil by hot irons in a machine specially adapted to the purpose. A particularly good insulation is effected in this manner, as all air spaces in the thickness of the insulation are eliminated. In the second case the insulation shown is of built-up mica backed with Empire cloth, perhaps the best combination where the wrapping has to be applied by hand.

External insulation—ends of coils.—The ends of armature coils are usually insulated by covering with some suitable tape. A plain cotton tape may be used and the coil afterwards impregnated with insulating varnish or compound, or a treated tape—as, for instance, a varnish-treated cotton tape—may be used and finished off by brushing or spraying with an air-drying varnish.

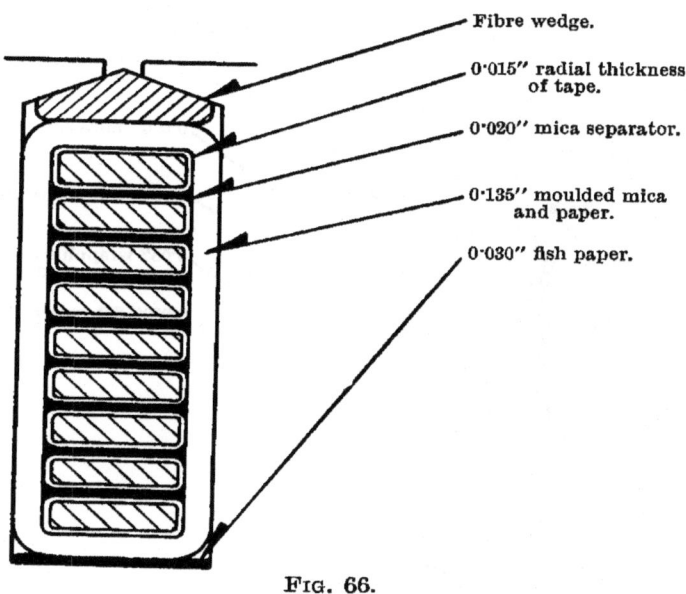

Fibre wedge.

0·015″ radial thickness of tape.

0·020″ mica separator.

0·135″ moulded mica and paper.

0·030″ fish paper.

FIG. 66.

Area of slot under wedge = 1·07 sq. ins.   Area of copper = 0·27 sq. in.
Space factor = 25·2 per cent.

For low voltage coils, such as shown in Fig. 49, a single layer of cotton tape, half-lapped, is usually employed, this being carried over the ends of the slot insulation to seal these up and then completely along the slot portions to hold the wrapping or other insulation in place. To economise in room it is usual to butt the turns of tape on these portions of the coil.

It will be noted in Fig. 49 that the insulation on the straight parts of the coil projects beyond the slots at each end so that the tape insulation on the ends of the coils is reinforced by the surface insulation thus provided.

For high voltage coils, such as shown in Fig. 54, the ends are usually insulated with several layers of Empire tape with a final covering of cotton tape. The Empire tape is made by cutting the cloth into strips, preferably on the " bias " so that the turns can be pulled tightly on to the coil. The varnish film on the tape is necessarily damaged to some extent, and each layer of tape as it is completed should be brushed over with a thin layer of varnish, this being allowed to set before the next layer of tape is applied.

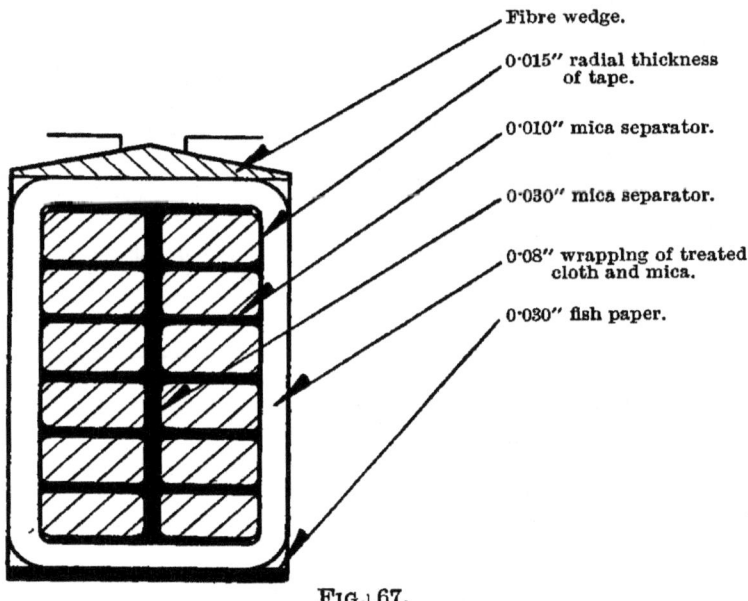

Fibre wedge.

0·015″ radial thickness of tape.

0·010″ mica separator.

0·030″ mica separator.

0·08″ wrapping of treated cloth and mica.

0·030″ fish paper.

FIG. 67.

Area of slot under wedge = 1·21 sq. ins.   Area of copper = 0·425 sq. in.
Space factor = 35·1 per cent.

It is unusual in high voltage work to depend entirely for insulation on the tapings on the ends of the coils, and the latter are usually spaced apart from each other and from the armature iron and end brackets of the machine so as to give additional insulation either as an air or surface distance. In general the figures given by the following formulæ for such distances can be used in designing armature insulation :—

For sparking distances, $\frac{1}{4}$ inch + $\frac{1}{4}$ inch per every 1000 volts.
For surface distances, $\frac{1}{2}$ inch + $\frac{1}{2}$ inch per every 1000 volts.

These figures apply to distances between bare copper parts and between these parts and "ground," and may be reduced when in addition solid insulation is used.

In cases where the total insulation consists of solid covering and a sparking or surface distance, the value of the solid insulation per mil can be considered to be roughly the same as already given for insulation on slot portions; so that the voltage to be borne by the sparking or surface distance can be approximately ascertained and an allowance made according to the formulæ given above. This is of course only a rough guide, since, as already pointed out, the distribution of voltage across the solid and air insulation is not uniform. In this connection care must be taken that the air insulation is not reduced below that equivalent to the sparking distance for normal voltage, as otherwise the distribution of potential may be such as to cause a continuous discharge to occur. Under such conditions, either the solid insulation must be increased so as to withstand the entire voltage and the air insulation dispensed with, or if ventilation requirements preclude this, the air and surface distance must be increased.

Connections between windings, or from windings to terminals, often afford the weakest points in the insulation of a machine, and care must be observed that the insulating value of the covering or the surface and air insulation conform to the rules laid down for the insulation on the coils themselves.

Voltage distribution over the projecting slot insulation of high voltage windings.—The voltage required to produce a breakdown over the surface of the insulation between two conductors *a, b* in Fig. 68 (*a*) is approximately the same as that for a similar distance in air, provided the surface of the insulation is quite dry and clean. In the case, however, of the projecting insulation surface of a high voltage machine winding between the points *A B* shown in Fig. 68 (*b*), where *A* represents the iron and *B* the winding, this relation no longer holds good. To appreciate the reason for this it is necessary to consider the distribution of the electrostatic field between these two points.

Assuming that the insulation around the winding *B* is removed, leaving an air space only between it and the iron *A*, the distribution of the lines of force will be as shown by the dotted lines in

Fig. 68 (*b*). When the insulation around the windings consists of a covering having high specific inductive capacity the distribution of field is altered to that shown by the full lines, the lines of force becoming crowded and more numerous close to the electrode *A*. It will be noted that in this respect the conditions are analogous to those that would exist if *A* and *B* were replaced by magnets and the insulation by a medium of high magnetic permeability.

If now the electrostatic field near *A* is intense enough for a local breakdown of the air to occur, the corona thus formed, being

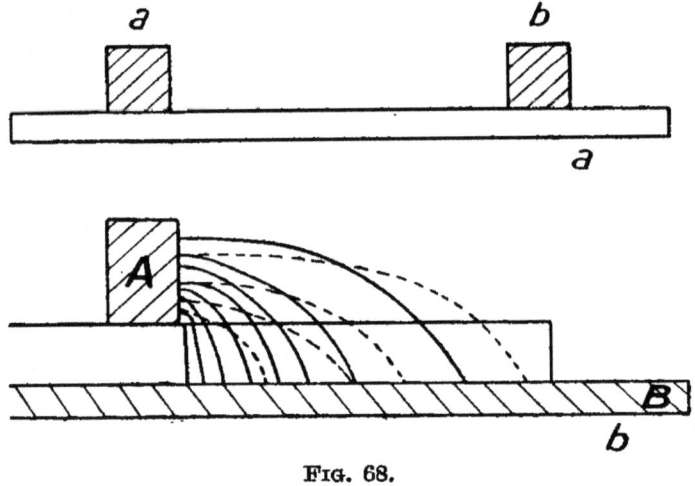

FIG. 68.

conducting, has the effect of shortening the surface distance by virtually moving *A* nearer to *B*, so that a fresh distribution of field is set up causing further local breakdown of the air, the process being continued until a flash-over between *A* and *B* occurs.

With conductors arranged as in Fig. 68 (*b*) it has been shown by Fortescue and Farnsworth [1] that the maximum value of surface insulation is obtained when the surface of the solid insulating medium between them is shaped so as to follow the direction of the lines of force.

[1] See *Proceedings of the American Institute of Electrical Engineers*, vol. xxxii., No. 3.

The conditions in machine insulation are so complex, due to the interference of the electrostatic fields set up around adjacent coils, and to the effect on the distribution of the field of the rotor when in place in the stator, that in practice very little advantage can be secured by the shaping of the end insulation.

The distortion of the electrostatic field serves to explain the fact that when a single coil in a machine is tested it will often stand up to a much higher voltage before flashing over at the ends than when a group of coils or the entire winding is tested together. Similarly, when stator windings are tested with and without the rotor being in place.

Attempts have been made from time to time to correct this non-uniform distribution of potential on the ends of high-voltage windings by inserting in the insulating wrapping on the slot portions, metallic foil projecting varying lengths beyond the ends of the slot so as to give a uniform potential gradient along the projecting surface, on the same principle as that of the well-known " condenser " terminal referred to later. This method, however, is not very extensively used in connection with machine windings.

Mechanical stresses on the end portions of windings.—On alternating current systems of such a size that a short circuit does not immediately pull down the voltage, there is a danger, should a short circuit occur either inside or outside the machine windings, of those portions of the coils projecting from the armature slots being distorted, due to the enormous electro-magnetic forces set up. The distortion may be specially severe if several large machines are operating in parallel, and in the case of motors that are not supplied through transformers, the reactance of the latter tending to reduce the short-circuit current which would otherwise flow into the windings.

To deal with the mechanical stresses set up by such conditions of service, very elaborate clamping devices are necessary to secure the ends of the windings. Unless these ends are so rigidly clamped as to prevent any movement, it is advisable to make the slot insulation as flexible as possible.

Special considerations in insulating high-voltage windings.— Although there are many exceptions, it is not at the present time the general practice on alternating current power systems to instal motors or generators operating at a normal voltage higher than about 8000 to 9000 volts between windings and ground—as for instance, a 15,000 volt star connected three-phase generator or motor—on account of the effect on performance due to poor space factor and the risk of internal insulation failure incident on the use of small slot conductors.

For very large units, however, these two factors to a large extent disappear, and the main reason why higher voltage machines are not more largely used is the lack of confidence in the reliability of the insulation, and consequently transformers are used to step up or down to the pressure required for the transmission lines and motors.

For machines operating at voltages between windings and ground of, say, 4000 volts or higher, the potential distribution radially through the dielectric surrounding the slot portions of the coils, must be very carefully considered, and also the shape of conductors and consequent distribution of the electrostatic field. This consideration is necessary, not only because of the liability of over-straining certain layers of the solid dielectric, but also on account of chemical action that may be set up.

The conditions governing the production of chemical action in high-voltage windings have been dealt with by the authors in a paper entitled "Chemical Action in the Windings of High-Voltage Machines,"[1] in which the following conclusions are set forth :—

1. Chemical action only occurs where air-pockets are present, and then only when the voltage across them is high enough to produce a discharge.

2. While the action commences on the surface of the insulation exposed to air-pockets, the gases produced by the discharge may be carried beyond the zone where they are formed, and produce action on other portions of the insulation outside the slots. While a discharge undoubtedly occurs between the outside of the insulation and the laminations, very little chemical action is to be expected on the exposed surface, since the gases formed

---

[1] See *Journal of the Institution of Electrical Engineers*, vol. xlvii., No. 209.

can freely escape, and, further, the insulation is not usually of a kind readily affected.

3. The action of the products of the air-gap discharge—whether these be ozone, oxides of nitrogen, nitrous or nitric acid —on the insulation is most commonly one of oxidation, and the effects produced on different materials are as follows :—

> Untreated cellulose materials have their fibrous structure readily destroyed, and disintegration follows.

> The oils and gums used in the preparation of insulating varnishes are practically all subjected to super-oxidation, and as a result yield organic acids. Of these materials, linseed oil is most readily affected.

> Certain asphaltum compounds are attacked only to a limited extent, and paraffin wax appears to be quite unaffected.

> Mica is itself unaffected, but the cements used in building it up are liable to attack on exposed surfaces.

4. The production of nitric acid is not essential for deterioration of the insulation to occur, although when it is produced the action is greatly accelerated.

5. The final disintegration of varnish-treated materials is greatly accelerated by the action of the released organic acids.

6. Failure due to chemical action is almost invariably the result of a short circuit between turns, and not, as is sometimes supposed, of a breakdown of the slot insulation between windings and ground. The short circuit is caused either by a destruction of the insulation on the conductors, which allows the turns to make actual contact, or by the hygroscopic, and therefore conducting matter formed between conductors when nitric acid is present. On this account mica or other material which is unaffected by chemical action should be used between turns.

7. Unless the air in the cavities of the winding is replenished by "breathing," the chemical action will cease.

8. For the range of voltages at present used, failure of machines from chemical action is not to be expected when the average stress across the slot insulation is less than about 35 volts per mil, with any of the methods of winding and insulating commonly employed. With windings having a voltage of less than 4000 to ground, the stress is usually kept below this limit by the ample thickness of insulation required for mechanical reasons.

9. A much higher average stress than 35 volts per mil of slot insulation is safe when the size and number of conductors permit the best method of grouping and insulating to be employed, and when special precautions are observed as to the kind of materials used and the proper filling of interstices.

10. While failure due to chemical action may be prevented by proper precautions, even when very high stresses are employed, there is in such cases some risk of producing a partial breakdown of the slot insulation when the ordinary pressure tests are applied. Such weakening is likely to occur when layers of material of high and low specific inductive capacity are used together, the insulation value of the latter being destroyed. In this connection it should be noted that a pressure test affords no criterion as to the safety of windings against chemical action, since the stress at which the latter takes place is usually far below that at which disruption of the insulation occurs.

11. The green discoloration which frequently occurs on coils of any voltage treated with linseed oil gum varnishes should not be confused with the chemical action due to the products of the air-gap discharge which takes place in high-voltage windings only. Such discoloration is quite harmless with the best makes of varnishes.

Electrostatic discharge may be prevented by using a split copper shield around and tightly fitted to the insulated coil, the shield being permanently grounded to the laminations. A similar shield should also be used underneath the insulation immediately around the coil and connected to one of its intermediate turns, being otherwise insulated from the winding sufficiently to prevent short circuiting of the turns. By this means the entire difference of potential is thrown on the dielectric between the two metal shields, thereby preventing abnormal stresses on the inferior insulation, such as the cotton covering generally used on the conductors themselves.

FIELD COILS.

Field coils seldom require insulating for a higher working voltage than 600, so that attention needs to be paid principally to the mechanical features of the materials used and the most satisfactory methods of applying them than to their actual insulation value. It is very important to wind field coils as tightly as possible, and to limit the amount of solid insulation to a minimum consistent with mechanical and insulation strength, so as to facilitate heat escaping to the core and frame and to leave as large an exposed surface as possible for radiation consistent with safety under service conditions.

Internal insulation—Cotton covering.—For field coils wound with round or rectangular wire the insulation generally employed is a single or double cotton covering on the wires. This may be treated during winding by running the wire through a bath of varnish or enamel or the completely wound coil may be dried and impregnated with varnish or asphaltum compound. For stationary field coils the latter is preferable, since it fills the interstices between the wires more thoroughly than varnish, and in this way assists heat dissipation.

Another alternative is to apply thick air-drying varnish or enamel to each layer as it is wound, and if this is done carefully it gives the most solid coil.

Asbestos covering.—For the series coils of railway motors asbestos covered wire is sometimes used. Its disadvantages are mechanical weakness and liability to absorb moisture unless well treated. It is also very expensive, and as a general rule cotton covering when properly treated has proved quite satisfactory.

Paper insulation.—Conductors insulated with one or more layers of thin paper have been used. The application, however, for this kind of insulation has been very limited, mainly on account of the difficulty of winding around sharp bends without cracking the covering.

Enamelled wires.—For low voltages a coating of enamel or varnish on the bare conductor is sometimes used. This insulation

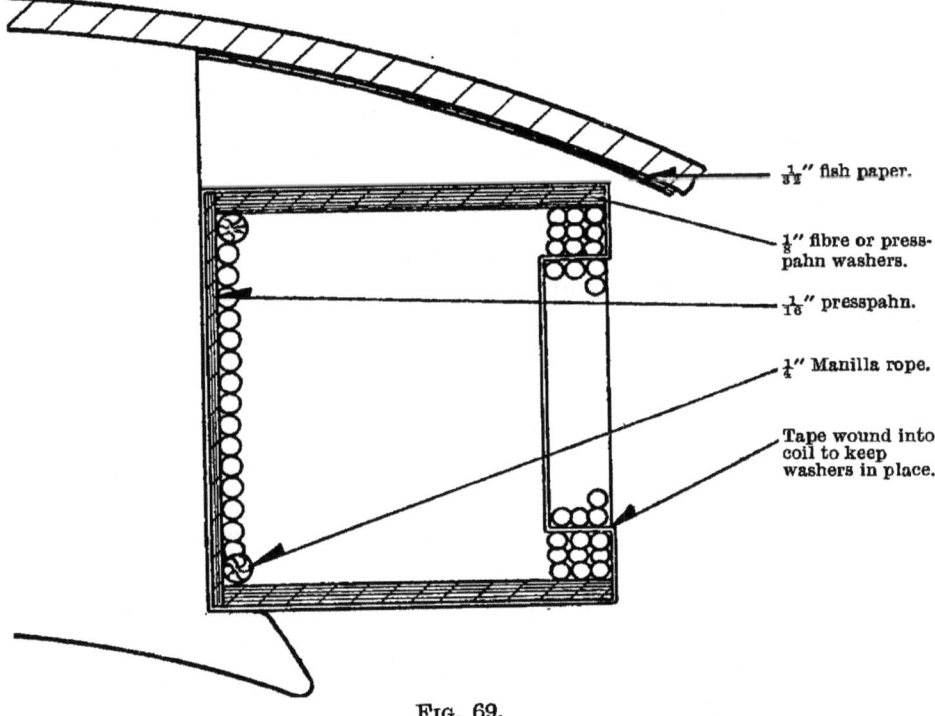

$\frac{1}{32}''$ fish paper.

$\frac{1}{8}''$ fibre or press-pahn washers.

$\frac{1}{16}''$ presspahn.

$\frac{1}{4}''$ Manilla rope.

Tape wound into coil to keep washers in place.

FIG. 69.

has the advantage of taking up considerably less room than cotton covering. It is, however, expensive and not mechanically good enough for use on other than small wires unless the coil to be formed is circular or elliptical and can be wound with very little hammering of the wires.

Oxide insulation.—Bare aluminium wire treated to give a surface covering of oxide of sufficient value to provide the insulation necessary between conductors is now being used to an increasing extent. It possesses the advantage of safety under temperatures sufficiently high to render cotton covering useless, and moreover shows some saving in cost. It is particularly useful for railway motor field coils where the temperature of the windings reaches a high value.

Heavy conductors.—Heavy strap coils for series and commutating pole windings may often be satisfactorily insulated by spacing the turns apart. The turns may be separated with strips of built-up mica or some fibrous material during winding, or these may be inserted after the coil is formed. A form of insulation between turns which is suitable for strap-wound coils for railway and for rotating field coil work, where a strong coil, mechanically, is required, consists of shellaced asbestos laid in between turns after the coil is formed. The turns are then forced together and the coil baked at a temperate sufficiently high to make the shellac run freely. As the coil is heated up the turns are forced closer and closer together until the shellac has been pressed right into the asbestos and any surplus varnish squeezed out, the coil then being allowed to cool. For work where the service conditions are not so severe, this method is rarely used on account of expense. A coil of only a few turns of heavy strap can be insulated very satisfactorily if the room permits by spacing the turns apart with small blocks of treated wood or fibre, so as to give a free passage of air between them.

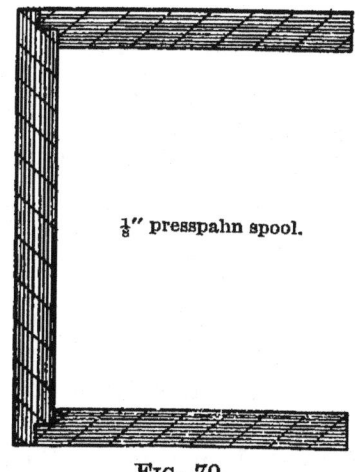

⅛″ presspahn spool.

Fig. 70.

External insulation. — Various methods of insulating field coils are shown in Figs. 69 to 74.

For the field coils of generators and a large proportion of industrial motors, the methods shown in Figs. 69 and 70 are quite satisfactory. Metal spools, lined with mica or some fibrous insulation, or spools made up entirely of mica, are sometimes used, but in general the additional cost is not justified.

Field coils for small two-pole machines are shown in Fig. 71.

The coils are wound, clamped to shape in suitable metal formers, and then impregnated in varnish or compound. They are then removed from the former, taped up and coated with air-drying varnish.

Fig. 72 shows a railway motor field coil, the conditions of service necessitating a substantial covering of tape completely over the coil.

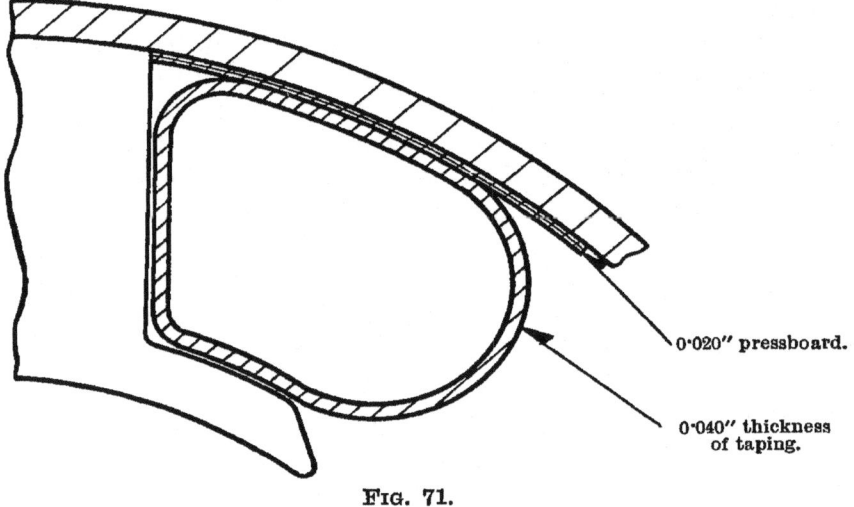

0·020″ pressboard.

0·040″ thickness of taping.

FIG. 71.

Figs. 73 and 74 show two types of ventilated field coils suitable for large generators.

COMMUTATORS AND COLLECTORS.

The greater part of the troubles occurring on commutators can be traced to insulation defects. These are due mainly to the difficulty of obtaining sufficiently accurate workmanship on the few insulating materials available for this class of work. In general, all designs of commutators are insulated on very similar lines. The commutator segments are assembled together with insulating strips between, then clamped in rings and baked out under heavy pressure to take up any give in the insulating material. The segments are secured from moving radially by V-shaped metal rings, which fit into grooves at each end of the segments, and which are, for high peripheral speeds, either strengthened or replaced by metal rings shrunk on to the outer face of the commutator. The V-shaped and shrink rings are suitably insulated from the segments with insulating bushes, and the commutator again baked and tightened up sufficiently to prevent any subsequent loosening of the segments.

Commutator segments are almost invariably insulated from one another by mica strips which, for all ordinary voltages, are

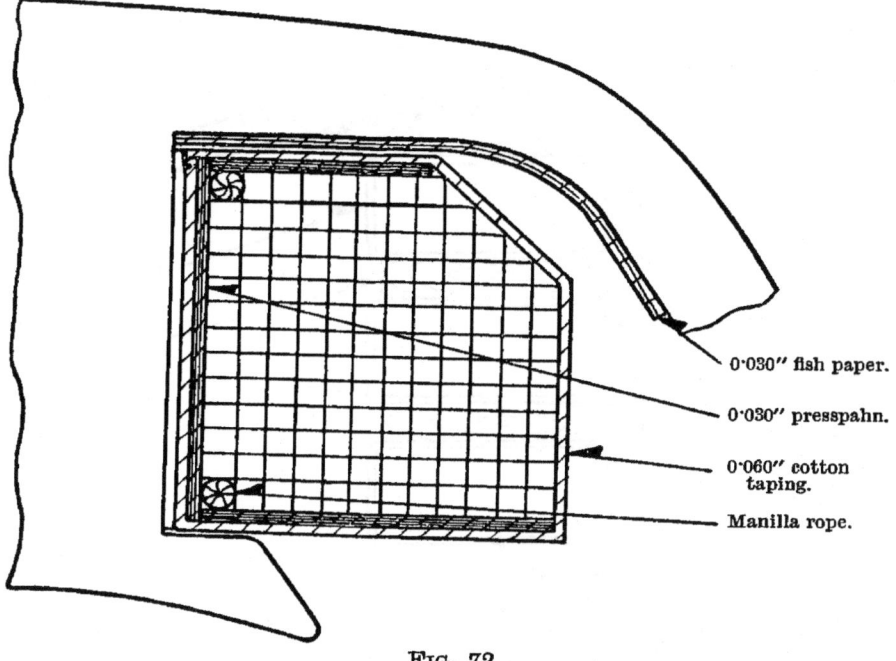

0·030″ fish paper.

0·030″ presspahn.

0·060″ cotton taping.

Manilla rope.

FIG. 72.

usually about $\frac{1}{32}$ inch thick. Fibre and various papers have been tried as substitutes, but these readily carbonise on their exposed surfaces, causing short circuits and pitting between segments. The mica strips are prepared as described in Chapter III.

The strips must be of uniform thickness, otherwise dirt may work down between adjacent copper segments, assisted by any oil that may creep from the bearings on to the commutator, and ultimately cause pitting along the edges of the strips. If there is an excess of shellac in the strips this may soften at the running temperature of the machine and allow the segments to slacken, causing "flats" in some places and "high-bars" in others. Further, if oil gets on the commutator, this, at the running temperature of the machine, will find its way into and ultimately completely permeate the strips. Evidence seems to indicate that this oil, due to centrifugal force, and to some extent to capillary attraction, is kept in motion and is continually being carbonised by sparking under the brushes until short circuits and consequent

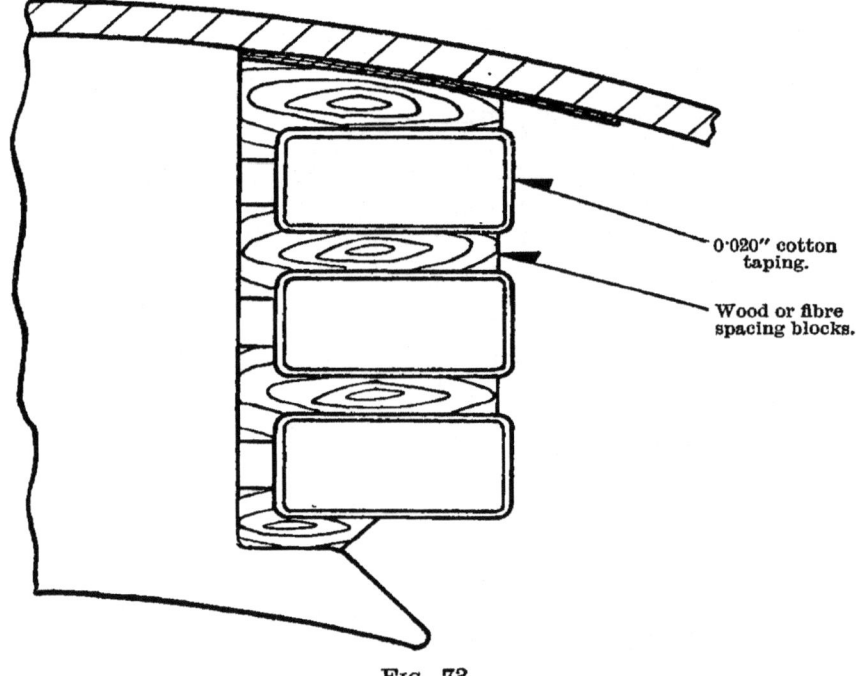

0·020″ cotton taping.

Wood or fibre spacing blocks.

FIG. 73.

pitting of the commutator occurs between the copper segments. Block mica is less liable to absorb oil, and in this respect is superior to micanite.

The only satisfactory method of dealing with this trouble is to keep oil off the commutator and in so far as this is due to creepage from the bearings, trouble may be overcome by a suitable design of oil thrower.

The insulation between commutator segments and ground

usually consists of moulded micanite bushings. Fibrous sheet insulating material is sometimes used, but there is difficulty in moulding this into the V-shape required, and further, there is always a danger of this material absorbing moisture, or becoming brittle when dried out.

It is very essential that the insulating bushings and rings be moulded and finished accurately to size, as high-bars in commutators can usually be attributed to poorness of manufacture and unevenness in thickness of these parts.

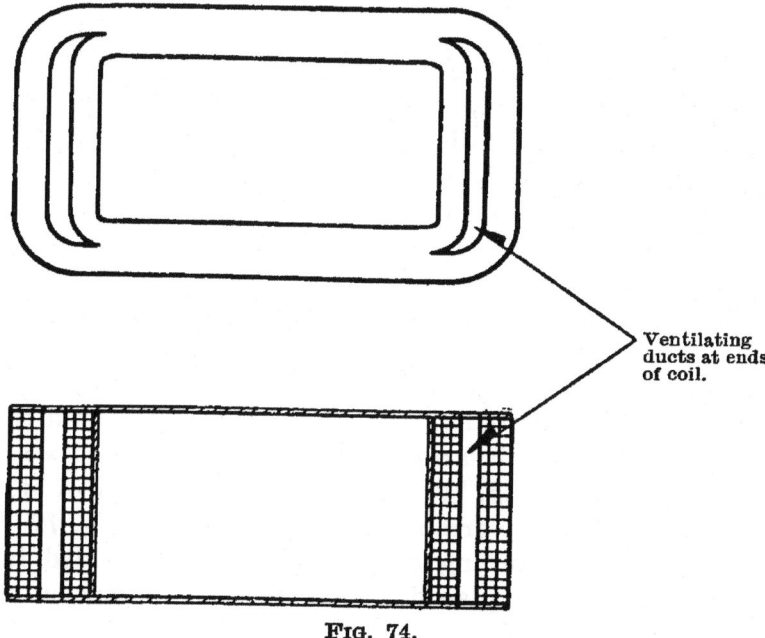

Ventilating ducts at ends of coil.

FIG. 74.

As regards the surfaces of the projecting insulating bushings, on account of the conducting particles resulting from the wear from the bushes and commutator, and the difficulty of cleaning the back portions, care must be taken that these surfaces are thoroughly well varnished and finished off as smoothly as possible to prevent lodgment of dirt, etc.

The allowance for surface insulation should be about 50 per cent. greater than the figures given in connection with machine windings.

Collector rings are usually insulated from "ground" by a micanite bushing, and from one another by spacing to give sufficient air and creepage distance. The insulation design resembles to some extent that of commutators, but as the surfaces are readily accessible for cleaning, the same difficulties are not encountered.

TRANSFORMERS.

General considerations.—Transformers may be divided into two types, core and shell, these again being subdivided into circular or rectangular core or shell, according to shape of core and consequent shape of windings. Single-phase transformers of these types for different arrangements are shown in Figs. 75 (*a*), (*b*), (*c*), and (*d*). As regards insulation details, polyphase transformers do not differ materially from similar types of single-phase units.

Types of winding.—Two arrangements of windings are commonly used, the *interleaved* or *sandwich*, and the *concentric*. With the former the high and low tension windings are subdivided into a number of coils, which are placed alternately along the core, as shown in Figs. 76 (*a*), (*b*).

In the *concentric* arrangement one set of windings, usually the low tension, is distributed the whole length of core and the other set placed over it. This arrangement, usually termed *single* concentric, is shown in Fig. 77 (*a*), and a modification of it, known as the *double* concentric arrangement, is shown in Fig. 77 (*b*). In this latter type of winding one set of coils is divided into two parts, one half being placed inside and the other outside the second winding.

In the concentric types the high-tension windings are usually subdivided into a number of coils or sections, as shown in Figs. 77 (*a*) and (*b*) to improve the ventilation and more particularly to facilitate insulating.

The choice of the winding arrangement depends to some extent on its general adaptability to the type of core; and the amount of interleaving of the windings on the extent to which it is desirable to reduce the magnetic leakage, and thereby improve the regulation of the transformer. Since the greater part of the insulation used is that which separates the high and low tension windings, it

will be appreciated that the more intimate the interleaving of
the windings, the greater will be the amount of room occupied

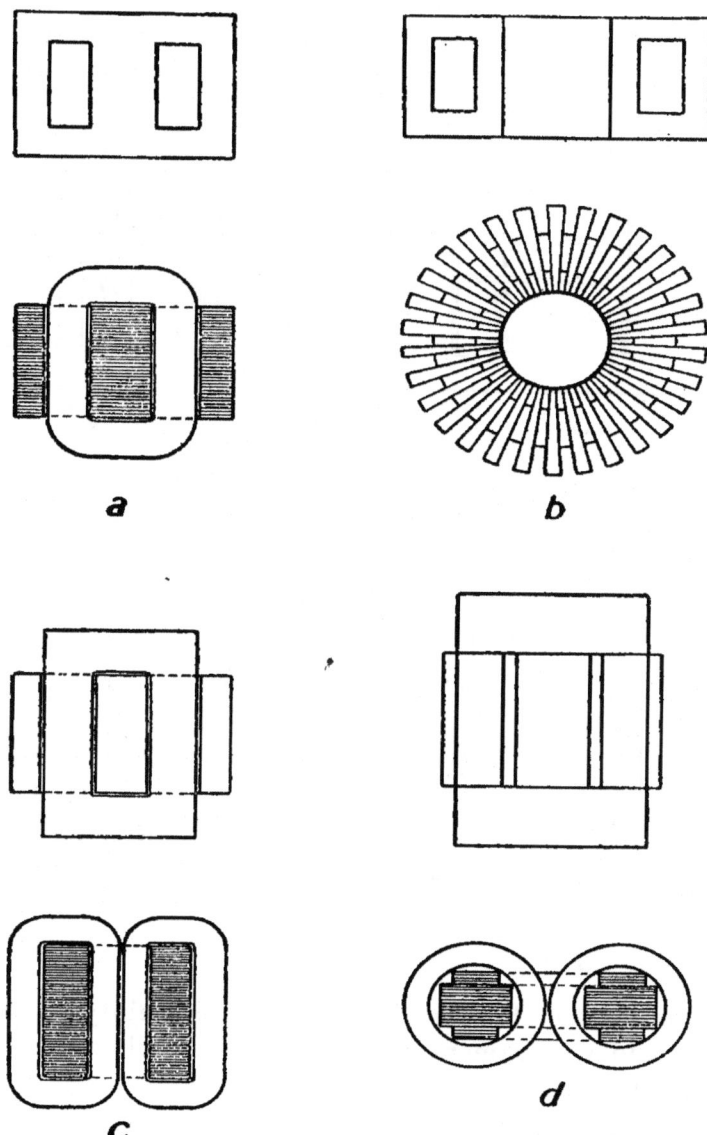

FIG. 75.

by the insulation, that is to say, the more the space factor will
be reduced.

Internal insulation.—The normal voltage per turn in transformers may be as high as 25 in the core type and about 80 in the shell type.

As regards the insulation between turns and layers of coils, the considerations apply that have been already generally dealt

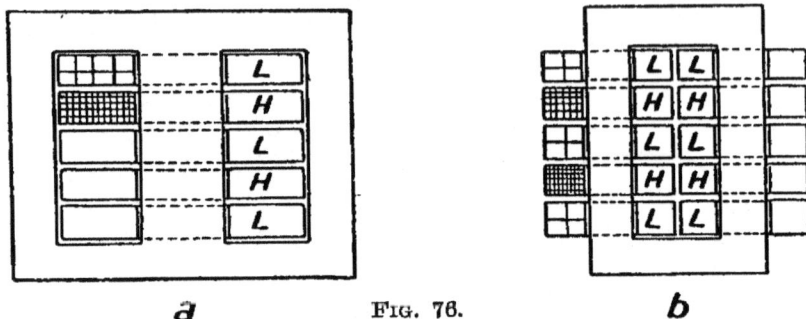

a   FIG. 76.   *b*

with in connection with machines, and in designing the windings it is most important to arrange them so as to reduce the normal voltage between adjacent conductors or portions of windings to a minimum.

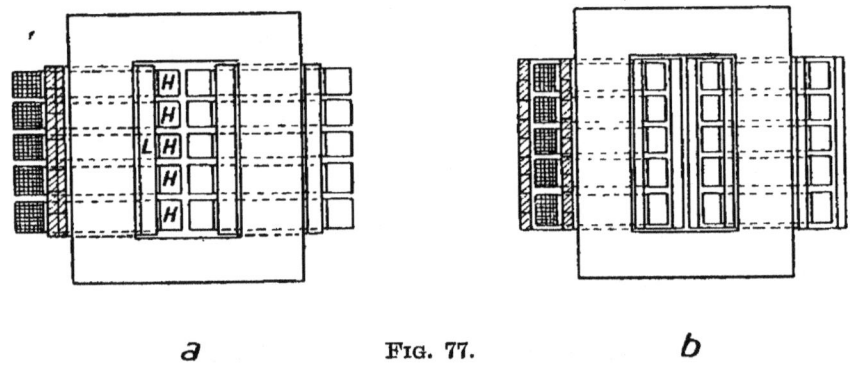

a   FIG. 77.   *b*

To what extent this can be done depends mainly on the size of conductor and arrangement of winding. The following methods of winding coils have been devised:—

    (*a*) Cross-over.

    (*b*) Layers wound in the same direction.

    (*c*) Spiral.

    (*d*) Sections.

Cross-over coils.—A type of cross-over coil is shown in Fig. 78 (*a*), in which there are five turns per layer, and the consecutive layers are wound in opposite directions, the cross-over from layer to layer being at the points marked *c, d, e*, etc., and from this Fig. it will be seen that with the number of turns per layer shown, the voltage between the adjacent turns at *b* is ten times the voltage of a single turn. In such coils it is necessary to insulate heavily between layers, not only on account of the normal voltage between the conductors having the maximum difference of potential as at *b*, but also, as pointed out later, on account of the possibility of abnormal rises of pressure. Further, this insulation must be

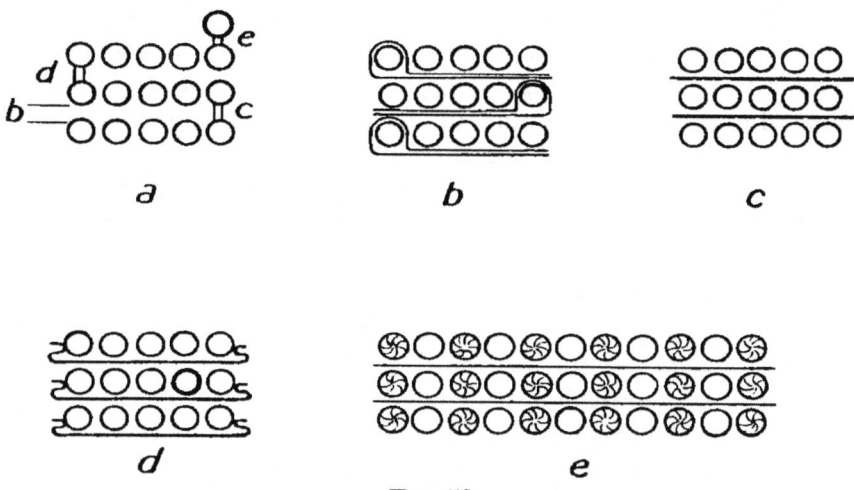

FIG. 78.

mechanically strong enough to withstand the tendency of crushing or cutting due to the tension on the conductors during winding.

This type of coil is used for both round or square conductors, but not usually for rectangular shapes. It is the most commonly employed and cheapest method of winding. For very small conductors it is the only practicable method. Where, however, the diameter of conductor exceeds about 0·1 inch, and rectangular section can be handled safely, the " section " method referred to later possesses many advantages ; on the other hand, where the voltage per conductor is small, wire up to a diameter of 0·2 inch round or square may be safely wound in this manner.

In order to prevent the coil becoming mis-shaped, the point at which the " cross-over " is made from layer to layer is usually distributed so that all the cross-overs do not occur one above the other.

At the point of crossing, a strip of fish paper or fullerboard must be used to prevent the conductors from cutting through the insulation at this point, especially where square conductors are used. Figs. 78 (b), (c), (d), and (e) show various methods of insulating between layers, the most common being to employ a flat strip of fullerboard, as shown in Fig. 78 (c), which may or may not project beyond the wire space. Where very high voltages per layer are used, the layers may be wound in sleeves as shown in Fig. 78 (b). This method is also employed to advantage in the case of very thin springy wires which are liable to become displaced if wound as in Fig. 78 (c). It will be noted that one of the conductors at the point of maximum potential is entirely enclosed in an insulating sheath. The material employed between layers is Empire cloth, treated paper, or thin untreated paper, according to the size of conductor and space allowable. Fig. 78 (d) shows a method whereby conductors are prevented from springing out of place, and suitable surface insulation provided at the edges of the insulation between layers. The insulation in such cases usually consists of one or more layers of thin paper which is folded back or crimped at the edges as shown. Fig. 78 (e) shows a method whereby each conductor is spaced from the next by a turn of cord, and the surface insulation between layers also secured in the same way. This method is often used where a very high voltage between turns is likely to occur. It is also employed on fine wire windings where bare instead of insulated conductors are employed.

Cross-over coils are seldom employed for transformers where the voltage per layer exceeds 125, *i.e.* where the maximum potential difference between two layers exceeds 250 volts. Even then, on terminal portions of windings, specially wound or protected coils are generally used.

Assuming, as is almost invariably the case, that double cotton covering is used on the conductors for voltages up to about 20 per layer, it is only necessary to use insulation between layers at sharp bends and underneath the starting and finishing turns for mechanical protection. For voltages above this, a thickness of well-treated fibrous insulation, such as varnished fullerboard, or if the conductors are small, Empire cloth or thin paper of 0·005 inch thickness for each 20 volts per layer should be used. Where heavy conductors are used this thickness should be increased; also, as pointed out later, additional reinforcement is necessary on the terminal portions of the winding.

Coils wound with layers in the same direction.—Fig. 79 shows this method of winding, from which it will be noted that the

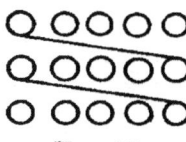

FIG. 79.

maximum voltage that can occur between any two layers is that of one layer only. This method of winding is seldom used other than on very high-voltage transformers wound with fine wire, such as testing transformers. The part where the conductor is brought across the layer requires to be very heavily insulated. Either of the methods of insulating described for cross-over coils may be used with this type of winding.

Coils wound in spiral form.—In the case of core type transformers with concentric form of winding, the low tension coils are usually wound in close spirals extending the whole length of the core. In order to avoid having two or more layers with, consequently, a high voltage between the conductors at one or both ends of the coil, the shape of conductor is usually chosen so that one layer only is used, thus making a very safe kind of coil. Where this cannot be done, however, or where for any reason it is necessary to bring the leads out at the same end, very heavy insulation must be used between layers and extended on the ends as shown in Fig. 80 (*a*), edge strips of wood or fullerboard being employed to support the projecting insulation. Windings of this type can be used up to a voltage between the end turns of adjacent layers of 5500, and, for such a voltage, $\frac{1}{16}$ inch radial thickness of insulation is required between layers, projecting at least $\frac{1}{2}$ inch at the lead end. Where very heavy conductors are wound in this way in two layers, the insulation between may conveniently be made of two split cylinders arranged as shown in Fig. 80 (*b*), so that any pressure on the cylinders tends to close up the gap, but not to crush the insulation.

Where possible spiral coils should be wound in a single layer, conductors of rectangular shape, wound on edge, being employed. Such an arrangement, giving a convenient size of conductor, is, however, somewhat difficult to fit into a given core length, especially where the number of turns is fixed between close limits.

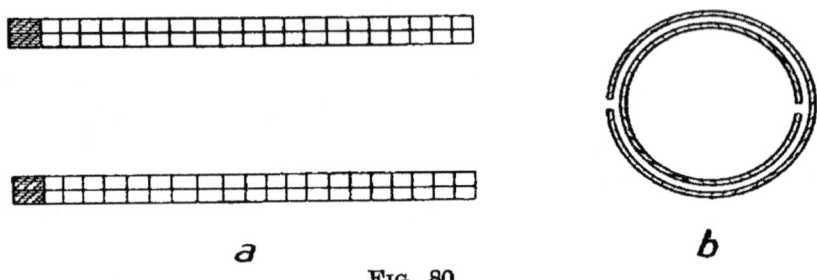

a   *b*

Fig. 80.

Section wound coils.—In the case of square or rectangular section conductors, and where the size permits, the safest form of winding is that in which only one turn per layer is employed, as shown in section in Fig. 81 (*a*). It will be readily seen that with

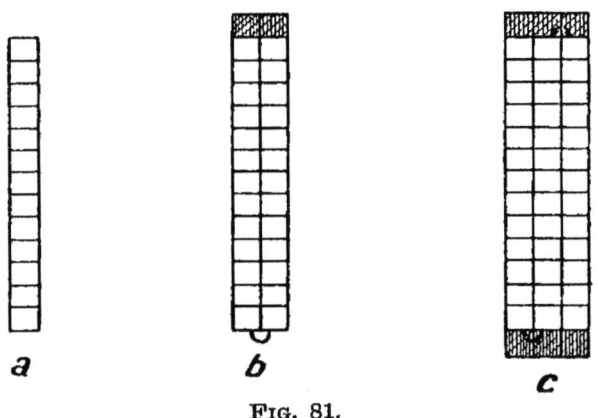

a   *b*   *c*

Fig. 81.

such a winding, the normal voltage between adjacent conductors cannot exceed that due to a single turn. This kind of winding applies equally to the core as to the shell type of transformer.

When the voltage per turn is high, insulating strips in addition to the covering on the conductors can be readily wound

M

between turns. In assembling two sections together, the insulation of the parts where the highest difference of potential occurs is done by extending the insulating washer, used between, beyond the edge of the coils and supporting it with edge blocks of fibrous insulation as shown in Figs. 81 (*b*) and 81 (*c*).

This type of winding is very largely employed, and in the case of small high-voltage transformers where the size of conductor is too small to permit of section winding, cross-over coils may be employed for all except the terminal coils, which may be wound in sections in a sufficiently large size of wire.

Where a number of sections are assembled together with insulating washers between, it will be readily seen that the points of highest potential difference occur alternately at the inside and outside edges, so that the insulation requires to be extended at these points. On account of the room taken up in this way, it is usually not advisable to design windings with a higher voltage per section than about 250 in core type transformers, and 1250 for the shell type.

Concentration of potential between turns at ends of winding.— As already pointed out, when the windings forming part of a high tension circuit are subjected to abrupt changes of potential, the voltage between conductors near the line terminals may be raised to many times the normal value, rendering it necessary to increase the insulation on the terminal portions to withstand such conditions.

The extent to which the reinforcement of the insulation of end windings must be carried, depends on the penetration of the potential surge or disturbance, and this again depends on the normal voltage per turn of the windings and the service conditions. The factors involved are too complex to enable any hard and fast rule to be given, but for voltages up to about 10,000, $2\frac{1}{2}$ per cent. at each end of the high-tension winding is probably sufficient for ordinary service conditions, and a further $\frac{1}{2}$ per cent. per every 10,000 volts may be taken as a rough guide.[1]

[1] In the case of a 125,000 volt transformer which was tested by grounding one side of the high-tension winding and raising its voltage to 50 per cent. above normal, and then short circuiting the high-tension terminals at 170,000 volts by causing an arc to be maintained between them intermittently, reinforcement of the windings $1\frac{1}{2}$ per cent. at each end was found too little, but with $7\frac{1}{2}$ per cent.

On such high-voltage coils section windings are almost invariably used, and the reinforcement is usually accomplished by increasing the insulation between conductors to several times the normal amount and allowing this to extend beyond the conductors, say $\frac{1}{16}$ inch each side. If, then, the coil is well varnished the conductors are sealed in, and a failure during the momentary rise in voltage can be readily guarded against. The insulation should be gradually graded down from a maximum at the end turn.

External insulation—general considerations.—The external insulation, that is, the insulation between high and low tension coils and between these coils and ground, consists mainly of either sheet materials or taping such as described in Chapter III., the kind depending on whether the apparatus is oil or air cooled, and on the type of core and winding employed. The thickness of insulation for a given normal voltage depends on specific conditions of service, test requirements, etc., but assuming that the materials are free from mechanical flaws and suitably treated and handled, a figure of 0·001 inch per 30 volts may be taken as a guide for voltages of 10,000 and upwards. This allowance holds good when the insulation consists partly of solid material and partly of an oil space, provided the latter does not exceed half the total insulation thickness.

For lower voltages, mechanical considerations have to be taken into account, and the safe limit per 0·001 inch may vary from 10 to 30 volts, depending on the size of apparatus and voltage. There are of course very many materials available which will permanently withstand much higher voltages in small thicknesses. When dealt with in bulk, and after being subjected to the handling required in application, their value is very considerably reduced, and the figures given above as working limits are shown by experience to be reliable, and may be considered the same for either air or oil cooled working.

The distances that should be allowed for surface insulation

of the windings at each end protected, the transformer satisfactorily withstood these conditions. See *Journal of the Institution of Electrical Engineers*, Part 194, Vol. xlii. "Transformers: Some Theoretical and Practical Considerations," by A. P. M. Fleming and K. M. Faye-Hansen.

depend very largely on conditions as to dirt and moisture, and figures can only be given for more or less normal conditions, and again, in view of the widely varying conditions that may be introduced, these can be considered as approximate guides only. For surfaces in air an allowance of ½ inch + ½ inch per every 1000 volts, and under oil ½ inch + 0·1 inch per every 1000 volts may be used. Surfaces under oil should be broken up as much as possible so as to prevent an accumulation of dirt from forming a continuous conducting path.

These figures are based on the assumption that the surface itself is non-hygroscopic, and that the material is such that a breakdown will not occur through the insulation parallel to the exposed surface, more readily than the surface breakdown occurs.

For direct breakdowns through air and oil an allowance of ¼ inch + ¼ inch per every 1000 volts in air, and ¼ inch + 0·07 inch per every 1000 volts in oil should be made.

These figures when considered in connection with the voltages at which air and good quality oil break down under test conditions and standard electrodes, may appear very liberal. The result of experience, however, under widely varying working conditions, taking into account voltage disturbances, impurities in oil, which tend to form a conducting chain under the influence of electrostatic stress, and the lack of precision observed ordinarily by workmen in the shops in obtaining proper spacing, indicate that these figures are reasonable.

From the figures given above, the design of the external insulation of any arrangement of winding and for any voltage may be determined.

In certain instances, such as between adjacent coils, the insulation may consist of sheet material in the form of a washer and a thickness of taping, or alternatively of a thickness of taping and a surface distance around the edge of the washer. In such cases the various elements of the insulation should be so proportioned that the alternative paths have the same insulation value, or where, for practical reasons, this is not feasible, care must be taken that the weakest path is strong enough.

Air-cooled transformers.—In the case of air-cooled transformers, the voltage for which insulation can be satisfactorily and commercially designed, is limited due to a destructive static discharge which takes place in the air ventilating spaces around and between the windings when the electrostatic stress reaches a certain intensity. On account of this it is not considered good practice to employ air-cooled transformers when the maximum voltage between windings and ground exceeds about 20,000, although transformers of this type have been built for higher pressures.

The insulation of the air-cooled type need not differ materially from that of other types, except that special ventilating ducts are required between coils which, however, cannot be relied upon entirely for insulation purposes, as moisture may readily be carried into the transformer and deposited on the spacing blocks, thereby forming a creepage path. For the same reason the coils should be very thoroughly impregnated to render them as moisture resisting as possible and also to limit the " breathing action " of windings, which, by expanding when hot, expel their occluded air, and by contracting during cooling suck in cool and possibly moist air. In high-voltage air-cooled transformers the proportion of air-ventilating ducts to solid insulation between high and low tension coils must, apart from ventilating considerations, be such that the air-gap will withstand the entire working voltage without the formation of a brush discharge, since, owing to the difference in specific inductive capacity of solid insulation compared with that of air, the voltage will probably be distributed so that the greater part of the stress falls on the latter.

Oil-cooled transformers.—This type possesses an advantage over the air-cooled in so far that it can be insulated satisfactorily and commercially for practically any voltage. While the oil is used primarily for cooling purposes it is of very considerable insulation value, not only on account of its high dielectric strength, but because of its self-healing properties, and except under very intense electrostatic stress, it prevents the formation of the static discharge which is so destructive to solid insulation in high-voltage air-cooled windings. Further, surface insulation can be utilised much more safely under oil; also in oil-immersed apparatus access of air to the insulating materials is prevented, and the slow oxidation and consequent deterioration of the varnishes used in the preparation of the insulation avoided. This enables oil-cooled windings to be operated at a higher temperature, without causing deterioration, than is possible in most air-cooled apparatus, where the insulating materials are freely exposed to the air.

In selecting insulating materials for oil-cooled transformers, it must be remembered that the oil slowly dissolves many of the varnishes and compounds suitable for air-cooled windings, and for

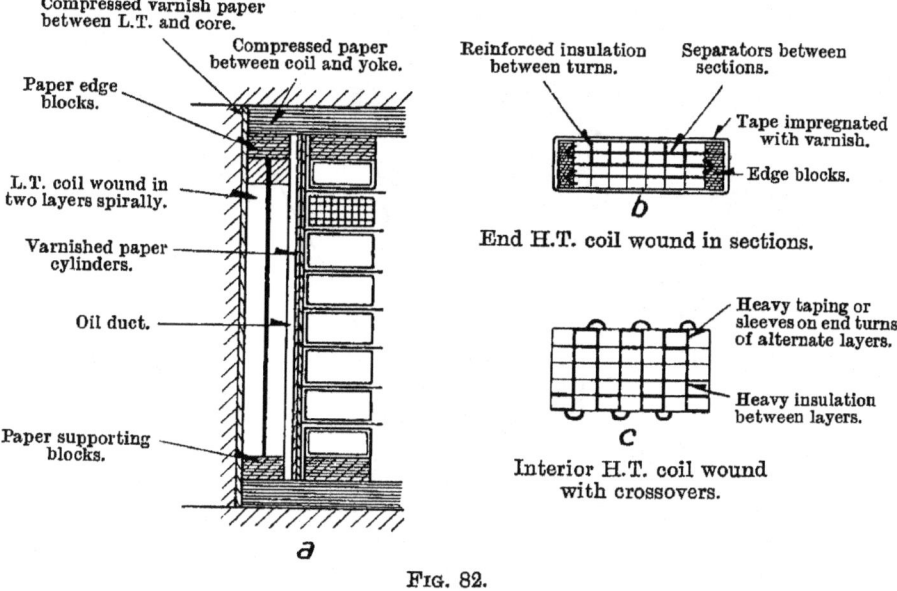

FIG. 82.

this reason the use of mica compositions particularly should be avoided.

Insulation details of principal types of transformers—Circular core type.—Figs. 82 (*a*), (*b*), and (*c*) show the insulation details of a typical oil-insulated transformer of the circular core type, with single concentric winding. It will be evident that very many alternative methods of insulating the various parts are possible, and this illustration serves merely as a guide as to the principal insulation features required.

In the case of very large high-tension transformers (as, for instance, of 2000 kw., 30,000 volts, 50 periods), the voltage per turn will be so high that the entire high-tension winding should be arranged in sections, since with cross-over coils the voltage between adjacent layers would be too high to deal with safely.

To avoid having to allow considerable space between windings on adjacent cores, a barrier of sheet insulation extending the whole length of the cores is supported between the top and bottom yokes.

In the double concentric winding of the circular core type transformer, the insulation details are very similar to those of the single concentric type, except that as the low-tension winding is

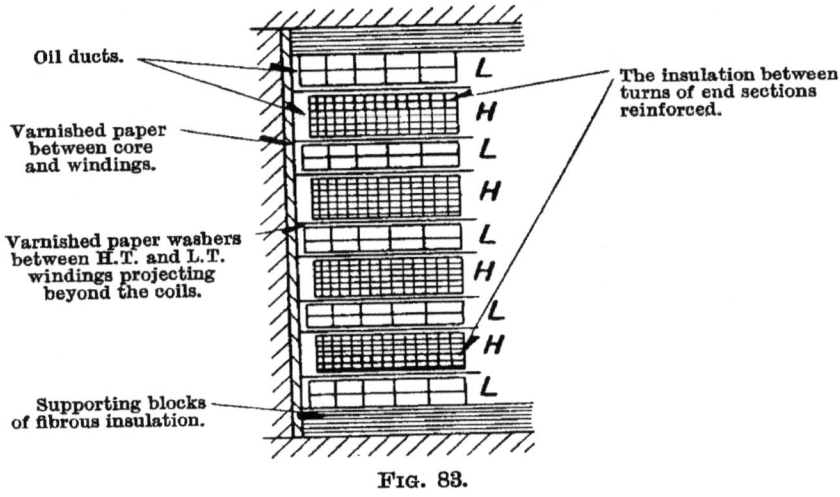

FIG. 83.

divided into two halves, one of which is placed outside and the other inside the high-tension winding, a second insulating cylinder is required between the high tension and outer portion of the low-tension winding. In other respects, except for a slight modification in the spacing blocks required between the coils and yoke, the description of the insulation of the single concentric type applies equally to the double concentric arrangement.

In the sandwich arrangement of windings the high and low tension coils are placed in alternate groups along the core. Fig. 83 shows the insulation details of a portion of the winding of this type.

This sandwich type of winding on circular or rectangular core type transformers is seldom used for voltages much above 10,000.

Circular shell type.—Circular shell type transformers are usually arranged with either single or double concentric windings. This type of transformer is frequently employed air cooled. The general arrangement of insulation does not differ materially from that already described for similar windings in the case of circular core type transformers, except that in the single concentric arrangement the outside of the high-tension coils must be protected from iron by a cylinder of insulation slipped over the windings or by taping heavily each coil.

Similarly in the case of the double concentric arrangement in which the outer low-tension coil is usually well insulated by taping.

Rectangular core type.—The rectangular core type may be wound with either the single or double concentric arrangement or with sandwich windings. For the concentric windings the insulation details given for circular core type concentric windings apply very closely and no further description is necessary.

Rectangular shell type.—In the rectangular shell type there is rather more difficulty in arranging the insulation satisfactorily than in the core type and circular shell transformers. This type is used for all methods of cooling, and when oil insulated may be designed for any commercial voltage. Figs. 84 (*a*), (*b*), and (*c*) shows the insulation details of this type.

The sandwich arrangement is almost invariably employed except for small sizes and low voltages, where economically the single concentric method is sometimes adopted for the sake of cheapness. Fig. 84 (*a*) shows a sectional elevation, Fig. 84 (*b*) a vertical section through one end of the winding, and Fig. 84 (*c*) a horizontal section through one side of the windings of a rectangular shell transformer of the sandwich type.

Where the rectangular shell type with sandwich windings is used for high voltages, say of 20,000 and upwards, the insulating wrappings and washers should be split up and provided with ventilating ducts to allow of oil circulation, otherwise the dielectric loss may be sufficient to cause heating, which will eventually destroy the insulation.

Space factor.—The percentage of the total space available that is actually occupied by copper varies considerably with the size

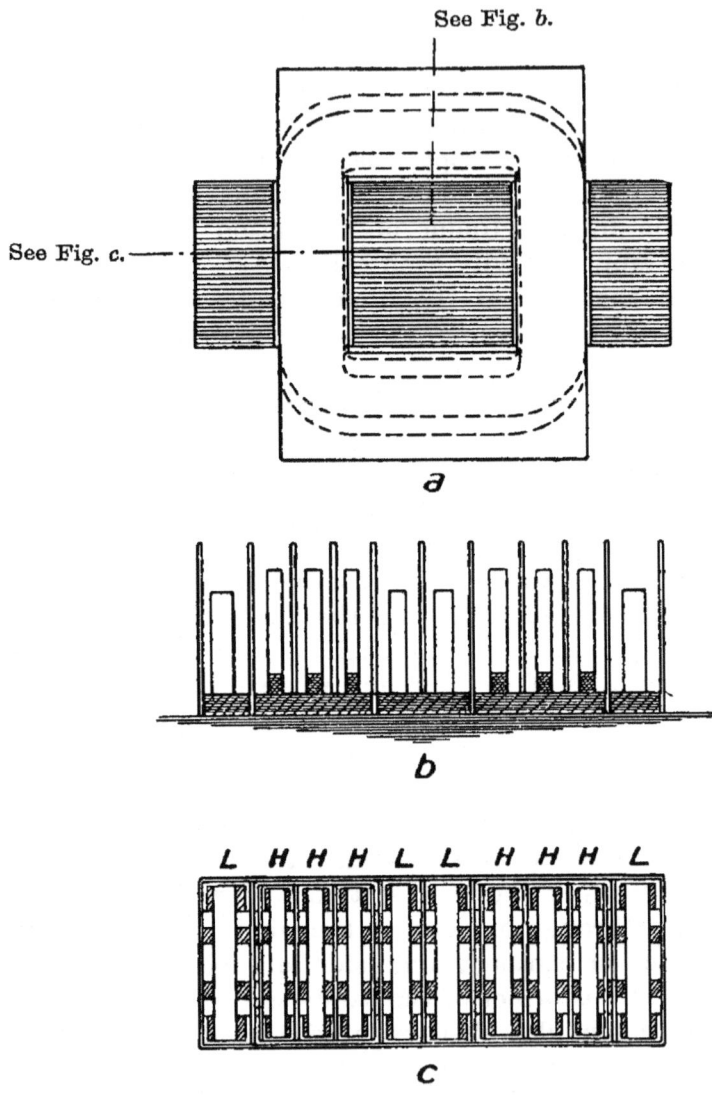

Fig. 84.

and voltage of the transformer. The curves in Fig. 85 show approximately this percentage, *i.e.* the "space factor," for the

circular core and for the rectangular shell types for various voltages in well-designed transformers.

Transformer terminal bushings.—It is usual either to bring out the high and low tension leads from the windings to suitably protected terminals mounted on the outside of the case, or to have these terminals mounted inside the transformer case and bring out the leads through insulating bushings.

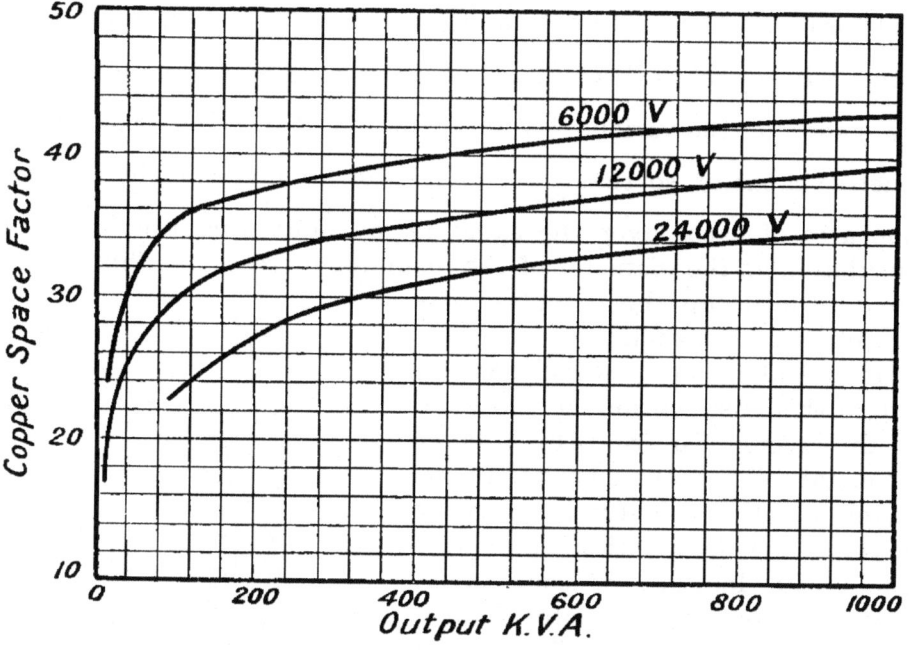

FIG. 85.

For voltages up to 20,000 no special insulation difficulty is presented in any type of transformer, and for oil-insulated types porcelain bushings suitable for working voltages up to 50,000 are easily obtainable. In such insulators one end projects below the oil level and the other is carried through the transformer tank cover far enough to allow sufficient surface insulation between case and projecting lead or terminal.

For higher voltages it is difficult to obtain porcelains entirely suitable and not too expensive, owing to the length required for surface insulation, which introduces a danger of cracking or warping. For such voltages it is usual to make up an insulator with heavily compressed varnished paper wound on to a central metallic rod or tube which forms the outgoing conductor. If such a conductor is insulated uniformly to a considerable radial thickness with homogeneous material, the electrostatic stress will not be distributed evenly across the radial thickness, but is much greater on the inner than on the outer layers owing to the smaller capacity of the former. The distribution is according to the law for condensers in series, *i.e.* $V \propto \dfrac{C}{K}$. This disadvantage may be overcome by using, for the various layers, materials of varying specific inductive capacity, so that $\dfrac{1}{K}$ is uniform for all layers, or by making the area of each layer the same, *i.e.* by shortening the layers of insulation as the diameter of the insulator increases. This would

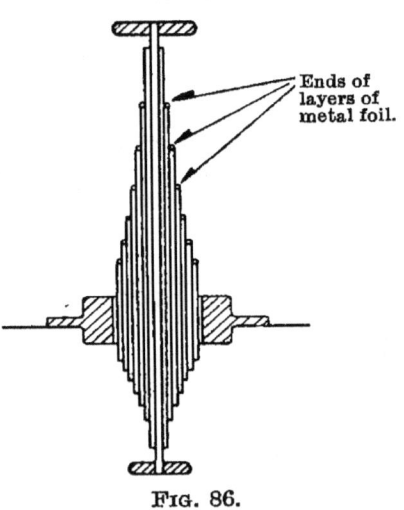

tend to even up the potential distribution across each layer but for surface leakage and discharge which alters this distribution at the ends of the layers. To avoid this, a layer of metal foil is wound between each layer or section of insulation, thereby making the distribution alike over the entire length of each layer. Fig. 86 shows an insulator known as the "condenser type" built up in this way. It will be noted that as the diameter of the insulator increases, the surface distance between adjacent metal cylinders becomes less and less, so that there is

Ends of layers of metal foil.

FIG. 86.

a danger of breakdown over this surface at the edges. To avoid this layers of material of different specific inductive capacity may be used, or the insulation extended somewhat beyond the foil, or even distribution of potential sacrificed on the outer layers. To prevent the tendency for a brush discharge to occur at the edges of the foil, which would upset the even potential distribution, metal discs may be used which, by offering a large radius of curvative, reduces the electrostatic stress at these edges, and the tendency to spark over the surface. Similarly the ends of the centre conductor should terminate in metal discs having a large radius of curvature.

The larger the number of metal cylinders employed, the more uniform will be the potential distribution. In practice, however, it is not usual to provide more than one cylinder per 5000 volts.

In addition to the "condenser" type, many other forms of high-tension bushings have been designed. One of the most prominent of these consists of a porcelain having an annular space around the central electrode. This space is provided because of the difficulty of making porcelain insulation a close fit around the electrode, and must be so dimensioned that it prevents a static discharge being formed, or so that it can readily be filled with compound.

In another form the annular space is filled with oil.

Either of these forms is much cheaper than the condenser type.

The principle of the "condenser" insulator has also been used in the insulation of very high-voltage transformers, the entire high-tension winding being wrapped with insulation into which is interleaved metal foil, the various cylinders of which may or may not be connected to equipotential tappings on the windings.

In the foregoing no specific mention is made of the insulation of shunt and series transformers. From the rules given, however, for larger transformers there is no difficulty in designing suitable insulation, as the type and windings conform very closely, although on a much smaller scale, to those already described. Mention might be made, however, of the use of compound in high-voltage series transformers. In these transformers the losses are very small, and there is, under normal working conditions, little fear of over-heating. In order to render such transformers immune from moisture troubles, the windings are sometimes impregnated under vacuum with compound and the containing case filled up solidly with similar material. The compounds used for impregnating machine windings are suitable for this purpose. Other transformers of this type may be either oil or air insulated.

DETAIL APPARATUS

The types of apparatus that will be considered under this head are switches, switchboards, and controllers, and only the insulation features peculiar to them will 'be considered at length. These features are very different to those presented by machines and transformers. As a rule materials of high insulating value can be employed, except in those cases where great mechanical strength or heat resistance is required, and it is seldom necessary to cut down insulation thicknesses to the minimum possible. Attention therefore has to be paid mainly to surface distances and air-gaps, due regard being given, as in the case of machines and transformers, to the conditions under which the apparatus operates, particularly with reference to dirt and moisture.

In any type of switch it is necessary to consider—
1. The safety of the operator.
2. The insulation from ground.
3. The insulation between switch contacts.

In low-voltage air-break switches the operator is usually safeguarded simply by a handle of hard rubber or some composition of a similar nature, while the insulation from ground and between contacts is obtained by distances over the surface of the insulating base. The mechanical design of the switch, and arcing considerations, usually necessitate more spacing between contacts than is required for insulation only, and similarly, the mechanical strength necessary, governs the thickness of material on the handle.

For voltages above about 1000, oil switches are generally used. The essential parts of practically any make of oil switch consist of fixed and movable contacts contained in an oil vessel, insulating supports for the metal contacts, and a handle for operating.

The safety of the operator depends on the insulation of the support for the movable contacts. As an additional safeguard the handle is usually insulated with hard rubber or a similar material. On account of mechanical strength the insulating support usually consists of a wooden rod, thoroughly seasoned and treated. The insulation to ground depends on the oil-gap between contacts and case, and on the insulation supports.

The fixed contacts are usually supported in porcelain or other insulating bushings. The points to be considered in designing the insulation are the thickness and surface of the insulating supports, and the length of oil-gap between contacts and from contacts to case. On account of the carbonisation likely to occur in the oil, the figures already given in connection with transformers should be increased by at least 50 per cent.

Air-break switches are usually mounted either on marble, slate or porcelain, and if these materials are dry, free from metallic veins, mechanically suitable, and, in the case of porcelain, properly manufactured, attention need only be given to the surface insulation and to the air-gaps separating parts of live circuits and these circuits from ground. A safe figure, under normal conditions for surface distances for marble and slate, is $\frac{3}{4}$ inch $+ \frac{3}{4}$ inch per every 1000 volts, and for porcelain $\frac{1}{2}$ inch $+ \frac{1}{2}$ inch per every 1000 volts.

When switchgear is for service in collieries and other places where it is liable to excessive dirt and moisture deposits, very much greater distances must be allowed, and in some cases the apparatus must be enclosed in a dirt and moisture-proof covering. Air-gaps should not in general be less than $\frac{1}{4}$ inch $+ \frac{1}{4}$ inch per every 1000 volts.

For low-voltage switchboards where apparatus such as switches is mounted directly on the panels, the figures already given for surfaces and air distances apply.

In high-voltage work the panels are mainly used as mechanical supports for fully insulated apparatus, and in such cases the main consideration from an insulation point of view is the spacing of bus-bars and live apparatus connected to different circuits.

In determining the surface distances and air-gaps between parts of apparatus, such as circuit breakers, and between contacts of switches where arcing is liable to occur, it must always be remembered that an arc is a good conductor and the insulation distances therefore should be measured from a line bounding the extreme range of the arc. The length of path taken by the arc depends mainly on the amount of power broken, and its upward tendency may be modified by draughts and by the mutual action between the magnetic field set up by the arc and that due to neighbouring bus-bars or other current carrying parts.

Full allowance must also be made for the ionisation of the air produced by the arcing, which will increase the conductivity of the air, and may thus cause further arcing between any bare conductors in the immediate vicinity.

In controllers and enclosed switches operating in air, the chief insulation difficulty is to prevent damage due to arcing and to confine the arcing within certain limits. This necessitates the use of fire-resisting materials which, as already pointed out in Chapter III., are in the main very poor insulators. These materials, consequently, must be backed with good insulation of low heat resistance and the latter depended upon entirely as regards the thickness and the surface insulation required.

When controllers are operated in oil, the surfaces and oil-gaps should be the same as those specified for oil-switches.

CHAPTER V

INSULATION TESTS

COMMERCIAL insulation tests may be divided into two main classes, viz. those on raw materials, including the investigation of new kinds of insulation, and those on finished apparatus. In addition, it is usual to test apparatus at various stages of manufacture by the momentary application of a voltage several times in excess of the working pressure, so as to detect flaws in materials and any mechanical damage due to bad workmanship, and to save thereby as far as possible the cost of dismantling finished apparatus on account of faults which might have been detected at an earlier stage. The grading of such tests and the special testing apparatus used for such purpose will be considered later.

Insulation resistance tests.—Many consulting engineers in their specifications to manufacturers pay special attention to insulation resistance measurements. While these are useful in determining the condition of the insulation of a machine as regards cleanliness and dryness, they afford no indication whatever as to the quality and reliability of the insulation employed. There is considerable misconception on this point, and it is frequently assumed that the insulation resistance of a machine is a measure of the quality of the materials used. That this is not the case is evident when it is understood that no matter which of the commonly used materials, such as cotton fabrics, papers, mica preparations, and asbestos, are employed, prolonged drying will raise the insulation resistance to an almost unlimited extent, provided always that the surfaces of the insulation are perfectly clean.

In Fig. 87 a comparison of curves A and B shows the increase in insulation resistance resulting from the drying out of the windings of a 2000 volt induction motor where the insulation consisted of paper, mica, and tape. The curves also show the effect of temperature on the insulation resistance, and are typical of machines irrespective of the kind of insulation used, although, as a general rule, the decrease in insulation resistance as the temperature is raised is greater where organic materials, such as varnished papers and fabrics, are used than where those of a partly inorganic nature, such as micanite, are employed.

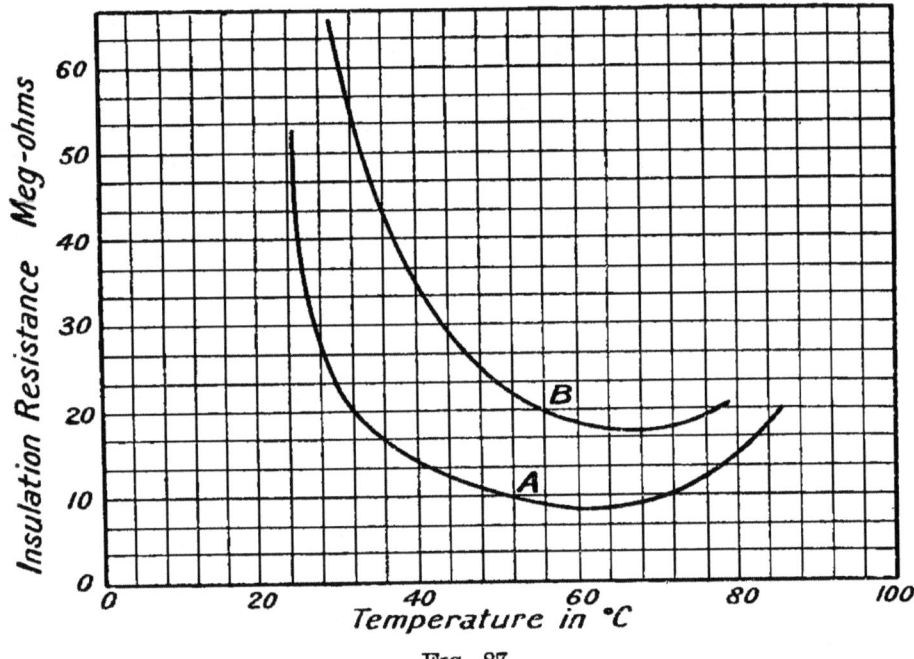

FIG. 87.

From the foregoing it might be inferred that a comparison of a number of insulation-resistance measurements obtained on machines over a certain period of time, and under similar temperature conditions, would afford a measure of the facility with which the insulation absorbs moisture. Such, however, is by no means generally the case, since in a moist atmosphere, long before the slot insulation has absorbed sufficient moisture to affect appreciably the insulation resistance, the exposed surfaces on the ends of the windings outside the slot portions will have become slightly

N

conducting, due to deposits of moisture. The resistance will then be found to be greatly reduced solely through leakage over the surfaces from lightly insulated portions of the winding, or from bare copper, as in the case of direct current machines. In the latter the insulation resistance is dependent almost entirely on the condition of the insulating surfaces between the commutator and iron, the actual leakage through the slot insulation usually being negligible. It will, therefore, be seen that insulation-resistance measurements of a machine are of negligible value as a guide to the quality of the insulating materials employed. On the other hand, both after erection and periodically during the operation of machines, they are of considerable value in indicating to what extent moisture and dirt are accumulating on the windings, and afford a warning as to the need for cleaning and drying.

Machines installed in chemical works may be cited as an example of this, where excessive leakage over end windings due to the formation of conducting deposits is particularly liable to cause failure. It must always be borne in mind, however, that it is the variation of insulation resistance from a well-seasoned condition, and not the value of the insulation resistance itself, which is of importance, and no hard-and-fast figure can be laid down as safe for machines under any particular condition. As a rough guide, however, the recommendation of the American Institute of Electrical Engineers may be taken, namely, "the insulation resistance of complete apparatus should be such that the rated voltage of the apparatus will not send more than $\frac{1}{1,000,000}$ of the rated full-load current at the rated terminal voltage through the insulation. Where the value found in this way exceeds one megohm, it is usually sufficient."

As regards investigations of the properties of insulating materials themselves, while insulation-resistance measurements are of undoubted value in establishing comparisons, the importance of such measurements is often greatly overrated. Measurements carried out with the necessary precautions taken to avoid surface leakage can be made to show the comparative facility with which different materials absorb moisture. It frequently happens, however, in the case of fibrous insulation, that those materials showing the highest insulation resistance, and being the least absorbent of moisture, are by no means those most suitable mechanically, and in general the mechanical characteristics, such as flexibility, are of the greater importance. Any fibrous insulating material can, of course, be made to show a high insulation resistance simply by prolonged drying-out. It should be noted, however, that this often results in the removal of certain of the natural moisture which is necessary to give a fibrous material strength, so that an excessively high insulation resistance may merely indicate that the material has been ruined mechanically.

Testing insulating materials.—The detailed tests of raw materials have already been discussed in Chapter III., from which it will be noted that, on account of the variety of characteristics and diverse qualities, only general rules for testing can be laid down. In testing raw materials it is important to keep in mind the particular function that the insulation has to fulfil, and the tests should be arranged to embody, as far as possible, the conditions occurring in practice. Of these tests the most important is that which determines the permanence or life of the material. While it is usually impossible to duplicate actual working conditions, sufficiently good results can often be obtained by intensifying the particular conditions which produce deterioration of the insulation, and in this way allowing the ageing tendency to be observed without undue expenditure of time.

Where an insulating material has been found satisfactory for some particular function after a long period of use, it should be considered a standard for comparison with newer materials. A close inspection of a new material, comparing it with the standard, will often enable a decision to be made without elaborate tests being required. In testing materials new features should be carefully noted. All tests on similar materials should, for purposes of comparison, be made as nearly as possible under similar conditions. For instance, the size and shape of electrodes, the time and method of applying voltage, the temperature, and such factors as frequency and wave shape, should be the same.

Tests on completed apparatus.—The established test for the insulation of completed apparatus is the application between the various current carrying parts, and between these parts and ground of a voltage considerably in excess of normal working pressure. It is obvious that such a test is in many respects of very limited value, since it has no bearing on the mechanical properties or permanence of the insulation, and consequently affords no guarantee that the apparatus will withstand actual service conditions. On the other hand, this test, in conjunction with the intermediate pressure tests, serves to detect flaws in the

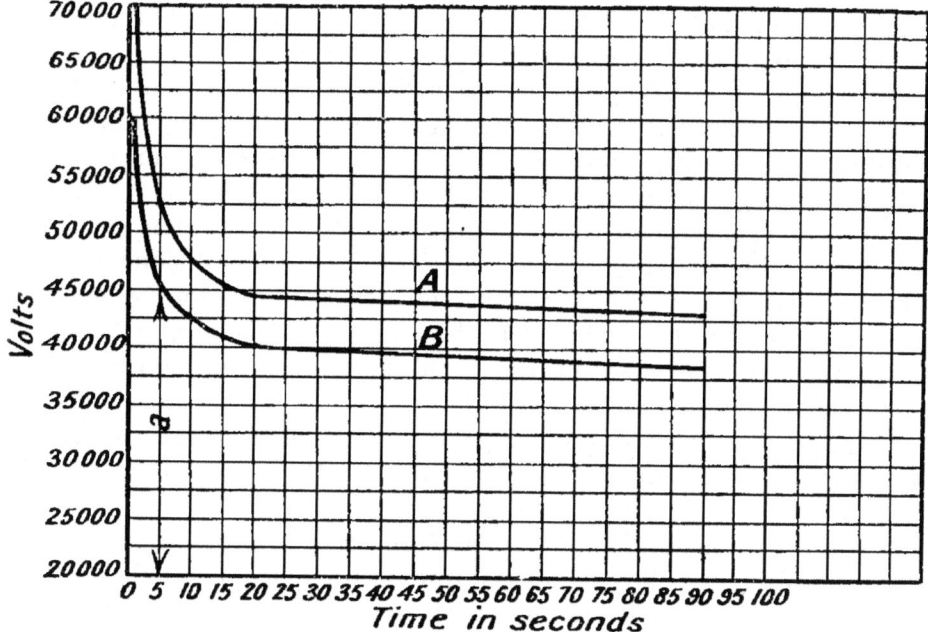

Fig. 88.

materials, and is a check on workmanship, and, to some extent, on the insulation design.

Pressure tests.—There is some risk of pressure tests weakening insulation, and the conditions under which such tests should be applied to prevent this have been the subject of much discussion among engineers in this country, on the Continent, and in America. The principal risk likely to occur is that of the charring of the insulation due to internal heating, caused by the dielectric loss which is set up in insulation when it is subjected to alternating electrostatic stresses, this heating being more or less proportional to the square of the voltage. In a lesser degree, also, chemical action set up in occluded air spaces, as the result of electrostatic stresses, may cause some deterioration. Further, an effect similar to overstraining may also contribute to this weakening.

Since all these effects are intensified as the voltage increases, many engineers have advocated a moderately high-pressure test applied for a long period, as preferable to a much higher pressure applied only for a very short time.

Considered solely from the point of view of weakening due to internal heating, the problem resolves itself into determining the correct relationship between varying periods of time and the corresponding voltage necessary to produce breakdown.

The curves shown in Fig. 88 indicate this relation for completely insulated coils tested under working conditions. From these curves it will be seen that a voltage *a* applied for five seconds produces the same tendency to breakdown—within the limits of uniformity of the valve of the insulation—as a voltage *b* applied for twenty-five minutes ; see Fig. 89.

Fig. 89 shows the same curves taken over a greater period of time. These curves are typical of all kinds of insulating materials.

An examination of the insulation thus tested indicated that the failures were in all cases due mainly to internal heating, the charring, however, being much more local in the short-time tests than where the voltage had been applied for a considerable time. While, therefore, a long-time test at a low voltage, or a short test at a higher voltage, may equally well cause a partial breakdown of the insulation, in actual practice cases of this kind are rarely experienced, since the factor of safety is usually very high, and, further, the insulation of the slot portions of the winding which are most severely stressed during testing is usually mainly of an inorganic nature, and, therefore, least affected by internal heating.

Effect of pressure test on composite insulation.—Where the slot insulation of the windings of a machine is made up of materials of widely differing specific inductive capacity, there is a danger, during the application of a high testing voltage, of actually causing disruption of the materials of lower specific inductive capacity without producing any apparent weakening of the rest

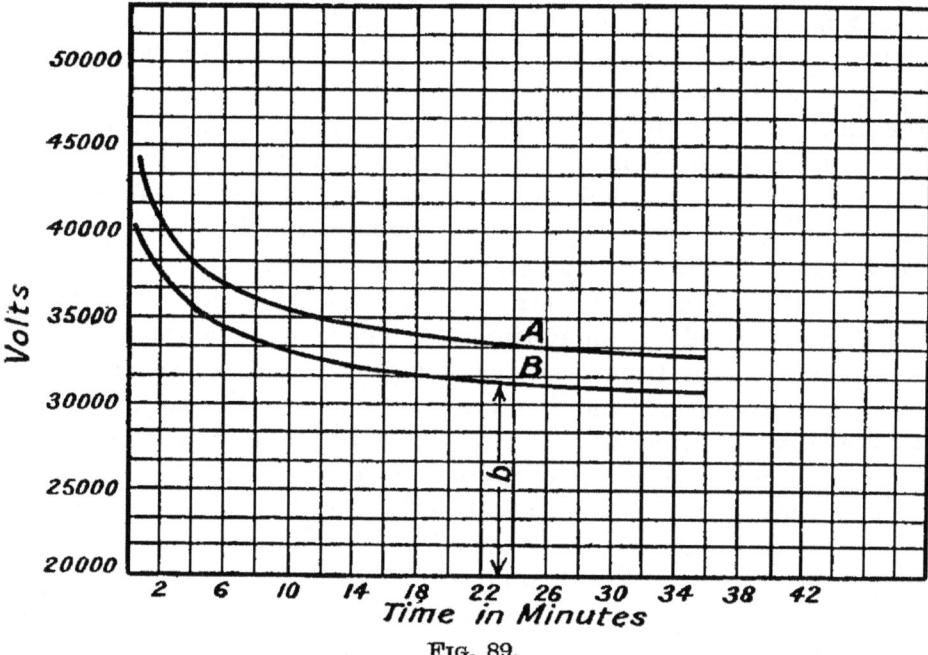

Fig. 89.

of the insulation. An experimental demonstration of this was made in the following manner :—Twelve sheets of paper, 0·008 inch thick, were sandwiched between two sheets of 0·06 inch

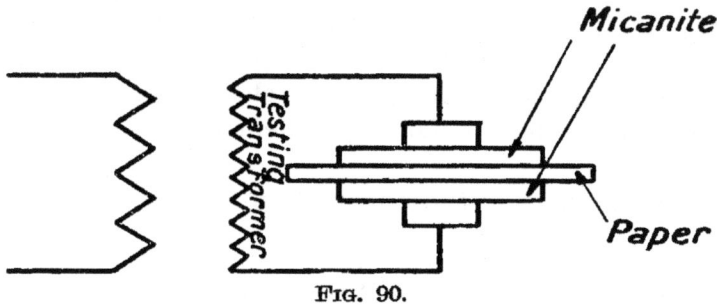

Fig. 90.

micanite, the whole being placed between two flat electrodes of small area with all corners carefully rounded. The arrangement is shown in Fig. 90.

An alternating E.M.F. of 20,000 volts was applied between electrodes for a few seconds. The paper was then removed and examined microscopically, and numerous minute perforations were found in the portions under the electrodes. These portions were separately tested between the electrodes, and broke down when a pressure of 3000 volts was applied, while those not coming under the electrodes required a voltage of approximately 10,000 to effect the puncture. It was, therefore, evident that the distribution of potential had been such as to impose a pressure exceeding half the applied voltage on the paper, though the latter constituted only one-third the total thickness of the dielectric.

Duration of pressure tests.—Considered from other points of view the high-voltage short-time test has some advantage over the low-pressure long-time test, inasmuch as it affords a better test of surface insulation, and is more likely to detect weaknesses due to defective workmanship. On the other hand, the duration of the test should not be so short that there is likely to be any serious error introduced in the time of application, since, as seen from Fig. 88, there is a very considerable difference in the voltage which insulation will withstand if the pressure is applied for one second or two seconds. It would therefore seem that the test duration of one minute now standardised by the German Normalien, as well as the American Institute of Electrical Engineers, is a reasonable one.

Standard insulation tests.—The insulation tests to be applied on finished apparatus have been fairly well standardised, both in Germany and in America. While for many years German engineers favoured long continued time tests as compared with the high voltage tests for a much shorter period advocated in America, there is now a fair agreement between the two sets of rules.

A brief summary of these insulation tests is given below.

German Standard Rules.

The measurement of the insulation resistance is not essential, and in preference to this, a test may be made of the soundness of the insulation by means of the application of a voltage test before the apparatus leaves the factory, and in the case of large units also, before it is put into service.

Machines and transformers must accordingly be capable of withstanding a test of this kind with an increased pressure relative to the normal voltage, according to that set forth below, applied for one minute. The test is to be applied when the windings are warm, and, in order to avoid the danger of subsequent damage, should only be repeated afterwards under exceptional circumstances.

Machines and transformers of from 40 to 5000 volts shall be tested at two and a half times the working pressure, but in no case at less than 1000 volts.

Machines and transformers of from 5000 to 7500 volts shall be tested at a pressure of 7500 in excess of the working voltage.

For voltages above 7500, the test pressure shall be twice the working voltage.

Transformers for testing purposes are excepted from these tests.

Machines and transformers of below 40 volts shall be tested at not less than 100 volts.

The above tests apply to the insulation between the windings and the frame, as well as to the insulation between windings electrically separated from each other. In the latter case, if the windings are of different voltages, the test specified for the higher voltage shall always apply.

Two electrically connected windings of different voltages shall be tested likewise between the winding and the frame with the testing pressure specified for the higher voltage.

When machines or transformers are connected in series, instead of the above test, the windings that are connected together shall be tested to earth at a pressure corresponding to the voltage of the complete group.

The above rules apply on the assumption that the test is undertaken with alternating current, the figures representing effective values. If the test is made with direct current, the pressures must be taken 1·4 times higher than those stated.

If a winding is normally electrically connected to the frame, the connection shall be broken during the insulation tests. The test pressure of such a winding to the frame to be determined in regard to the maximum voltage that can occur in service between any point of the winding and the frame.

For separately excited field magnet coils the test pressure shall be three times the excitation voltage, but not less than 100 volts.

Short circuited rotors do not require testing.

Machines and transformers in operation should be able to stand an increase in pressure of about 30 per cent. for five minutes. In machines this excess pressure test may be combined with a raising of the speed to about 15 per cent. above normal, provided, however, that the machine is not overloaded at the time. These tests are merely intended to give assurance of the soundness of the insulation, and should be commenced at such a temperature that the permissible temperature rise is not exceeded.

STANDARDISATION RULES OF THE AMERICAN INSTITUTE OF ELECTRICAL ENGINEERS.

The following voltages are recommended for testing all apparatus, lines and cables, by a continued application for one minute.

The test should be with alternating current having a virtual value given in the table, and preferably for tests of alternating apparatus at the normal frequency of the apparatus.

Rated terminal voltage of circuit.	Rated output.	Testing voltage.
exceeding 400 volts	Under 10 kw.	1000
,, 400 ,, ...	10 kw. and over	1500
and over, but less than 800 volts .	Under 10 kw.	1500
,, ,, ,, 800 ,, .	10 kw. and over	2000
,, ,, ,, 1200 ,, .	Any	3500
,, ,, ,, 2500 ,, .	,,	5000
. . . .	,,	Double the normal rated voltage.

Exceptions—Transformers.—Transformers having primary pressures of from 550 to 5000 volts, the secondaries of which are directly connected to consumption circuits, should have a testing voltage of 10,000 volts, to be applied between the primary and secondary windings, and also between the primary winding and the core.

Field Windings.—The tests for field windings should be based on the rated voltage of the exciter and the rated output of the machine, of which the coils are a part. Field windings of synchronous motors and converters, which are to be started by applying alternating current to the armature when the field is not excited and a high voltage is induced in the field windings, should be tested at 5000 volts.

INSULATION TESTS USED IN ENGLAND

In England no rules have been officially put into force, but the British Electrical Manufacturers' Association has provisionally adopted a scheme of tests according to the following plan :—

High-pressure tests.—Commercial high-pressure tests are to be made on the completed apparatus while it is in good condition and before it is put into service. In the case of apparatus which has been in service, reduced tests only are to be applied.

Unless otherwise specified the high-pressure tests are to be made at the maker's works.

The test is to be made with a pressure of approximately sine wave form, preferably at the rated frequency of the apparatus, but in general any frequency between 25 and 100 is satisfactory.

Prolonged tests at high pressures are undesirable, since they permanently weaken the insulation.

The following tests are to be applied for one minute between the windings and the frame and core when the apparatus is at normal working temperature.

Rated terminal pressure of circuit.	Test pressure.
Not above 333 volts	1000 volts.
Above 333, but not more than 1500 volts	3 times rated voltage with a minimum of 1500 volts.
,, 1500, but not more than 2250 volts	4500 volts.
,, 2250 volts	Twice rated voltage.

NOTE.—In the case of machines driven by water-wheels and exposed to runaway conditions, or otherwise exposed to possible excess pressure, it is recommended that pressure-limiting devices shall be provided, otherwise the test must be based on the highest pressure to which the windings may be subjected. High-pressure tests on field windings are to be based on the excitation pressure. Field windings of synchronous machines intended to be started from the alternating current side are to be tested at a pressure of 5000 volts, unless the field windings are provided with a "break-up" switch, or will always be short-circuited at starting. Transformers are to have the same test between high-pressure winding and core as between high-pressure and low-pressure windings. In making such tests the low-pressure winding should be connected to the core.

In general, constant current apparatus and apparatus used for series operation, is to have the test pressure rating according to the maximum pressure which may be imposed upon the apparatus.

Insulation resistance.—Very high insulation resistance (megohm test) should not be specified on electrical machinery, since in order to obtain it, long baking at high temperatures may be required, which may permanently damage the insulating material.

Insulation resistance tests are of value in showing the condition of the insulation with special reference to moisture and dirt, and it is usually advisable to measure the insulation resistance before making high-pressure tests.

In general, an insulation resistance of one megohm for windings

above 350 volts, or 0·25 megohms for low-pressure wind-·
ings, is sufficient evidence that the windings are in condition
to receive the high-pressure test.

Tests during manufacture.—As already pointed out, it is
necessary to test the insulation of various parts of apparatus at
different stages of manufacture. For example, in the case of a
direct current machine, the armature and field coils should be
tested for short and open circuit immediately after they are wound
and before they are insulated. The insulated armature coils
should be tested to " ground " in temporary metal slots, and then
placed in the armature slots and again tested to ground and for
short-circuits, before connecting up. With direct current machines
the commutator should at this stage be tested for grounds and
short-circuits between bars. A further test to ground should be
made both on field and armature coils after connecting up, and
the details such as brush-holder gear and terminal boards also
tested. Finally, another ground test is necessary before shipment
and after the machine has had its temperature run and is still hot.
These tests should be graded in about 10 to 15 per cent. steps.
For instance, if the final test is 3000 volts, the test after assembling
and connecting should be about 3500 volts, before connecting
4000 volts, and on individual coils 4500 volts.

Methods of applying tests to machine windings.—The tests to
be applied for insulation on machines are : Direct current
machines — windings, etc., to ground. Alternating current
machines—windings, etc., to ground and between phases, the
phases being for this purpose temporarily disconnected from one
another.

In all cases the final tests should be made while the machine
is hot and when in as dry a condition as possible. In the case of
alternating current machines for test voltages up to about 10,000,
no special precautions are necessary if suitable appliances are
used in making the test. For higher voltage tests on large
machines, however, the combination of distributed capacity and
self-induction of the windings may produce abnormal pressure
rises at the various parts of the winding, and thus tend to cause
breakdown, usually in the nature of vicious static discharges over
the surface of the insulation from windings to frame.

A danger not often recognised in applying pressure tests between windings of machines and ground lies in the possibility of causing short circuits between adjacent turns of the coils. This is likely to occur if the test produces a breakdown to ground at a point in the winding, or if a flash-over occurs from the end of the winding to ground,

This will be appreciated if reference is made to Fig. 91. The entire winding of the stator is represented diagrammatically by AB, and connection from the testing transformer to winding and ground is shown made at the two points C and D. If now failure occurs to earth at the point E, either through the breakdown of the insulating materials surrounding the coils, or by a flash-over from the windings across the air-gap to the armature

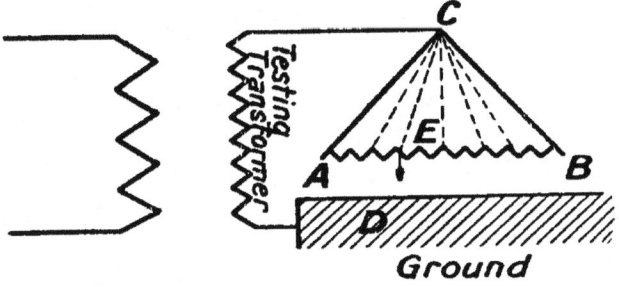

FIG. 91.

iron, the potential at the point E is suddenly reduced to zero, and the full testing voltage is thrown across the portion of the winding AE and BE, the slope of potential being greatest across those turns nearest the point E. The momentary voltage across these turns may easily be sufficient to puncture the insulation between them, and such cases of failure have from time to time been observed.

The risk may be minimised by connecting the testing lines to as many points as possible on the winding, as indicated by the dotted lines. This also affords similar protection against the effect of surges liable to be set up if the testing voltage is suddenly switched on or off.

Insulation tests on transformers.—The insulation tests required on a finished transformer are :—

(a) H.T. to L.T. windings and terminal gear.

(b) H.T. to ground.

(c) L.T. to ground.

(d) Between circuits where there is more than one high-tension or low-tension winding.

(e) Between phases H-H or L-L according to whichever are adjacent.

All tests should be made directly after the load run while the transformer is at its maximum temperature, since, as already pointed out, the insulation is at its weakest under these conditions, and further, the tests should be made as far as possible under the same conditions as those occurring during operation.

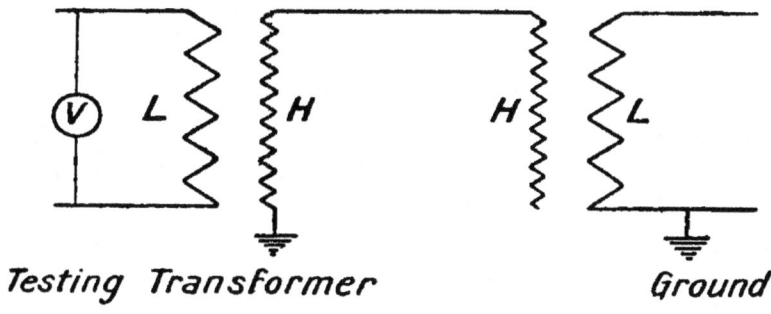

Testing Transformer   Ground

FIG. 92.

In oil-insulated transformers the oil, after frequent usage with different transformers during tests, gets dirty and is liable to contain moisture, and consideration should be given to this in testing very high voltage apparatus. One of the means of drying and cleaning oil, referred to in Chapter VI., should be employed periodically to maintain the oil in good condition. Further, before making the test, care should be taken that air bubbles are not rising from the windings. In testing from high-tension to low-tension windings of finished apparatus, care must be taken to ground the low-tension winding, otherwise its potential above that of ground will be raised to half the applied voltage, and a breakdown of this winding to ground may occur.

The test may be made with voltage derived from an external source and applied as shown in Figs. 92 and 93, in which case the difference of potential between all parts of the high-tension and low-tension windings is the same, or the test may be made by applying more than normal voltage to the low-tension winding and grounding the terminals of the high-tension winding alternately, as shown in Fig. 94. In the latter case the stress between

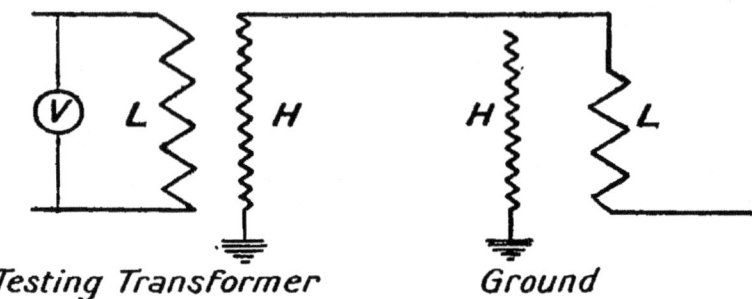

Testing Transformer   Ground

FIG. 93.

various parts of the winding and ground are in the same proportion as in a transformer operating with one side grounded. It is obvious that this is the best method of testing, since the voltage is applied where it is wanted, and permits in some cases saving of insulation space, since the interior portions of the winding need

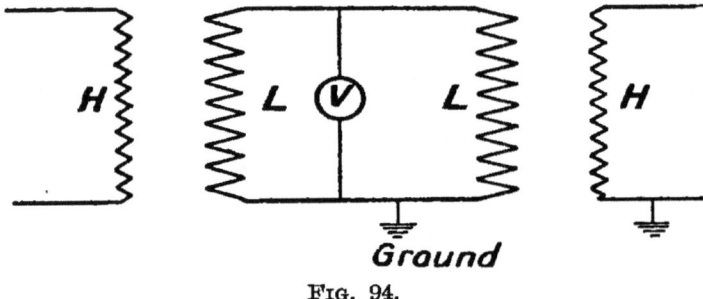

Ground

FIG. 94.

not be so heavily insulated to ground, and further, the insulation between adjacent turns and coils is tested. It must be remembered, however, that should one side of the high-tension winding of a step-down transformer be connected to the high-tension system, and the other terminal disconnected, the whole of the winding assumes the same potential, and consequently the same tendency to break down at all parts.

In applying test voltages up to 10,000, in the case of ordinary apparatus the pressure may be switched on suddenly, and while there is some danger of a concentration of voltage at the terminal portions of the winding, this is equally likely to occur during normal switching operations. For much higher testing voltages, however, it is advisable to raise the voltage gradually by means of some controlling device in the testing circuit, as apparatus for such high voltages will in practice be protected against sudden applications of pressure by suitable protective devices.

Insulation tests on detail apparatus.—The insulation testing of control and detail apparatus does not in itself entail any special precaution. The materials employed in such apparatus are usually of such a nature that a breakdown of their surface insulation is more likely to occur than a break through the thickness. The magnitude of the tests on instruments should be decided by the conditions under which they are to be used. For . instance, alternating current ammeters or voltmeters operated on the low-voltage side of instrument transformers should be tested in accordance with the voltage to which they will actually be subjected, and similarly the transformers. Further, when the instruments are supported on marble switchboards, they need not necessarily be insulated or tested as heavily as when mounted, say, on a grounded framework.

In the case of switchboards, a careful inspection of surface distances and a thorough test on each piece of apparatus used on them is more satisfactory than a pressure test. On the other hand, a high voltage test is useful in picking out any flaws or metallic veins in the marble or slate, and also. indicates its condition as regards moisture by the amount of surface discharge.

Testing Apparatus

The first consideration to be observed in the selection or design of testing apparatus is the safety of the operator. The continual handling of high-tension apparatus leads to carelessness and negligence of the ordinary precautions which should be observed in such work, so that every care should be taken to render the accidental touching of live bare parts an impossibility.

Short-circuit testing devices.—Individual windings may be tested for short and open circuit by means of the apparatus shown in Fig. 95. This consists of a laminated E-shaped core A on which are placed exciting coils B and indicating coils C symmetrically disposed and connected to a voltmeter or other indicating device, a telephone receiver being used to advantage for frequencies of 50 and upwards. A removable yoke D is used to complete the magnetic circuit. The coil to be tested is placed on either of the limbs E. If any of the turns are short-circuited, the distribution of the flux is rendered unsymmetrical and the induced currents in the two indicating coils become unbalanced, causing a deflection in the voltmeter.

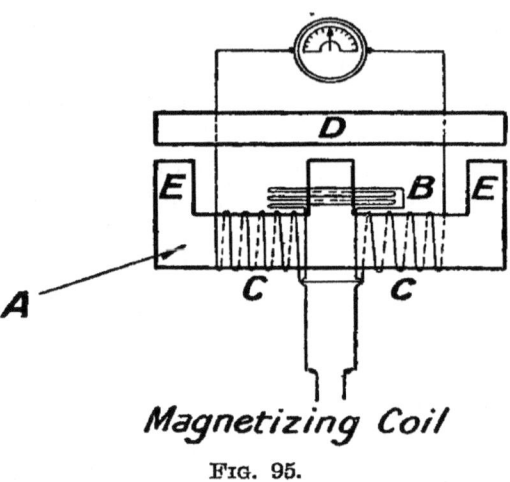

Fig. 95.

An open circuit in the coil can be detected by connecting the terminal leads of the coil together and noting if this causes an indication of short circuit.

If a coil containing short-circuited turns is placed over the middle limb and the yoke placed into position, the short-circuited turns will form the secondary of a transformer of which the exciting coil on the core is the primary. The induced current then set up in the short-circuited turns will cause local heating, and this may serve to indicate the position of the fault.

In the case of armature coils which are liable to be damaged when inserted into the slots, the complete winding is tested by means of the apparatus shown in Fig. 96. This consists of a laminated pole piece A on which is placed a coil B of sufficient number of turns to create a strong field. The armature is placed against the pole face and the flux produced threads the various coils as the armature is slowly rotated by hand. If any coil is

O

short-circuited, it will behave as the secondary of a transformer, and the current induced in the short-circuited portion will produce back ampere turns, tending to cause considerable leakage flux between this secondary winding and the primary winding represented by the coil on the field pole. This leakage flux can be detected by the pull on a loosely held piece of lamination used as a feeler around the armature.

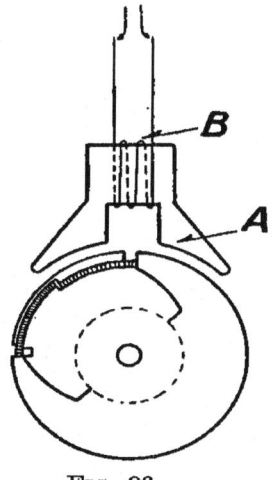

Fig. 96.

A rough method of testing for open circuits in the different armature coils is to slowly rotate the armature against the pole face, using a strip of metal to bridge at least two of the commutator segments. If sparking occurs as each segment is passed, the coils have no open circuit. A more exact method is to apply a definite voltage to those commutator bars falling under the positive and negative brushes of the machine and to measure the drop across adjacent bars by means of a low-reading voltmeter.

Portable testing transformers.—In the high-voltage testing of apparatus in course of manufacture, when the electrostatic capacity is small, a portable testing transformer of from 5 kw. to 10 kw. capacity with necessary L.T. switches, fuses and circuit breaker is required. The windings should be provided with tappings on the high-tension side so that voltages from 250 to 10,000 may be obtained in 250 volt steps, the low-tension winding being arranged for any convenient voltage. The arrangement of connections should be as shown in Fig. 97. The voltage on the high-tension side is adjusted by means of the two dial switches, one giving 250 volt steps and the other 2000 volt steps. A limiting resistance should be provided in the low-tension circuit if it is desired to burn out a fault in the insulation.

It is not necessary with such a transformer to provide a high-tension voltmeter, since, if the low-tension voltage is fairly steady, the testing voltage can be ascertained from the position of the dial switches, the transformer ratio not being appreciably altered by such a small capacity load. Such a transformer is very suitable for flash, *i.e.* momentarily applied, tests—or even for time tests when the charging current is not sufficient to overload its windings. It does not provide for any gradual variation of the testing voltage, but this is seldom wanted for such comparatively low-testing voltages.

Testing transformers for apparatus of large electrostatic capacity.—When the electrostatic capacity is high, as for instance

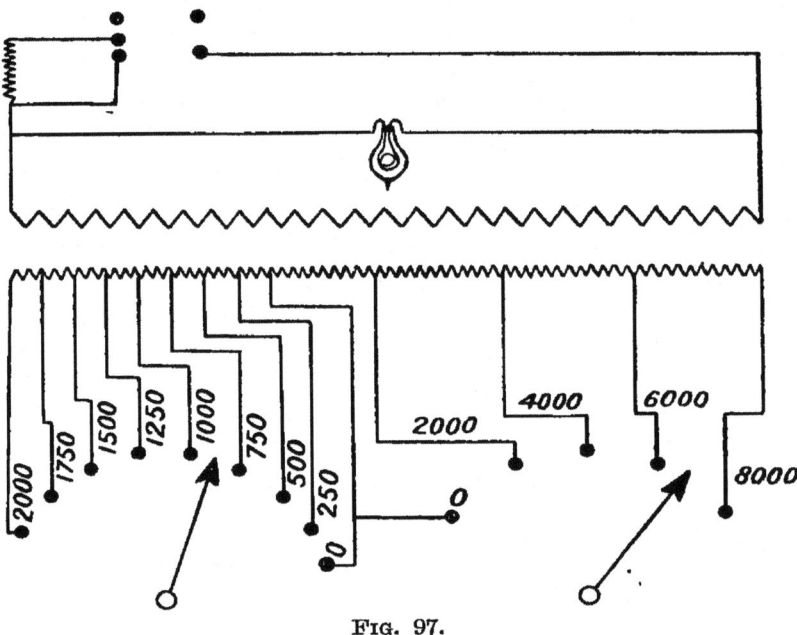

Fig. 97.

in finished apparatus having a large exposed surface of windings, it is necessary to provide a larger transformer to take care of the charging current, particularly for very high voltage testing. In such cases, *i.e.* above 10,000 volts, it is advisable to raise the high-tension voltage gradually, either by means of a suitable rheostat in the low-tension circuit or by operating the testing transformer from an alternator whose field excitation can be varied between wide limits without, however, causing any marked change in wave-form even with loads having leading or lagging power factor. The size and weight of such a testing set preclude the use of portable apparatus. It is therefore convenient to instal the testing transformers where they will be convenient for testing finished apparatus, and arrange a permanent switchboard for fuses, circuit breakers, switches, etc., and the necessary voltage regulating device in the low-tension circuit. Transformers for this purpose should be not less than 100 KVA capacity, and capable of giving voltages up to 100,000. It is usually convenient to arrange the high-tension windings in four groups arranged for series, series-

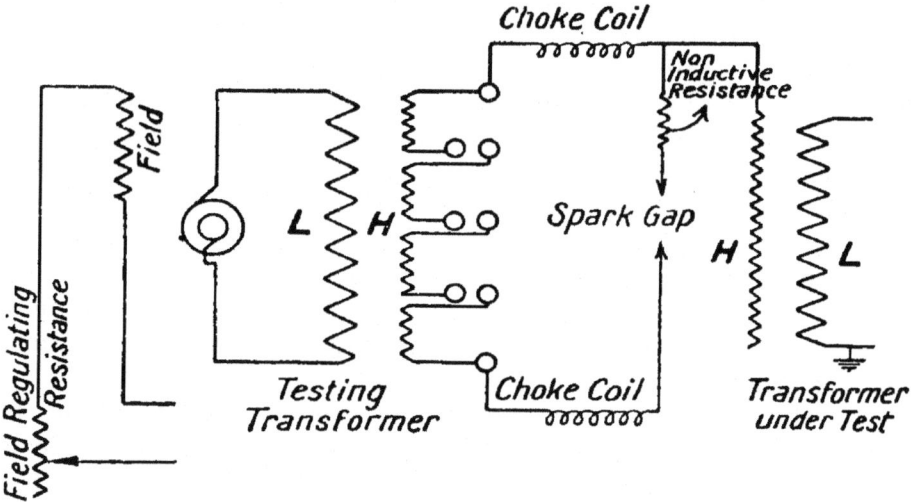

Fɪɢ. 98.

parallel, or parallel connection, by means of links on a terminal board, as shown in Fig. 98.

In applying a high-tension insulation test to apparatus, especially that having a large electrostatic capacity, care must be taken that the testing voltage is not pulled down due to the charging current taken by the apparatus under test, and that, on the other hand, the combination of this capacity and the transformer reactance does not produce a change in ratio tending to increase the testing voltage. The transformer should, therefore, be of ample KVA capacity to deal with the charging current without having too high an ohmic drop, its reactance should be low, and it should be operated from a circuit with plenty of power behind it. This gives a combination which will behave practically as though the testing voltage was derived directly from a large high-tension source of supply, without there being any intermediate transformer, and consequently little fear of either ohmic drop or increase in testing voltage resulting from the effect of the capacity of the apparatus. At the same time it is necessary, in this case, to interpose between the transformer and the apparatus to be tested a choke coil in each line, so that in the event of failure of the insulation comparatively little current will flow through the fault, thereby minimising the chance of damage to the windings. The choke coils also will have the tendency to smooth out any pressure ripples due to rapid variations in the supply voltage. Voltage should be measured preferably on the high-tension side, either by an electrostatic voltmeter—for very high voltages the compressed air type may be most suitable—by a voltmeter supplied from a step-down potential transformer, by a voltmeter in series with a high non-inductive resistance, or by spark gap. Of these the electrostatic voltmeter is the most accurate. Where a spark gap is used it should have in series with it a high non-inductive resistance to damp down any high frequency oscillations that are otherwise likely to occur when a spark passes.

In all cases one side of the low-tension circuit should be grounded, since otherwise, as already pointed out, if one side of the high-tension winding is grounded, the potential on the low tension may be raised to a dangerous degree.

CHAPTER VI

THE DRYING AND HANDLING OF ELECTRICAL WINDINGS

THE proper care of the insulation of electrical apparatus subsequent to the final tests in the maker's works requires sound judgment rather than expert knowledge. In the packing and shipment of machines and transformers, special regard must be given to the fragile nature of the insulating materials and adequate precautions taken to protect windings against mechanical damage and against accumulation of dust and dirt.

The precautions to be observed in handling during erection depend mainly on the nature of the apparatus and local conditions.

As regards electrical machines there are two classes to be considered, namely, industrial motors and generating plant.

As regards the former, where the machines have not been subjected to ocean transport, and provided there is no evidence of the windings having been exposed directly to rain or moisture, it is usually unnecessary to make any special arrangements for drying. As a precaution, however, the insulation resistance between the windings and ground should be ascertained, and if this when measured cold is lower than half a megohm on either the field or armature windings separately, or the stator or rotor (excepting short-circuited windings), drying should be carried out in the manner described later. In cases also where motors have to be subjected to an insulation pressure test they should be dried before the test is applied.

In the case of generators, particularly those of large size and for high voltages, attention to drying prior to putting into service is usually essential.

Frequently such machines have to be installed in newly or

even partially erected buildings, and under such conditions there is every possibility of absorption of moisture as well as mechanical damage to the insulation, and of the accumulation of dust and dirt on the windings.

Absorption of moisture is one of the most fruitful sources of insulation failure, and no commercial insulating material of a nature suitable for use on windings can be considered entirely immune from this weakness.

Suitable care in packing is to some extent a safeguard ; but as apparatus may often be left in damp surroundings for a long time before being installed, it is essential, except under very favourable conditions, to thoroughly dry out the windings before putting them into service.

Methods of drying windings.—Drying may be accomplished either by passing current through the windings ; by placing the apparatus in an oven heated by steam or hot air ; by surrounding it by charcoal stoves, or electric radiators, or by heating over a gas stove.

Drying electrically.—Where windings are dried out electrically the method adopted depends mainly on whether alternating or direct current is available, and whether suitable regulating devices are at hand for varying the current so as to control the heating over a wide range of temperature. Whatever the method adopted, however, the temperature should be brought up very slowly to about 70° to 90° C. and maintained for a period of 24 to 48 hours.

The maximum temperature permissible depends on the depth of winding and thickness of insulation ; and the time of drying, on the size and voltage of the apparatus, that is to say, the volume of material to be dried.

The following methods of drying apply specifically to different types of machines.

Alternating current machines.—In the case of generators, the armature winding should be short-circuited and an ammeter placed in at least one phase. The machine should then be brought up to speed and the field current varied until about 25 per cent. above normal full-load current flows through the armature winding. When the maximum safe temperature is reached, the field current should be adjusted to maintain this at a steady value. In the case of synchronous motors the same procedure should be followed, except that the machine must be driven by external means. Slip-ring motors may be treated as generators by short-circuiting the stator winding, and applying direct current to two of the rotor slip rings, the rotor being driven by external means. The stator winding must not be opened while there is voltage on the rotor.

In the case of motors having short-circuited rotors, the rotor may be locked to prevent rotation, and a low voltage applied to the stator winding. About 10 per cent. of the normal voltage should be sufficient to produce the required degree of temperature.

As an alternative to the above procedure, direct current may be passed through the windings, but in general this is less easy to regulate and is much more wasteful as regards the energy dissipated outside the windings undergoing the drying process.

Direct current machines.—The armature should be short-circuited through an ammeter and driven at a slow speed with a weak field, motors being treated as generators. The temperature should be measured at intervals and the field current and the speed adjusted to give the required temperature. In general, due to the greater simplicity in insulation, field coils are much less vulnerable to moisture than the armature windings, and consequently the greatest attention should be paid to the drying of the latter.

Very great care is necessary in measuring the temperature during the drying operation. If the thermometer can be placed in contact with the copper the higher temperature limit noted above may be allowed. If, however, there is much insulation intervening, a lower temperature should be maintained to allow for the difference between the temperature indicated and that attained by the windings, otherwise the internal insulation may become carbonised. Thermometers should be inserted in the windings wherever possible so as to ensure that there is no danger of local over-heating. The temperature may also be ascertained by the increase in resistance of the windings where suitable measuring instruments are available.

The voltage used when drying out should be as low as possible and applied in such a way as to keep the stress on the insulation down to a minimum.

Drying by means of a heater.—If it is not feasible to dry out the windings by circulating current through them, or to place the apparatus in a heater, external drying stoves must be used. These should be placed underneath or in close proximity to the windings, and a housing built round the whole apparatus, arranged so that a natural draft of air enters underneath the apparatus and the heated air rises through the windings, and escapes moisture-laden from the top. Ample facilities should be provided for the free inlet of air. Drying under these conditions should be continued for three or four days, and the average temperature controlled at as nearly 100° C. as possible. Great care should be taken that no fuel is used which gives off smoke or carbon dust, and charcoal will generally be found most suitable for this purpose.

If a suitable hot-air or steam heater is available for drying, a temperature of 100 to 110° C. may be permitted and should be maintained for about fifteen to twenty hours. During the drying period the air should be changed occasionally and, if possible, a continuous draught be allowed through the heater.

Drying by vacuum.—The best and safest method of drying is with a vacuum oven, by which means moisture may be removed much more quickly and at a lower temperature than with an ordinary heater, and consequently there is much less danger of embrittling the insulation by over-heating. With a vacuum oven drying can be accomplished satisfactorily in about half the time, and at a much lower temperature, than with the ordinary heater, due to the drop in boiling-point of water as the pressure is reduced. The temperatures at which water will boil for various conditions of vacuum are shown in Fig. 99.

In drying-out apparatus it must be remembered that to remove absolutely all the moisture absorbed by the insulation it is necessary for the temperature to reach or exceed the boiling-point of water, that is to say, 100° C. at atmospheric pressure, or, as already noted, a lower temperature if the air pressure is reduced, as in a vacuum chamber. On the other hand, the ordinary surface moisture which, except under very bad conditions, is all that should be taken up by well-insulated apparatus, may be removed at a much lower temperature than the boiling-point, even at atmospheric pressure. Where, however, moisture is actually absorbed by the insulation, the drying requires to be very thoroughly done, otherwise the moisture becomes merely distributed in a vapour form throughout the material, and the attempts at drying will be harmful rather than useful.

The evaporation of moisture from a substance depends on the condition and temperature of the surrounding air, and ceases as

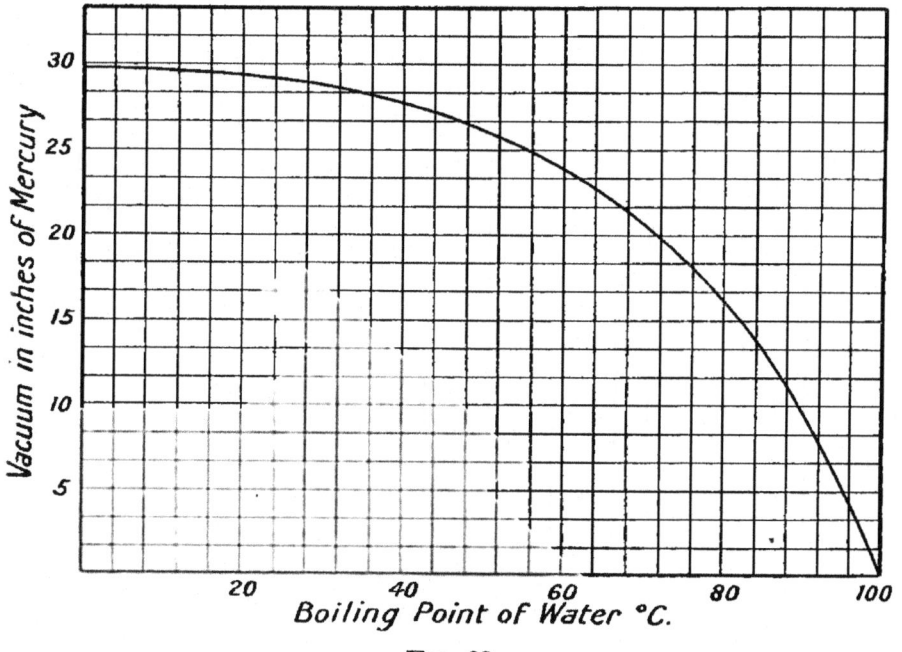

FIG. 99.

soon as the air becomes saturated. The capacity of air for containing moisture increases very rapidly with the temperature.

The curve in Fig. 100 shows the maximum vapour pressure in air at different temperatures and illustrates relatively the maximum amount of moisture that air is able to contain at these temperatures. It will thus be seen that in many cases drying may be accomplished without the trouble and risk of employing a high temperature.

Insulation resistance as an indication of the dryness of insulation.—The condition of apparatus as regards moisture, and the effect of drying, may to some extent be ascertained by measuring the insulation resistance between windings and frame. This measurement repeated occasionally during the drying period will give some indication as to how long the drying process should be maintained. Care must be taken, however, that all measurements are made at the same temperature, since, as already pointed out

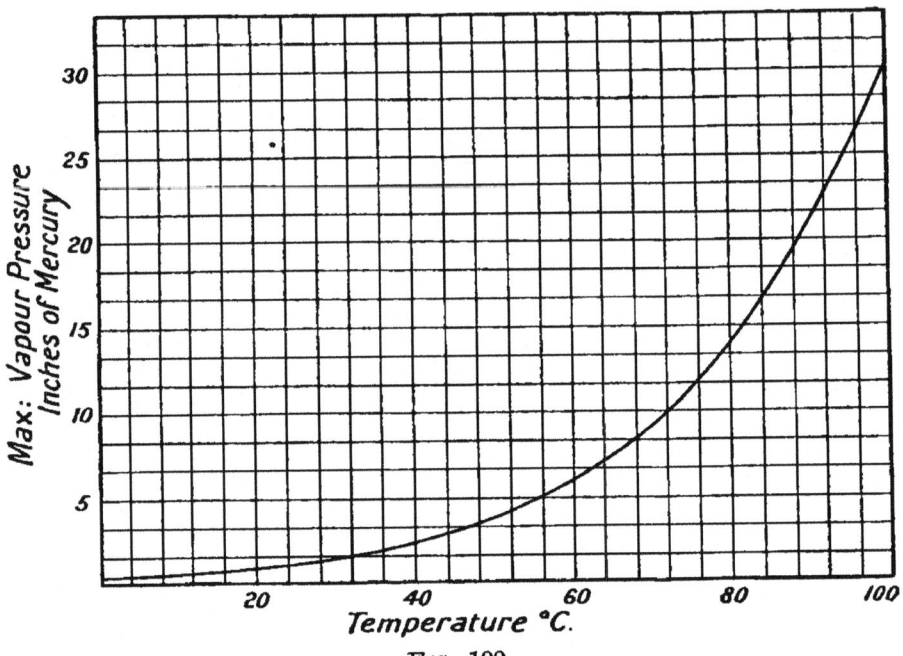

Fig. 100.

in Chapter I., the insulation resistance of commercial insulating materials varies very considerably with temperature.

The American Institute of Electrical Engineers some years ago put forward the rule that a machine might be considered satisfactory for service if its insulation resistance is such that at the working voltage the leakage current does not exceed one-millionth part of full load current. Such a rule is useful as giving an approximate figure to work to, but no hard and fast rule can be laid down, as it is obvious that two machines of equal output, but of greatly different speeds, may have very different insulation resistances, there being fewer coils and less total surface area of insulation in the case of the high-speed than in that of the low-speed machine. The insulation resistance may be ascertained by means of an ohm-meter or by the use of direct current and a high-resistance voltmeter.[1]

Precautions to be observed in drying.—It is extremely important that a very close supervision be kept on apparatus while it is being dried out, especially if the drying is done electrically, since with this method there is always a danger of over-heating, particularly on the inner portions of the winding where the temperature cannot readily be measured.

If apparatus is left out of service for any length of time there is always a danger of its windings absorbing moisture, since, owing to the mass, there may be a considerable temperature lag between it and the surrounding air, and moisture will tend to be deposited on the cool surfaces. Whenever possible, therefore, current should periodically be circulated through the windings of apparatus that is out of commission to dry off any such surface moisture.

Importance of keeping windings clean.—In addition to drying-out windings, it is extremely important to see that they are kept clean, dirt deposits being a frequent source of trouble, causing surface leakage to ground often accompanied by a burning of the insulation on the ends of windings.

Protection against effects of external chemical action.—Special attention is necessary in this respect in connection with gas-engine driven generators and machines operating in chemical works or where chemically active fumes are prevalent.

With the increasing application of gas-engine driven generators, insulation troubles peculiar to these machines are receiving more and more attention. That such troubles are still experienced is mainly due to an entire misconception of the root cause of the failures.

---

[1] Method of measuring insulation resistance by means of a direct current voltmeter. Read voltage V across line. Connect voltmeter in series with the insulation to be measured and take the resulting voltage reading V_1. Then, if r is the resistance of the voltmeter, the insulation resistance $R = \dfrac{r(V - V_1)}{V_1}$.

The opinion generally held is that the chemically active fumes from the gas engine attack the insulating materials on the windings and destroy their protective value, and this has led to the extended use of special acid-resisting varnishes on all exposed portions of the windings.

From the fact that practically all the troubles experienced occur on direct-current machines, it is clear that other factors have to be taken into account.

A number of insulation failures on gas-engine driven machines have been investigated by the authors. While in some instances the insulating coverings, particularly the varnished surfaces, have

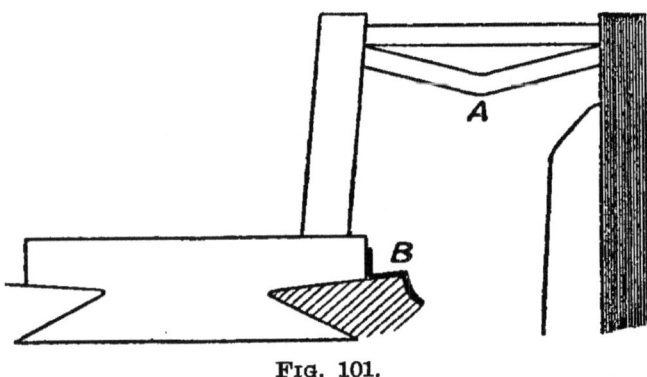

FIG. 101.

been attacked to a slight extent, no cases of breakdown traceable to this cause were found.

Trouble is first indicated by a gradual reduction of insulation resistance. Finally the windings become grounded, due to surface creepage and burning. This invariably occurs on the commutator end of the windings, and can be traced to the formation of a conducting surface from the commutator to " ground." The surface creepage usually takes place from the commutator necks across the under side of the insulated ends of the coils to the armature iron, though occasionally " grounding " may occur over the commutator bushing. The two paths are shown at A and B respectively in Fig. 101.

If the trouble is taken in hand in time, a thorough cleaning of the surfaces affected is sufficient to restore them to their original condition, as shown by a high insulation-resistance measurement.

In an actual case, the insulation resistance of an armature, taken over a period of three months only, fell from 10 megohms to less than 0·1 megohm. In the latter condition a voltage of 250 applied directly between the windings and the armature iron was sufficient to cause a leakage and burning across the taped ends of the windings for a distance of 8 inches, which, under normal conditions, would be good for thousands of volts. That this deterioration was due solely to the accumulation of conducting deposits, and not to chemical action on the insulation, was shown by the fact that merely cleaning the surfaces was sufficient to restore the insulation to its normal condition. An insulation resistance was then obtained in excess of 10 megohms, and a pressure test of 2000 volts was applied without causing any creepage.

The conducting deposit is formed by the action of fumes on the wearing surface of the commutator, the sulphide or other salt formed being worn off by the brushes, and, together with carbon dust, carried by windage on to the surfaces already referred to.

Failure may be prevented by frequent cleaning, the insulation resistance of the winding not being allowed to drop below a certain minimum figure. Usually, however, the affected surfaces are very difficult to get at, and the cleaning becomes an expensive and tedious undertaking. The difficulty of cleaning is frequently increased by the presence of an oil film, which causes the deposit to adhere to the insulation and renders an air-blast practically useless.

Attempts have been made to obviate the trouble due to this deposit by heavily varnishing the commutator necks and also the armature iron, this being done in the case of small armatures by completely immersing them in varnish. In service, however, the expansion and contraction is sufficient to crack the varnish film just where the protective value is most needed, *i.e.* where the coils leave the slots.

A drastic, but efficient, remedy is to completely house in the generator and provide a pure air supply. This, however, is expensive and cannot always be arranged. It therefore becomes necessary to prevent the deposit having access to the windings. This can be done by entirely enclosing the windings at the commutator end, or by so designing the armature as to create a draught from the rear end of the machine. The first of these alternatives has the great disadvantage of destroying ventilation, and for this reason is comparatively seldom adopted on large units.

Another remedy which has proved eminently satisfactory in practice is to break up the exposed under surfaces of the winding by means of insulating barriers so arranged as to prevent the formation of an unbroken layer of conducting deposit.

In all cases it is desirable thoroughly to fill the insulating tapings and provide a smooth glossy surface so as to afford as little lodgment for dirt as possible. Other than in this respect, it is not necessary to use any special kind of insulation on gas-engine driven generators.

While the trouble is mainly confined to armatures, field coils are also sometimes affected where surfaces are depended upon to any large extent for insulation.

Troubles such as the above are by no means confined to gas-engine driven generators, but are likely to occur on machines subjected to any chemically active fumes, such as those met with in alkali works or in the vicinity of gas-producer plants.[1]

Drying of transformers.—Drying out is particularly essential in the case of high-tension transformers. Such apparatus is usually oil insulated, and, when in service, the oil provides the requisite moisture resisting covering. During transit, however, the oil is often shipped separately, and there is consequently a danger of the windings, which are otherwise ill provided against moisture absorption, becoming damp.

Methods of drying electrically.—Drying may be conveniently done by short circuiting the low-tension winding of the transformer, and applying to the high-tension side sufficient voltage

[1] The information under this heading is contained in an article by the authors, entitled "The Insulation of Gas-engine driven Generator Windings," published in the *Electrical Review*, Vol. 69, No. 756. The permission of the Editors to reproduce it is hereby gratefully acknowledged.

from an alternating current circuit to cause from half to full load current to circulate through the windings. Unless the impedance of the transformer is very high—*i.e.* the regulation very poor—a voltage of from 2 per cent. to 4 per cent. of the high-tension voltage will be sufficient for this purpose. It should be noted that it is immaterial whether the high or low tension windings are short circuited. If the former, the voltage required to circulate the current will be less in proportion to the ratio of transformation. An ammeter should be inserted in one of the windings during the whole time of drying. Fig. 102 (*a*) shows the connections for drying a single-phase transformer in this manner.

Where it is required to dry out several transformers at the same time they may be coupled in series on say the high-tension side and each low-tension winding short circuited on itself as shown in Fig. 102 (*b*), provided the transformers are similar in all respects.

Figs. 102 (*c*), (*d*), (*e*) and (*f*) show the connections for drying out three-phase star and delta transformers with three-phase current, and Figs. 102 (*e*) and (*f*) show the required connections when only a single phase supply is available for this purpose.

Drying by vacuum.—The most desirable method of drying a transformer is by means of a steam-heated vacuum chamber. Manufacturing firms building very high-voltage transformers adopt this method, since it is the only one whereby all the moisture can be removed from the windings, and usually after drying in this manner the insulation and windings are impregnated with transformer oil. Transformers contained in stout boiler-iron cases can often be dried out under vacuum on site, where an air-pump is available. When this is done it is necessary to heat the windings to a temperature of about 80° C. by passing current through them, and also to heat up the inside of the tank, by means of resistances, to a temperature above that of the boiling-point of water at the vacuum obtained, otherwise there is a serious risk of moisture being removed from the insulation and condensed on the sides of the tank only to be taken up again when the oil is eventually put into the tank. Where a condenser is available, this affords a means of determining how long drying should be continued. When it is remembered that fibrous insulation may

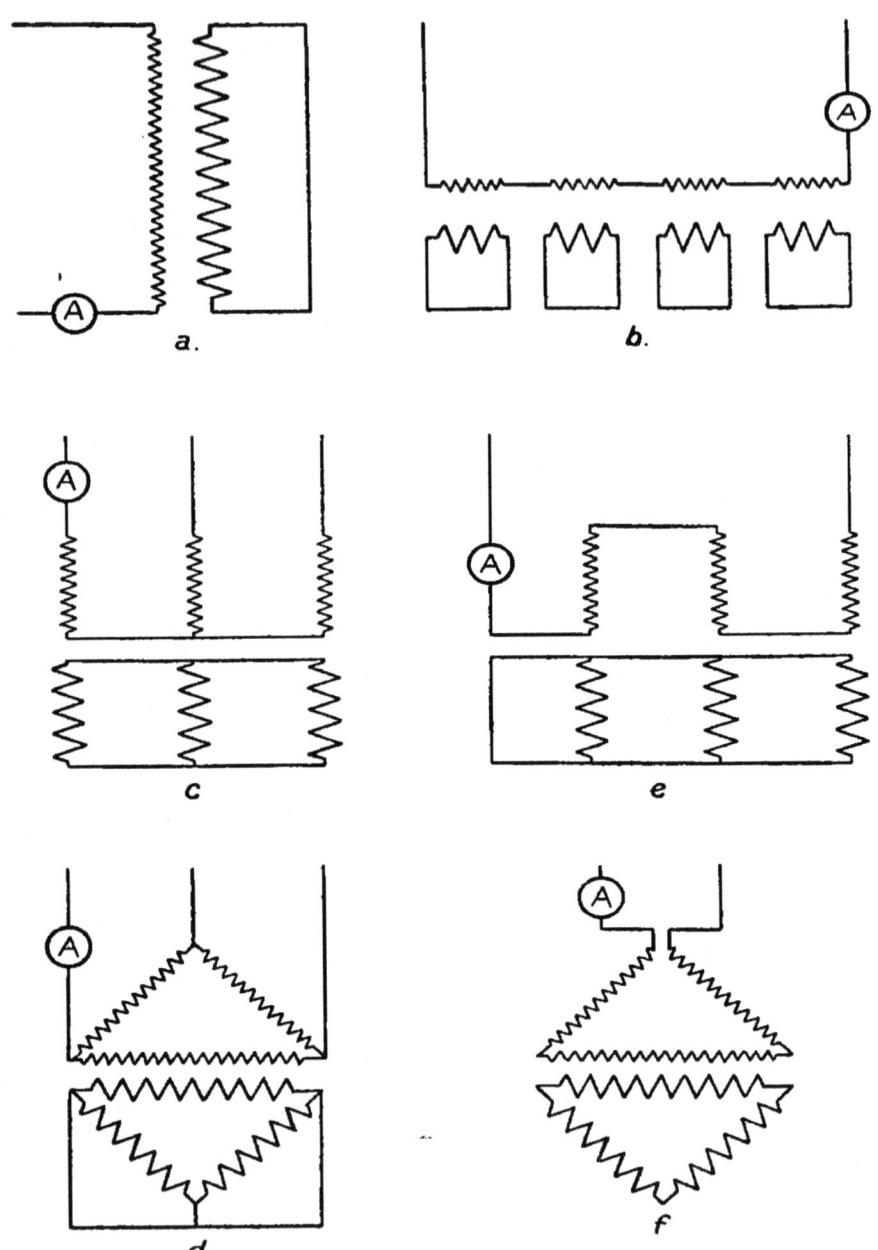

FIG. 102.

P

contain, even when treated, 5 per cent. or more of moisture, and that a high voltage transformer of say 1000 kw. insulated for 50,000 volts contains, according to the type, upwards of 1000 lbs. in weight of insulating material, so much as 5 or 6 gallons of water may be removed from the insulation. In such a transformer it is almost impossible to dry out thoroughly by merely passing current through the windings and without the aid of a vacuum, since to heat up the mass of poorly conducting insulation requires so much energy that the windings themselves become over-heated before a high enough temperature is reached to drive off the moisture.

Drying with heated air.—Where means are not available for drying out such transformers under vacuum, very good results may be obtained if a steady flow of air is passed through the windings. If, for instance, an air-pump is available, and the cover of the tank can be rendered sufficiently air-tight, air may be drawn through a suction pipe let into the cover and fresh air admitted through the oil valve at the bottom of the tank. This inlet air may be heated by passing it through a short length of piping on which a gas flame is played. The air being heated will have its capacity for containing moisture increased. Alternatively, if such means are available, the temperature of the inlet air may to advantage be reduced by freezing, and the moisture it contains thereby removed, and in this manner its capacity for absorbing further moisture, when in contact with heated transformers, increased.

In drying out transformers by means of current circulating through the windings, a variable impedance or resistance should be employed in the supply circuit so as to control the heating within the necessary limits, and so that, by passing more current through the windings at the commencement when the apparatus is cold, the time required to reach the drying temperature may be reduced as much as possible. In so doing, however, precautions must be taken not to over-heat the windings internally.

Transformers of the oil insulated type preferably should be removed from their cases, except when dried under vacuum in the manner described above, and during the drying process should be freely exposed to the air.

Such transformers usually have their windings unprotected by taping, whereas the natural draft or air-blast transformers are usually heavily protected with such insulating covering; hence in drying out the latter types, care must be taken to allow plenty of margin for the difference in temperature which will exist between the windings and that measured on the outside of the insulation.

Drying of transformer oil.—Transformer oil should be separately dried out, and this may be conveniently done by one of the following methods :—

Chemically, by means of a dehydrating substance, such as calcium chloride, unslaked limes, sodium, etc. Of these calcium chloride is the most effective.

Heating, by means of a resistance placed in the oil which raises the temperature of the oil to about 105° C. from 24 to 48 hours. This process is very commonly employed but is very slow, and there is a risk of injuring the oil by over-heating and causing the formation of a deposit, as mentioned in Chapter III. The use of a vacuum in order to reduce the boiling-point of water is advantageous in this respect.

Air, by means of heated air bubbled through the oil. This also is liable to produce sediment which, as already pointed out in Chapter III., is to some extent due to oxidation.

Separation.—Heating the oil causes the moisture to sink to the bottom, when it may be removed by drawing off the lower portion of the oil.

Filtering through absorbent material such as blotting paper, which takes up the moisture and also serves to cleanse the oil. The fact that such papers will permit oil, but not water to pass through them has been utilised on a commercial scale in oil-drying outfits comprising a series of chambers containing blotting-paper diaphragms through which the oil is forced by means of a motor driven pump, and this method of drying is probably the most satisfactory and practicable that has yet been devised. In connection with transformer work it is useful not only in dehydrating the oil when it is first used, but can also be used for further drying and cleaning it during service, the oil being pumped through the filter from the bottom of the transformer tank and returned again at the top.

By suitably drying transformer oil it is usually possible to improve its breakdown voltage 100 per cent. or more above the normal value. For instance, a sample of transformer oil, which after storage for some months in an open tank broke down at 15,000 volts between needle points ⅛ inch apart, withstood 31,000 volts after drying by the filter method.

The subject of drying transformer oil has been fully dealt with by H. W. Toby.[1]

Whatever method of drying is employed, the effect of the drying can only be readily determined by making a breakdown test. The breakdown value of oils varies considerably, differing mainly according to the viscosity and origin of the oil, so that comparison should be made with figures obtained with different oils that are known to be in a thoroughly dry condition.

Before being used, the dried oil should be very carefully filtered through several thicknesses of very fine mesh muslin so as to remove any dirt, and particularly the deposit which is liable to occur in oil of this kind when heated, as well as any iron oxide scale from the drums in which the oil is shipped. The oil should be piped to the bottom of the transformer tank, as this tends to prevent occlusion of air in winding pockets. Transformer oil should always be shipped in metal drums, as when kept in barrels it is liable to absorb moisture from the wood. The drums must be free from dirt and rust inside.

The newly dried out transformer should be put into the hot oil, and full voltage should not be applied, except in low-voltage transformers, until all air bubbles have ceased to rise from the windings. In very high-voltage transformers the windings should be heated up again after immersion in oil so as to expel occluded air, and enable all interspace in the windings and insulation to be filled with oil.

Care of apparatus in service.—After apparatus has been put into service, every care must be taken to keep the insulation of

---

[1] See *Transactions of American Institute of Electrical Engineers*, vol. xxix., No. 7.

windings, and all exposed parts, clean and dry and that adequate ventilation of the buildings is provided to ensure that the apparatus does not overheat. This latter point does not seem to be sufficiently recognised and is most important, since it is the actual temperature to which insulation is subjected which determines its life, and while the temperature rise of the apparatus above the surrounding air is quite normal, and within the makers' guarantees, if the air temperature is very high, it may be unsafe to operate the apparatus at its normal load.

In the case of railway motors and such apparatus which is continually exposed to damp, the armatures should be removed occasionally and cleaned, dried out, and the exposed insulation re-varnished. For this purpose, where a large number of machines are in use, a small heater should be installed for drying purposes.

The occasional revarnishing of the insulation of all machines is advantageous, and for this purpose a quick-drying insulating varnish may be used.

CHAPTER VII

INSULATION FAILURES

THE thorough investigation of insulation failures is a matter of considerable importance, both as regards the modification and improvement of designs, and to indicate where a change in the operating conditions is desirable.

Such an investigation frequently presents considerable difficulties, since a burn-out often obliterates the evidence of the cause of the failure, and it is only by experience, and by taking all the factors that enter into the case in their logical sequence, that erroneous conclusions can be avoided.

Industrial motors.—In the case of industrial motors, by far the greatest number of failures occur due to the accumulation of dirt or moisture on the exposed portions of the winding. Such machines are frequently installed in damp or dirty situations, and receive very little skilled attention.

Failures due to dirt, moisture, etc.—In the case of such failures the faulty winding should be cut out, and the condition of the rest of the insulation ascertained by measuring the insulation resistance between windings and ground. The effect of cleaning the various insulating surfaces should be noted by checking the insulation resistance after each part has been attended to, and finally, the resistance should be measured after the windings have been completely dried out, care being taken always to measure the resistance at the same temperature. In this way the most vulnerable portions of the insulation when subjected to those particular conditions can be ascertained, and some guidance obtained as to the best means of overcoming the trouble.

In general, alternating-current machines, whether having squirrel-cage or wound rotors, are more immune from failure due to dirt and moisture than direct-current motors. In the latter the projecting bushings of the commutator, and the connections at the front end, afford a considerable amount of exposed surface.

Over-heating.—Where general over-heating has occurred, this may be caused by overload or be due to poor conditions of ventilation.

The question of overload should be determined by the kind of service and by direct measurement of the power required of the motor, and a measurement of the temperature rise under known conditions of load also indicates whether the ventilation is sufficient. It must always be remembered that it is the ultimate temperature attained, not the temperature rise, that determines the life of the insulation, so that if the initial air temperature is high the maximum temperature may cause overheating, although the temperature rise is normal.

Again, since the heating of the windings increases as the square of the current, if the conductors are already rated nearly up to their limit as regards current density, a comparatively small overload is sufficient to cause dangerous heating.

Generators.—As regards generating plant, this is usually installed in a clean and dry station, and is under the supervision of a skilled attendant, consequently failures due to dirt and moisture are comparatively rare.

External chemical action.—In the case of direct current generators driven by gas engines or installed in the vicinity of gas producers, or where liable to be exposed to chemically active fumes, failures due to deposits of conducting materials are liable to occur on the commutator end, as already fully dealt with in Chapter VI.

Over-heating.—The remarks already made as regards over-heating in connection with industrial motors, also apply here, except that the conditions of load are much more under control, and the ventilating conditions are usually much more suitable.

Failures due to concentration of voltage between turns.— Failures of this kind are likely to occur on alternating-current machines, especially high-voltage motors, on switching in, and the local nature of such failures usually affords a clue as to the cause of breakdown. Such failures are only likely to take place on high-voltage motors of, say, 3000 volts and upwards, and can only be prevented by either reinforcing the insulation on these turns, or using an external choke coil having its conductors heavily insulated from each other.

Internal chemical action.—The conditions governing this have been fully described in Chapter IV. Where failures take place due to this cause, the evidence is usually unmistakable, and while the discoloration of the insulation, due to its effects, occasionally may be mistaken for the greenish discoloration commonly produced by certain varnishes, the examination of a few coils taken at intervals between the points of maximum and minimum voltage to ground will show by the consistency or otherwise of the discoloration whether the effect is due to chemical action. Such troubles are unlikely on machines of lower voltages than 4000 between the points of maximum potential and ground.

Failures due to mechanical troubles.—Excessive vibration may cause local disintegration of the insulation. Where generators are subjected to very heavy sudden overloads, short circuits, or switching-in out of phase, particularly when operating on large power systems where current from other sources can flow through the short circuits, enormous mechanical forces may be set up, tending to distort the portions of the winding projecting from the slots. In large turbo-alternators the windings are very heavily braced on the ends to withstand such conditions, but even so, the stresses may be sufficient to cause a slight movement which, if repeated often, may ultimately result in a failure at the point where the coils leave the slots.

In the case of large motors, used, for instance, in rolling mills, where rapid and sudden reversals of rotation occur, there is a risk of the coils being racked on the ends, and the insulation damaged at the ends of the slots.

Where mechanical conditions such as the above are likely to occur, a certain degree of flexibility in the insulation on slot portions is more or less essential.

Special causes of failure.—When a machine has once broken down in the slot portions, the laminations adjacent to the point of failure may become welded together, and thereby cause local heating, which may destroy the insulation of any new coils used in such slots if care is not taken to separate the laminations.

Transformers.—In analysing the failures likely to occur on transformers, the various types have to be taken into consideration.

Moisture.—Failures due to moisture are likely to occur on dry-type transformers, but more often on the oil-immersed type, due to the moisture absorption during transit when the transformer is without its protective covering of oil. In the case of oil-insulated water-cooled transformers there is a risk of leakage from the cooling coils into the oil, and of moisture being condensed on the inlet piping of the cooling coil which drains into the transformer tank. To prevent this condensation the inlet pipe is usually lagged with some heat insulation.

Mechanical troubles.—Due to the low reactance of transformers a short circuit on the secondary side will permit often as much as fifty times full load current to circulate through the windings, provided the supply system is of sufficient capacity. Since the mechanical forces on the windings, set up electro-magnetically, vary as the square of the current, the forces may be sufficient to distort the windings and destroy the insulation, not only between conductors, but also between high and low tension windings. To avoid failures of this kind, the windings of all transformers used on very large power systems should be thoroughly braced and also arranged so that any shrinkage of the insulation, due to heating or compression resulting from the weight of the coils, can be taken up and thus prevent a hammer blow of the loose coils should a short circuit occur.

Over heating.—Where a number of transformers are operated in parallel, and they are not all of the same reactance, those of lower reactance take a heavier load, and *vice versâ*. If the division of load is very unequal, over-heating of the unloaded transformers may result.

Transformers are frequently placed in poorly ventilated sub-stations, and in such cases over-heating is liable to occur. A sub-station having a capacity suitable for, say, four 500 KVA transformers with total losses of 30 kw. would require a displacement of air equal to 6000 cubic feet per minute to keep the sub-station temperature to within 10° C. of the outside air temperature.

With transformers having half these losses, well designed roof ventilators and louvres in the walls near the bottom of the transformer tanks will afford sufficient ventilation. For dealing with one-fourth the losses the natural dissipation through the walls should be sufficient, provided there is ample space between the transformers.

Where sludging of the oil occurs, this is liable to set up local heating due to the formation of a heat insulating covering on the windings. In the case of water-cooled transformers, such a covering may be formed on the cooling coils, in which case over-heating rapidly follows.

INDEX

THE END

PRINTED BY WILLIAM CLOWES AND SONS, LIMITED, LONDON AND BECCLES.

ImTheStory.com

Personalized Classic Books in many genre's

Unique gift for kids, partners, friends, colleagues

Customize:

- Character Names
- Upload your own front/back cover images (optional)
- Inscribe a personal message/dedication on the
  inside page (optional)

Customize many titles Including
- Alice in Wonderland
- Romeo and Juliet
- The Wizard of Oz
- A Christmas Carol
- Dracula
- Dr. Jekyll & Mr. Hyde
- And more...

Emily's Adventures in Wonderland

Ryan & Julia

Lightning Source UK Ltd.
Milton Keynes UK
UKOW06f1949050517

300619UK00015B/392/P